# The Mediated Presidency

# The Mediated Presidency

## TELEVISION NEWS AND PRESIDENTIAL GOVERNANCE

Stephen J. Farnsworth and S. Robert Lichter

ROWMAN & LITTLEFIELD PUBLISHERS, INC.
*Lanham • Boulder • New York • Toronto • Oxford*

ROWMAN & LITTLEFIELD PUBLISHERS, INC.

Published in the United States of America
by Rowman & Littlefield Publishers, Inc.
A wholly owned subsidiary of The Rowman & Littlefield Publishing Group, Inc.
4501 Forbes Boulevard, Suite 200, Lanham, Maryland 20706
www.rowmanlittlefield.com

P.O. Box 317, Oxford OX2 9RU, UK

Copyright © 2006 by Stephen J. Farnsworth and S. Robert Lichter

British Library Cataloguing in Publication Information Available

**Library of Congress Cataloging-in-Publication Data**

Farnsworth, Stephen J., 1961–
     The mediated presidency : television news and presidential governance / Stephen J.
Farnsworth and S. Robert Lichter.
        p.   cm.
     Includes bibliographical references and index.
     ISBN 0-7425-3677-7 (alk. paper)—ISBN 0-7425-3678-5 (pbk. : alk. paper)
     1. Presidents—United States—History—20th century.   2. Presidents—United States—
History—21st century.   3. Presidents—Press coverage—United States—History.
4.   Mass media—Political aspects—United States—History.   5. Press and politics—
United States—History.   6. United States—Politics and government—Press coverage.
7. United States—Foreign relations—Press coverage.   8. United States—Military policy—
Press coverage.   9. United States—Economic policy—Press coverage.   I. Lichter, S.
Robert.   II. Title.
     E176.1.F228   2005
     070.4'49320973—dc22                                                                        2005008333

Printed in the United States of America

♾ ™ The paper used in this publication meets the minimum requirements of American
National Standard for Information Sciences—Permanence of Paper for Printed Library
Materials, ANSI/NISO Z39.48-1992.

# CONTENTS

# TABLES

# ACKNOWLEDGMENTS

The centerpiece of this book is a content analysis that compares news coverage of the first year of the Reagan, Clinton, and George W. Bush administrations. This analysis was developed from a study originally commissioned by the Council for Excellence in Government (CEG) as part of its ongoing Government in the News program. The Council is a nonpartisan, nonprofit organization that works to improve the performance of government and government's place in the lives and esteem of American citizens. One of its principal goals is to increase citizen confidence and participation in government through better understanding of government and its role.

Along these lines, CEG's Government in the News program is designed to help journalists better understand and cover government by providing workshops for journalists and conducting research on media portrayals of government. Its projects are guided by a program advisory board, which represents some of the most respected names in the media and political arenas. The board is chaired by David Broder of the *Washington Post*. Its other members are: Tim Clark, *Government Executive* magazine; Marlin Fitzwater, former press spokesman, Presidents Reagan and Bush; Tom Hamburger, the *Wall Street Journal*; Peter

Harkness, *Governing* magazine; Stephen Hess, The Brookings Institution; Albert R. Hunt, the *Wall Street Journal*; Kathleen Hall Jamieson, Annenberg School for Communication, University of Pennsylvania; Marvin Kalb, Shorenstein Center, Kennedy School of Government, Harvard University; Susan King, Carnegie Corp. (former TV journalist and government spokesperson); Mike McCurry, former press spokesman to President Clinton; Doyle McManus, *Los Angeles Times*; Guy Molyneux, Peter D. Hart Research Associates, Inc.; Charles Peters, *Washington Monthly*; Walter Pincus, the *Washington Post*; Tom Rosenstiel, Project for Excellence in Journalism (and a former journalist); Terence Smith, *The NewsHour with Jim Lehrer* (PBS); Basil Talbott, *Congress Daily*; Judy Woodruff, CNN; and David Yepsen, *Des Moines Register*.

The overall parameters of the study, from the sampling frame to the focus of the content analysis system, were developed in close consultation with the board. We are grateful to its members for their hard work and valuable suggestions in helping to bring the study to fruition. But our greatest debt of gratitude is to Pat McGinness, president and CEO of the Council, who conceived of the study and offered her unyielding support through the vicissitudes that inevitably accompany a project of such wide scope and lengthy duration. Pat was assisted in this endeavor by an able team that included Carl Fillichio, Sue Ducat, Caryn Marks, David Roberts, and Tim Seidel. We are all indebted to the Pew Foundation, which provided funding for this study as part of its ongoing support for the Government in the News program.

The research itself was conducted under the auspices of the Center for Media and Public Affairs (CMPA). It was directed by Mary Carroll Willi and benefited from the extensive contributions of Dan Amundson, Raymond Shank, Amy Shank, Matthew Curry, Trevor Butterworth, Irina Abarinova, and numerous student coders. The research discussed in this book also goes beyond the CEG study to encompass material from ongoing CMPA content analyses of the presidency on broadcast television news since 1988. That project was first overseen by Richard Noyes and is currently overseen by Mary Carroll Willi. It has involved many other researchers over the years; we thank them collectively for their work.

We thank the editors of *Presidential Studies Quarterly*, *Congress &*

*the Presidency*, and *The Harvard International Journal of Press/Politics* for permission to reprint tables and portions of our arguments previously presented in their publications. We also thank these editors and their manuscript reviewers for their thoughtful ideas along the way. In addition, we acknowledge the financial support of the University of Mary Washington and Georgetown University.

Thanks are also due to Jack Kramer, Lew Fickett, and Jason Davidson, all of the University of Mary Washington, who generously provided advice and helpful evaluations of the arguments presented here, and to Chris Wright, Renée Legatt, and April Leo, who provided research and production assistance. Thanks are due as well for the inside perspective on journalism provided by the reporters and editors of the Washington Bureau of the *Los Angeles Times*, the *Kansas City* (MO) *Star & Times*, the *Burlington* (VT) *Free Press*, and the *Rutland* (VT) *Daily Herald*.

Special thanks are due to Tanya DeKona and to Margaret and Willis Farnsworth for their many years of support and encouragement, and to Diana Owen, whose patience, encouragement, and insight helped make this work possible.

Finally, we would continue to sing the praises of our longtime editor Jennifer Knerr, but after several acknowledgments of her many virtues, we have begun to worry that competitors might begin to discover this precious resource and overexploit her. Like the travel guide authors who leave the very best places out of their books, we want to keep her as editor for ourselves.

As always, any errors or oversights are our responsibility.

# CHAPTER 1

## U.S. PRESIDENTIAL GOVERNANCE AND TELEVISION NEWS
### Studying Media Content

### Recent Presidencies: A Struggle over Presidential Roles

On January 20, 1981, almost at the moment Ronald Reagan became America's fortieth president, two planes took off from Iran
with dozens of ecstatic U.S. citizens aboard. They had been held as
hostages since November 1979, taken prisoner when the U.S. Embassy
in Tehran was overrun by Islamic revolutionaries. The optimistic new
president and the newly freed Americans shared the media spotlight, a
sign that a very different presidency was under way.

A former actor and governor of California, Reagan saw himself as
leading a cavalry charge from the frontier West to rescue the country
from the ineffectual Jimmy Carter, whose term had been marked by the
Iranian hostage crisis, energy shortages, and economic distress (Brinkley 1998). In the wake of Richard Nixon's lies and Carter's apparent
impotence, Reagan's first role on the national stage was as the new
sheriff in town. Domestically, he prepared to do battle with Congress,
which dominated a White House diminished by more than a decade of
scandal and incompetence. Internationally, he vowed to get tough on

the Soviet Union, which he famously branded an "evil empire" (Abramson et al. 1982; Kellner 2002; Woodward 1999).

Ronald Reagan's early public image—part Gary Cooper and part John Wayne—was established in the public's mind on March 30, 1981, when he responded to an assassination attempt with courage and humor. (The grievously wounded president joked to his surgeons that he hoped they were Republicans [Gergen 2000].) Comic timing also served Reagan well in his reelection campaign in 1984. During the second presidential debate, he dispatched charges that he had grown old and out of touch with the quip: "I am not going to exploit for political purposes my opponent's youth and inexperience" (Pomper 1985:77). Even his opponent, Democratic nominee Walter Mondale, had to chuckle.

But issues of Reagan's competence during his second term were no joke. Concerns about his fitness to serve resurfaced in 1987 during the Iran-contra affair, when the somewhat disengaged president appeared unaware of lawbreaking and cover-ups by his trusted aides (Neustadt 1990). To make matters worse, Reagan's foreign policy team broke the president's promise to the American people never to negotiate with hostage-takers (Gergen 2000). By 1988, the tough frontier sheriff had become a shadow of his former commanding presence. (It was revealed several years later that he had been diagnosed with Alzheimer's disease.)

After eight years as Ronald Reagan's vice president, George H. W. Bush sought the White House in 1988. But first he had to erase public doubts over whether he was tough enough for the job. Bush toured American flag factories and ran an aggressive campaign that charged his opponent, Michael Dukakis, with being an extreme liberal who was soft on criminals (Farah and Klein 1989). He further sought to dispel his media image as a "wimp," and to reprise Reagan's tough-guy-role rhetoric, by proclaiming at the Republican National Convention, "Read my lips, no new taxes."

Bush's tough-guy approach backfired, however, when he increased taxes two years later in response to budget deficits (Hershey 1989). Bush's approval ratings briefly soared in the wake of the Gulf War of 1991, when the United States liberated Kuwait, but his popularity quickly fell again as the nation's economic troubles became the focus of public attention. Voters sacked Bush in 1992, largely for failing to preside over a healthy economy (Germond and Witcover 1993; Gillon 2002).

Bill Clinton, who followed George H. W. Bush as president, fashioned his public image as a working class hero from an Arkansas community he described as "a place called Hope." The nation's forty-second president came to office facing numerous challenges. Although the Cold War was over, it had been replaced by a series of foreign policy difficulties involving such diverse nations as Haiti, Somalia, and Iraq, along with the former Soviet Union, which had splintered into more than a dozen struggling republics. The federal budget deficit had more than quadrupled since 1980, and Congress, which often hesitated to take on Ronald Reagan, was challenging the executive branch with renewed vigor (Campbell and Rockman 1996; Drew 1994; Woodward 1994).

Bill Clinton tried to cast himself in the Horatio Alger role of an all-American small-town boy who succeeded by his own skill and hard work. But the role was a less-than-perfect fit. Although he grew up in far less privileged circumstances than either President Bush, Clinton attended some of the world's leading academic institutions: Yale, Georgetown, and Oxford, where he was a Rhodes Scholar. He had also acquired a reputation in some circles as a political opportunist. Clinton's opponents dubbed him "Slick Willie," a political grifter who was loyal to nothing and no one but himself (Edwards 1996).

Thus, Clinton's political enemies tried to rewrite his personal narrative as that of an arrogant and out-of-touch liberal elitist who had lost touch with his childhood roots. In 1995, Newt Gingrich of Georgia became the first Republican Speaker of the U.S. House in four decades after portraying Clinton in just this fashion, using the president's mammoth health care plan as exhibit A (Burnham 1996; Skocpol 1997). In his second term, Clinton handed his partisan enemies even more ammunition when citizens learned of a dalliance with Monica Lewinsky, a twenty-one-year-old White House intern (I. Morris 2002; Sabato et al. 2000).

Eight years after voters fired his father, George W. Bush campaigned for the role of national "best buddy," offering a friendly demeanor and promises of moderately conservative policies, higher moral standards, and lower taxes (Ceaser and Busch 2001; Dimock 2004; Hershey 2001). Following a Supreme Court decision that halted a recount in Florida, Bush took office at the end of the most controversial presidential selection process in over a century (Bugliosi 2001; Sunstein and Epstein 2001). The second President Bush faced a deeply divided public but initially enjoyed Republican majorities in the House and Senate—until Sen. James Jeffords left the GOP, giving control of the upper chamber back to the Democrats (Jeffords 2003).

However well the role of national "best buddy" may have fit Bush, it was not to be the dominant image of his public presidency for very long. Before his first year as president was out, the United States suffered the most devastating terrorist attack in its history. Almost immediately, Bush's public image was transformed into that of a warrior president. Under Bush's direction, the U.S. military helped Afghan rebels destroy the Taliban, driving its remnants and those of al Qaeda's terrorist militia into hiding (Abramson et al. 2002; Booth 2002; Sabato 2002; Woodward 2002). Bush then led the country into a quick military victory over Iraq and deposed its dictator, Saddam Hussein.

As the 2004 election approached, however, criticism of Bush mounted over whether he told the public the truth about Iraq's alleged stockpiles of chemical and biological weapons of mass destruction (Pollack 2004). The continuing loss of life among U.S. troops and the problem-filled occupation of Iraq also raised questions about the president's capacity to manage foreign policy (Fallows 2004). The public presentation of Bush as a warrior president (cf. Woodward 2002; Frum 2003) was also undermined by Democrats who alleged that the president had failed to fulfill his duties in the National Guard during the Vietnam War (Roig-Franzia and Romano 2004).

## Channels of Communication: Presidents Face the Camera

Whatever roles recent presidents tried to play, or had thrust upon them, they sought to craft their public images through a common channel: an independent news media dominated by the big three television networks (ABC, CBS, and NBC) and—to a lesser extent—by national newspapers like the *New York Times* and the *Washington Post*. Since the 1960s, the networks' evening news shows, the national newspapers, and the other news organizations that followed their lead have been the lenses through which many citizens view government (T. Cook 1998; Farnsworth and Lichter 2003a; Graber 2002; Iyengar 1991; Sparrow 1999).

Of course, the media environment has changed markedly since the Reagan era. The most visible changes include the rise of cable news, talk radio, and the Internet. Nonetheless, the broadcast networks and the elite newspapers remain the loudest voices amid the growing media cacophony. The new outlets did not displace the older ones; they simply offered a wider variety of choices for contemporary news consumers (Davis 1999; Davis and Owen 1998; Farnsworth and Lichter 2003a; Farnsworth and Owen 2004; Seib 2001). From the perspective of newsmakers, however, the media became an echo chamber that never stopped reverberating as the various organs amplified and sometimes distorted each other's messages.

Today we live in a dizzying world of media "spin," in which politicians, journalists, and interest groups continually compete to define the public agenda by shaping the news. Nowhere are the stakes higher than at the White House, where political operatives and journalists battle over the mediation of the presidency (Bernstein and Woodward 1974; Deakin 1983; Fitzwater 1995; Han 2001; Kurtz 1994). Presidents dominate television news coverage of government; they are the communicators in chief of contemporary American politics (Waterman et al. 1999). Sometimes, but less frequently than they wish, they also are the interpreters in chief of the political scene.

White House staffs have sought to manipulate media coverage for decades, recognizing that a president who looks good in the media is more likely to succeed. To that end, they present events in ways designed to maximize media coverage of good news and minimize coverage of bad news, to substitute their boss's perspective for the "framing" done by reporters and producers (Dimock 2004; Hollihan 2001; Paletz 2002; Patterson 1994). Since the vast majority of information about presidential performance received by ordinary citizens is mediated information, the television networks play a vitally important linkage role in the process of governance—arguably more important than the government officials themselves (cf. T. Cook 1998).

Presidents who mastered the media arts of the public presidency—such as Kennedy, Reagan, and Clinton—enjoyed considerable popularity during much of their time in the White House. Their personal popularity helped boost their legislative agendas and sustain them in crises, such as the Bay of Pigs invasion, the Iran-contra affair, and the Clinton-Lewinsky scandal, respectively (Han 2001). Other presidents, such as Carter and George H. W. Bush, have been less successful in shaping perceptions of the policy environment. Instead, they ended up being defined by the media. Thus, the first President Bush's inability to present himself as an articulate, compassionate leader helped doom his 1992 reelection campaign (Han 2001).

## Presidents as Communicators in Chief: From Partisan Newspapers to "Dot-Gov"

In the beginning of presidential communication, there was the word. Even before the United States became a nation, our founders sought to transmit their message to the world through the very deliberate use of language. The Declaration of Independence spelled out their vision of the new nation in its second paragraph: "We hold these Truths to be self-evident, that all Men are created equal, that they are endowed by their Creator with certain unalienable Rights, that among these are Life, Liberty and the Pursuit of Happiness." The founders realized, like so many political leaders before and since, that a political movement not defined clearly at the outset will be defined later by others.

Indeed, the wording of the Declaration demonstrates how badly the delegates wanted to present themselves as reasonable men, who rebelled only because conditions under Britain's King George III had become intolerable. Once the American Revolution was won, the Constitution demonstrated the same commitment to a clear public presentation: it begins, "We the people of the United States," establishing the bedrock principle that political authority in this new land rests with the people, not a king. The founders also explicitly rejected the thought in some quarters that political authority rests with the individual states that ultimately became part of the "more perfect union" they envisioned (Carey 1989).

The nation's first president did not have to struggle to create a public persona. George Washington was already recognized as the hero of the age—the commanding general of the Revolutionary War who could have seized power but did not, because of his love for republican government. The presidential office itself was not particularly well formed in the Constitution. As the new nation's first president, Washington helped create the public image of a president as a dignified "national father" who was above the petty partisan squabbles of Congress (Genovese 2001). He also lacked the temperament of a demagogue or populist agitator—a personality type that generated grave concern among the nation's founding intellectuals (Tulis 1989). Indeed, many historians believe Washington's most important contribution to the new government was to leave it peacefully and with dignity after two terms, establishing the precedent that the office is greater than the person who occupies it (Genovese 2001).

We cannot say how Washington would have fared facing the microphones and cameras of today's electronic media. As a national icon, however, he was treated far gentler by the newspapers of his day than were his immediate successors (C. Smith 1977). Both John Adams and Thomas Jefferson were fierce partisans who led tribes of loyalists no less hostile toward each other than Republicans and Democrats in today's so-called red versus blue America. Adams was so outraged by criticism from his opponents' partisan newspapers that he secured passage of the Alien and Sedition Acts, which called for fines and imprisonment of those who published "any scandalous or malicious writing or writings against the Government of the United States" that could bring government officials "into contempt or disrepute" (C. Smith 1977). Jefferson ran for president partly in opposition to the acts, and they fell into disuse after he took office and pardoned those who had been convicted under its provisions.

As much as Adams's successors may have been tempted at times to criminalize dissent, the ability of the president to manipulate the press expanded with the growth of the White House staff in the latter two-thirds of the twentieth century. While the presidency always provided a "bully pulpit," public presidencies for most of U.S. history relied largely on the public relations skills of the president himself (Tulis 1987). In the pretelevision era, there was some disagreement over how much the media even mattered. Richard Neustadt's *Presidential Power*, arguably the most significant study of the presidency ever written, treated the news media almost as an afterthought when it was first published in 1960 (Neustadt 1990).

Before the expansion of the executive branch during the New Deal, presidents had few aides, and their aides rarely had much experience in public relations (Burke 2003; Hess 1996). Of course, the less combative press of the past needed less tending. At times journalists went so far as to hide from the public vital information on the state of the president's health (R. Smith 2001). In 1944, reporters failed to warn the nation of the precarious health of a rapidly declining Franklin Delano Roosevelt. In 1960, reporters failed to follow up on claims by Richard Nixon that John F. Kennedy had a variety of debilitating health problems (Burns and Dunn 2001; R. Smith 2001). Of course, the public never saw photos of Roosevelt in a wheelchair during his lifetime; reporters and photographers were complicit in efforts to minimize public awareness of the president's severe paralysis (Goodwin 1994).

Despite aggressive coverage of the Clinton sex scandals, throughout much of U.S. history the press did not report on personal foibles of political leaders, including cases of alcoholic senators and affair-prone presidents (Sabato 1993; Sabato et al. 2000). For example, John Kennedy's affair with a woman with organized-crime connections could have seriously compromised his presidency. Thus, if journalists sometimes go too far in pursuing scandals today, they may not have gone far enough in the past.

The media environment of the twenty-first century provides new opportunities for presidents and other political leaders to reach the public by going over, under, and around the mainstream press. Internet-savvy citizens can read presidential statements and administration position papers online, free from any editing by reporters. Fans of C-SPAN can spend hours watching unmediated events as they take place in Washington, from daily on-camera appearances by administration officials to the daily slog of legislation through the legislative labyrinth of Capitol Hill. While efforts to use the 24/7 cable news channels have been a prominent part of political media strategies at least since Ross Perot's independent presidential campaign of 1992, political figures can be both beneficiaries and victims of the new media environment.

Table 1.1 offers comparisons for news media use patterns among citizens from 1992 through 2004. As you can see, television has dominated the public's news attention throughout the period, with more than three-quarters of respondents saying that television was their dominant news source in 2004. Newspapers remain in a clear second place, well ahead of radio, the Internet, and newsmagazines like *Time* and *Newsweek*. (Because respondents can list up to two news sources, the results do not add up to 100 percent.) The greatest gains over the past four years were found in the online arena, where the number of people using the Internet as an important news site nearly doubled.

| TABLE I.I | Media Use Trends, 1992–2004 |
|---|---|

Question: "How did you get most of your news about the presidential election campaign—from television, from newspapers, from radio, from magazines, or from the Internet?" [Accept two answers. If only one response is given, probe for one additional response.]

[If the respondent answered television, ask:]

(2004) Did you get most of your news about the presidential election campaign from: (randomized list) local news programming, ABC Network news, CBS Network news, NBC Network news, CNN cable news, MSNBC cable news, the Fox News cable channel, CNBC cable news?" [Accept up to two answers.]

(1992–2000): "Did you get most of your news about the presidential campaign from network TV news, from local TV news, or from cable news networks such as CNN or MSNBC?" [Accept up to two answers.]

(Results in Percentages)

|  | 2004 | 2000 | 1996 | 1992 |
|---|---|---|---|---|
| Television (overall) | 76 | 70 | 72 | 82 |
| Network | 29 | 22 | 36 | 55 |
| Local | 12 | 21 | 23 | 29 |
| Cable | 40 | 36 | 21 | 29 |
| Newspapers | 46 | 39 | 60 | 7 |
| Radio | 22 | 15 | 19 | 12 |
| Magazines | 6 | 4 | 11 | 9 |
| Internet | 21 | 11 | 3 | n/a |
| Other | 2 | 1 | 4 | 6 |
| Don't Know/Refused | 1 | * | 1 | 1 |

*Less than 0.5 percent.
*Source:* Pew Research Center for the People and the Press (Pew 2000b, 2004c)
*Note:* Because two answers were accepted, columns do not add up to 100 percent.

But the range of material found online can be dramatic. Some Internet journalists, exemplified by Matt Drudge, see themselves as avatars of a new media age in which everyone can be his own editor and publisher (Drudge 2000). Drudge, who rose to prominence by breaking the Clinton-Lewinsky scandal, has come under fire for publicizing erroneous information that is subsequently spread by mainstream media outlets (Hall 2001; Seib 2001). The absence of gatekeepers that Drudge loves about cyberspace also calls into question the credibility of some material found online (Seib 2001). Other online media sources are simply the cyberspace offshoots of off-line media, like washington post.com.

In addition, the ability of online media to critique the content of off-line media offers a new way for more critical voices outside mainstream media to be heard, and researchers are only beginning to consider how these online critics—known as "bloggers"—can affect public relations strategies of government officials and individual politicians (Hall 2001; Klotz 2004). We will return to the opportunities and pitfalls presidents may face in this new media environment in our final chapter.

## The Contemporary White House Communications Operation

The business of promoting the president and his agenda has come a long way since President Franklin Roosevelt's "fireside chats" in the early 1930s. During the Great Depression, Roosevelt took advantage of the then-new medium of radio to speak to the nation over coast-to-coast broadcasts to reassure the troubled country (Goodwin 1994). Two decades later, television greatly enhanced the opportunity for political leaders to reach the citizenry. Despite being known for his "hidden-hand presidency," President Dwight Eisenhower pioneered the use of television for both campaign advertising and presenting policy initiatives (Greenstein 1982; Kumar 2003b).

But Eisenhower's understudy was even more aggressive. When Richard Nixon's position as Ike's running mate was threatened by charges that he improperly accepted gifts, Nixon responded with the famous Checkers speech. In that nationally televised appeal, Nixon portrayed his critics as partisan grinches who would even prevent his little daughter from keeping a dog (a spaniel named Checkers) that she had received as a gift (Aitken 1993). After losing the 1960 election to a more media-savvy John F. Kennedy (Druckman 2003), Nixon was elected president in 1968, partly because of an aggressive media management strategy that scripted his television appearances (McGinniss 1969).

Today nearly all White House officials must consider public communication matters as part of their workday. But three high-ranking officials in particular assist the chief executive in disseminating the president's message—the chief of staff, the director of communications, and the press secretary (Kumar 2001, 2003a). The press secretary is the official spokesperson for the White House. He or she meets with reporters regularly—sometimes several times a day—to answer questions about the latest issues in the news. Press secretaries and their deputies try to direct reporters' attention toward stories the president wants covered and away from those he wants to avoid.

In addition, they try to frame stories in ways that benefit the administration and selectively provide information in ways designed to advance the president's legislative and political priorities (Kumar 2003a, 2003b; Nelson 2003). The position is a challenging one. A press secretary risks angering the president by saying too much about an unpopular topic, and he may anger reporters by saying too little (Kumar 2001). If a press secretary is seen as uninformed or dishonest, reporters lose trust in the administration's pronouncements, and that can lead to critical news coverage (Kumar 2001; Nelson 2003).

The press secretary's frequent availability to the press makes it difficult to engage in long-term communications planning. The White House director of communications and the chief of staff take the lead in this longer-term framing of presidential communications (Kumar 2001). These plans showcase the president, tout administration accomplishments, and emphasize presidential priorities.

If a public event can be designed to produce emotionally powerful pictures—like Ronald Reagan speaking at Normandy, France, to commemorate the fortieth anniversary of D-Day, or George W. Bush speaking atop the rubble of the World Trade Center after the 9/11 attacks—it can have a powerful effect on public opinion (Frum 2003; Gergen

2000). Similarly, meetings with foreign leaders serve to remind citizens that the president is America's head of state rather than merely its most powerful politician. Indeed, every public meeting and "photo opportunity" with the president is scheduled with the intent to build political capital one way or another.

If an administration does not have a strong media operation, the president risks losing control not only over his public image but also over his administration's political agenda. Indeed, most presidents invest great care to use the great natural media advantages the executive branch has over the legislative branch. Above all, the administration speaks with a single voice, while Capitol Hill can sound like a disorganized din of 535 disparate individuals. Even a unified party in Congress represents only part of the legislative branch, while the president's position always carries the day in the executive branch. As an officeholder elected nationwide, a president also commands far greater media interest than even the House Speaker or Senate Majority Leader. As presidential scholar Martha Kumar writes,

> A president needs an effective communications operation for both defensive and offensive reasons. He needs to define himself and his programs and to keep to a minimum threat level the efforts of others to portray him in terms not of his choosing. (Kumar 2003b:675)

Failure to manage the media effectively deprives a modern president of one of his greatest advantages over the divided legislative branch. Troubles with media management sometimes produce desperate responses. Bill Clinton's rocky first few weeks in the White House led to his decision to hire David Gergen, a moderate Republican, to assist the first Democratic administration in twelve years in getting its message out. Several senior members of the Clinton administration, particularly the more liberal ones, objected to the influence that Gergen and White House pollster Dick Morris had over the president's media and policy strategies (Blumenthal 2003; Gergen 2000; Reich 1998; Stephanopoulos 1999; Woodward 1994, 1999). Similarly, when President George W. Bush seemed to be losing the public relations war to Democratic presidential candidates in early 2004, he proposed a manned space mission back to the moon and ultimately to Mars. However, that effort to rekindle the Kennedy-era spirit of a "new frontier" failed to capture the public's imagination and quickly faded from view.

Presidential events are often carefully scripted to play to a president's natural advantages. Bill Clinton, who possessed a quick mind and engaging demeanor, frequently used town hall meetings to get coverage for his projects (Kurtz 1994, 1998; Kumar 2003b). George W. Bush, who is less comfortable and less articulate in unscripted settings, held roughly half as many press conferences during the first three years of his term as did Bill Clinton (Kumar 2003b). Bush favors more-planned events—such as appearances before crowds of military personnel, whose presence emphasizes the president's responsibilities as commander in chief (Dimock 2004). Any appeal to the "symbolic politics" of the presidency may be beneficial, especially in the emotionally charged political environment since September 11, 2001 (Gregg 2004; but see Adler 2003 and Jacobson 2003 for alternative views).

Of course, reporters do not simply accept whatever information they are given and pass it along to their audience (Kurtz 1994). White House reporters are among the most experienced journalists in the country. They can be quite aggressive in their questioning of the press secretary, whom they see regularly, and the president, whom they can question far less frequently. Journalists and scholars both speak of a vigorous tug-of-war between the White House and the press corps over the release of information, particularly when it comes from the president himself (Jacobs 2003; Kurtz 1994). Some researchers even argue that we should envision the news media as the fourth branch of government, comparable in influence and in independence to the executive, legislative, and judicial branches (cf. T. Cook 1998).

Thus, there is a natural "life cycle" to relations between the president and the media, just as there is between the White House and Congress. This cycle is described by presidential scholar Stephen Hess, who also served on the White House staffs of two presidents:

> The start of a presidency is a time of fermentation. New people and new ideas arrive in Washington, and, from a reporter's point of view, this is a good time to get stories. From the president's vantage point, these stories tend to be favorable. Then the administration has its first foreign crisis or its first domestic scandal, weaknesses in personnel and organization begin to appear, and the novelty of new personalities wears off.

These things make for good stories for reporters, but they are no longer favorable to the president. Ultimately, president and press, having mutual needs, learn to live with each other like an old married couple who can no longer surprise one another. Finally, the reporters will begin to look forward to the next president, and the process will start again. (Hess 1996:122–23)

## Past Research: Coverage of Government

Previous studies of government coverage have established some findings that provide a baseline for our research. First, political news has fallen dramatically in recent decades. For example, in 1977 nearly three-quarters of the stories on ABC's evening newscast focused on political news; in 1997 fewer than half did (Graber 2002:274). Among seven national media outlets examined in that study, only the *New York Times* increased its political coverage (Graber 2002:274).

Second, the presidency routinely receives the bulk of the coverage. As commander in chief of the world's sole remaining superpower, as legislator in chief when it comes to setting the agenda, and as the head of a largely unified branch of government (particularly when compared to a Congress divided by partisan conflict), the president and his staff are very useful sources of the information reporters need for their stories (Lowi 1985; Waterman et al. 1999). Much of what Congress does, in contrast, is tentative or ambiguous, and therefore less newsworthy. A presidential pronouncement about a policy is far more definitive than a lawmaker's unveiling of a bill that may not pass in either chamber of Congress, or survive a conference committee, or be signed into law by the president (Graber 2002).

For example, a study of one year during the Clinton administration found that the president received 60 percent of all television news coverage of the national government. That was twice as much as Congress received, leaving less than 10 percent of the government news hole for the Supreme Court (Graber 2002:275). Earlier research likewise found patterns of far more extensive media coverage of the executive than the legislative branch, with the judicial branch functioning as an afterthought, especially for television reporters (Grossman and Kumar 1981; Hess 1981; Kaid and Foote 1985; Lichter and Amundson 1994).

The executive branch's dominance is not as overwhelming in print. A study of *New York Times* and *Washington Post* articles in 1979 found that the president was the focus of 51 percent of the news reports on the federal government and Congress 36 percent, with the remainder dealing with both branches (Rutkus 1991). This trend may be even less apparent in papers located far from the corridors of power. One study of Washington stories that appeared in twenty-two newspapers during 1978 found that slightly more articles focused on Congress than on the president (Hess 1981:98).

The third major finding of past research is that the news about the president has become more negative in recent decades (cf. Farnsworth and Lichter 2003a; Kerbel 1995; Patterson 1994; Sabato 1993). One strong current of research in this area has developed under the concept of "media malaise," the idea that exposure to contemporary media, and particularly television, can increase citizen cynicism and negativity regarding government (cf. M. Robinson 1976).

Historical studies provide a powerful contrast with the negativity that has dominated media coverage of government during the past quarter century. One study found that print coverage of the president from 1953 to 1978 and network news coverage from 1968 to 1978 showed a consistently favorable portrayal of the president (Grossman and Kumar 1981). At CBS, for example, there was almost twice as much positive as negative coverage—45 percent to 24 percent (with the rest neutral)—from 1974 to 1978 (Grossman and Kumar 1981:265). This is particularly notable for a period that included such polarizing stories as the Vietnam War, Watergate, and the oil crisis and stagflation of the 1970s. Another study of the *CBS Evening News* from 1968 to 1985 found a trend of rising negative coverage for presidents, regardless of their party (Smoller 1986).

The tone of presidential news coverage can vary substantially from one outlet to another. For example, Ronald Reagan's proposals to cut taxes were treated far more negatively in the *New York Times* than in a local newspaper, the *Durham (NC) Morning Herald* (Paletz and Guthrie 1987). Similarly, the three broadcast networks took different approaches to reporting rising and falling presidential approval poll ratings from 1990 to 1995 (Groeling and Kernell 1998).

Contemporary presidents have a powerful incentive to use the media to build public support. "Going public" is an increasingly popular way to break up legislative logjams that tie up a president's initiatives on Capitol Hill, by helping to convince uncertain lawmakers to support the White House (Kernell 1997). An individual lawmaker, even a party leader, is far less able to attract sufficient press attention (and consequent voter interest) than a president who uses his domination of the nation's airwaves and news columns to advance his agenda (Alger 1996; Lowi 1985). However, this does not mean that the president consistently prevails on Capitol Hill. Much of the research on presidential-congressional relations suggests that presidential influence is not dominant, but is found "on the margins" of policymaking (cf. Edwards 1989, 2003; Edwards and Wood 1999).

## LEGISLATIVE BRANCH COVERAGE

Television news coverage of the legislative branch has been falling as well, according to several studies. Network television news presented more than two hundred stories mentioning Congress during April 1975, but less than one hundred during April 1985 (Ornstein and M. Robinson 1986). The number of congressional stories on evening newscasts during the month of April dropped by two-thirds from the 1972–1978 to the 1986–1992 period (Lichter and Amundson 1994). Similarly, the networks ran only half as many stories about Congress during the summer of 1989 as they did during the summer of 1979 (Rutkus 1991).

Like that of the executive branch, the tone of congressional coverage has also turned more negative over time (Asher and Barr 1994; T. Cook 1989). On the network evening newscasts, three-quarters of all evaluations of Congress were negative in 1972, as were seven-eighths of all such statements in 1982, and nine-tenths in 1992 (Lichter and Amundson 1994:135–37). This trend toward greater negativity has also been documented for stories in weekly newsmagazines like *Time*, *Newsweek*, and *U.S. News & World Report* and in elite papers like the *New York Times*, the *Washington Post*, and the *Wall Street Journal* (Rozell 1994).

Some studies have found periods with less negative trends. A comparison of newspaper coverage of Congress in 1979 and 1989, for example, found negative coverage outnumbered positive coverage by a

10-to-1 ratio in 1979 but only a 2-to-1 ratio ten years later (Rutkus 1991). However, the bulk of the evidence points in the opposite direction. As political scientist Mark Rozell concludes, "Over the years, press coverage of Congress has moved from healthy skepticism to outright cynicism" (Rozell 1994:59). Given such pervasive media negativity, it should come as no surprise that Congress is a favorite target for citizen discontent with government (Craig 1993, 1996; Hibbing and Theiss-Morse 1995; Farnsworth 2001, 2003a, 2003b).

While coverage of Congress in the news media may help or hurt individual politicians, it may be especially damaging to the institution itself: "By treating Congress poorly but its incumbents relatively well, [the media] may be strengthening incumbents but weakening their institution" (M. Robinson 1981:92–93). Indeed, much of the academic research relating to public opinion regarding Congress pays great attention to what is known as "Fenno's paradox," after Richard Fenno's observation that citizens dislike Congress as a collective but feel much more favorably toward their own representatives (Craig 1993; Farnsworth 2003a, 2003b; Fenno 1975; Hibbing and Theiss-Morse 1995). In fact, members frequently blame the institution of Congress for their problems in their own districts (Craig 1993). Media coverage of Congress reinforces this negative image of the congressional collective, even as coverage tends to present individual members in a favorable light (Arnold 2004; Asher and Barr 1994; T. Cook 1989; Lichter and Amundson 1994; M. Robinson 1981).

Of course, not all lawmakers are treated equally in the media. National news outlets focus their coverage on senators with leadership roles, such as the majority and minority leaders, committee chairs, and ranking members (Hess 1986). The same pattern of focusing on dominant lawmakers holds for network news coverage of the House (T. Cook 1989). As a result, most members of Congress receive little national coverage, though they are much more likely to be featured by their local media (Alger 1996). Their "hometown" coverage is usually far more positive than that of the national media (Hess 1991).

## JUDICIAL BRANCH COVERAGE

The judiciary attracts only a fraction of the coverage afforded the two more publicly oriented branches of government. The media take little notice of any courts other than the Supreme Court, which itself receives surprisingly little media attention. For example, during a yearlong period in 1999 and 2000, ABC devoted 280 minutes to presidential stories, 165 minutes to congressional stories, and only 46 minutes to stories involving the Supreme Court (Graber 2002:310–11). An earlier study found that from 1969 to 1983, the judicial branch received only 4 percent of the national government coverage on CBS, 10 percent in the *Los Angeles Times*, and 8 percent in the *Syracuse Post-Standard*, an important regional paper in upstate New York (Davis 1987).

Many important legal stories and judicial decisions are missed in such a low-coverage environment. One study found that fewer than one in four Supreme Court rulings were reported on any network evening newscast in 1989, and this fell to one in six rulings in 1994 (Slotnick and Segal 1998). Even the nation's "newspaper of record," the *New York Times*, did not report on nearly one-quarter of the Supreme Court's decisions in 1974 and failed to provide what the researchers considered "essential" information for an additional one-third of the Court's decisions (Ericson 1977).

Many scholars have argued that the refusal of the Supreme Court to admit cameras into the courtroom, together with the justices' unwillingness to hold on-the-record news conferences, discourages television coverage of the Court (Davis 1994; Graber 2002). Ironically, this strategy of minimizing the Court's public profile may help explain why the Court has unusually high citizen support, far higher than that of the executive or legislative branches (Farnsworth 2003a). In contrast to the negative and sometimes voyeuristic coverage of the inner workings of the White House and Congress, the Supreme Court has preserved some aura of mystery.

## Consequences of Coverage: Declining Political Knowledge and Trust?

There is no definitive survey or critical experiment that shows how much news, how many details, or how much exposure to government is "enough" to produce either a minimally or optimally informed citizenry. But the existing evidence shows that even small changes in television news content can influence perceptions of issues and governmental figures (Cappella and Jamieson 1997; Farnsworth and Lichter 2003a, 2003b; Iyengar and Kinder 1987; Iyengar 1991).

Changes identified by past researchers, to be sure, are not small. The declining volume of governmental news has negative consequences for the polity, according to many media analysts (cf. Edelman 1985; Jamieson 2000; Patterson 2000; Postman 1985; Putnam 1995, 2000). Experimental evidence strongly supports the proposition that less substantive news coverage increases public cynicism. "When journalists frame political events strategically, they activate existing beliefs and understandings; they do not need to create them" (Cappella and Jamieson 1997:208). But research in this area has not identified a precise threshold where audience effects become observable in experimental settings.

The single most important trend in public opinion regarding the national government over the past several decades has been the steady public conviction that government officials are not worthy of much respect. Starting with public frustration over government deceit during the Vietnam War, and deepening in the wake of the Watergate scandal, growing numbers of Americans decided that the government simply could not be trusted. In the 2000 American National Election Study (ANES), only 44 percent of those surveyed said the national government could be "trusted to do what is right" most of the time, down from 78 percent in 1964. And even this figure was an increase from the 32 percent who expressed trust in government in 1996. In fact, the 1972 ANES survey marked the last presidential election year when at least half the people surveyed thought the government could be trusted to do the right thing most of the time (Farnsworth 2003a).

The downward trend is found among all generational groups, and the nation's youngest voters—those in their twenties and thirties who grew up after the baby boom—were the most likely to distrust government in 2000. The baby boomers, who were born between 1943 and 1960, were the second-most-negative generational group (Farnsworth 2003b). Public support for government increased in the immediate aftermath of the 9/11 terrorist attacks; but within months of the destruction of the World Trade Center, bin Laden was replaced by the economy as the voters' top concern (Stevenson and Elder 2002; Kohut

2002). By the time George W. Bush sought reelection in earnest, both his personal approval and trust in government had fallen to where they were before the attacks (Edwards 2004).

More than three decades ago, political scientists looking at discontent with government concluded that a well-functioning government relies on two kinds of support from its citizens. The first is "diffuse support," a fundamental attachment to the political system as a whole. The second is "specific support," explicit evaluations of governmental performance in particular areas, like the economy or national defense (Easton and Dennis 1969). Frustration and anger with government officials and their policies may reduce support for these particular officeholders, without affecting an underlying belief in the institutions of the American political system.

In fact, a diffuse but profound emotional attachment to political institutions more or less holds the society together, permitting it to survive crises and to tackle difficult problems (Easton 1975). High levels of diffuse support enable government officials to convince citizens to undergo inconvenient and sometimes dangerous personal hardships, ranging from paying taxes to military service, for the sake of advancing or maintaining the political system (Easton and Dennis 1969:62–64).

Increasingly, researchers have looked to the mass media for possible explanations of growing citizen distrust and alienation from government (cf. Hetherington and Globetti 2003). However, no consensus about this possible link has yet emerged. Part of the reason for the continued debate among scholars stems from a shortage of content analysis data that analyzes the media images of individuals and institutions separately—a deficiency that we try to address in this book.

Some scholars argue that mass media outlets undermine public respect for government through their trivialization of news and their growing skepticism toward government officials (cf. Bennett 2001; Cappella and Jamieson 1997; Neuman 1986; Patterson 2002; Postman 1985; Putnam 2000; Sabato 1993). Others assert that the news media maintain public support for government by helping citizens make rational evaluations of their government and its leaders (cf. Graber 1988; Page and Shapiro 1992; Popkin 1991).

A third school of thought, more critical of the current political system, argues that the media protect the political system even as reporters criticize individual politicians. From this perspective, television news and newspapers act as "boundary-maintaining" institutions that declare certain types of criticism too threatening for mass dissemination. Any media enhancement of public support for government excludes and therefore marginalizes critical voices outside the official power structure (cf. Gitlin 1980). So, by calling on only a narrow range of sources, media outlets mold the views of the mass public to reflect elite values (Ginsberg 1986; Iyengar and Kinder 1987).

The "episodic" nature of news conventions keeps television in particular from becoming an agent of serious criticism, according to political scientist Shanto Iyengar (1991). Because news on television is often disconnected from previous or subsequent events that might provide some context, it is more difficult to assess the government's performance than it would be if coverage were more "thematic," that is, one that contextualizes the new information (Iyengar 1991). Other researchers, however, argue that voters receive enough information to engage in "gut reasoning" and therefore know enough to make effective decisions (Popkin 1991).

Finally, the media's role in creating distrust in government may be limited by the growing mistrust that the public also feels for the media. For example, every four years, the Pew Research Center asks the public to grade the performance of the participants in the presidential election that just ended. They routinely give the news media lower grades than the parties, the candidates, the pollsters, and even the much-criticized campaign consultants (Pew 2000c). From 1988 to 2000, on a scale from zero (F) to four (A) reporters' "grade point average" varied from D+ (1.7) to a straight C (2.0), hardly a vote of public confidence (Farnsworth and Lichter 2003a:7).

## Research Design

This book examines news media coverage of the four most recent presidents: Ronald Reagan, George H. W. Bush, Bill Clinton, and George W. Bush. The primary research method is content analysis, a social science technique that classifies (or "codes") information in a systematic and reliable fashion. Content analysis uses a set of explicit rules and procedures to minimize subjective judgments. This approach replaces everyday anecdotal media criticism, which may be based on unrepresentative examples or subject to personal preconceptions and partisan allegiances.

The conclusions of our content analysis are based on a sentence-by-sentence examination of a systematic sample of news stories. The examinations were conducted by trained coders whose judgments follow the same specified procedures, and the results were tested to make sure that different coders came to the same conclusions, regardless of their personal backgrounds and beliefs. It is possible to obtain high levels of agreement between coders, formally called intercoder reliability, because they are following rules rather than expressing their own opinions. For all variables in this study, intercoder agreement was at least 80 percent, and it was usually much higher. Among the topics we covered were the amount of coverage, the individuals and institutions upon which the news focuses, the issues that are dealt with, the sources who are cited, and the nature and tone of all evaluations of officials and institutions.

Our study draws from extensive content analyses of television coverage of presidential governance conducted over the years by the Center for Media and Public Affairs, a nonpartisan media research institute based in Washington, DC. These data, which cover various periods from Ronald Reagan's presidency through George W. Bush's, provide a quantitative portrait of how government news has changed over the past quarter century.

This book emphasizes the news content of the first year of three distinctly different administrations: 1981 (Reagan administration), 1993 (Clinton administration), and 2001 (George W. Bush administration). All three years marked a change in partisan control of the White House. Two Republican presidents (Ronald Reagan and George W. Bush) took office following Democratic defeats in 1980 and 2000, and a Democratic president (Bill Clinton) took office after a Republican defeat in 1992.

The first year of a presidency is a time of heightened media attention to the government's agenda and activities, especially after a partisan turnover that redirects government policy. We studied all coverage of the federal government, including the president and his staff, the cabinet, any agency of the executive branch, the U.S. Congress, the Supreme Court, and all other federal courts. We excluded the uniformed military services but included all civilian bodies involved in military affairs, such as the Department of Defense. We included coverage of both institutions and the individuals who staffed or represented them.

Although presidents do not take office until January 20, presidents-elect become the focus of governmental coverage well before the inauguration ceremony. We therefore include stories about the incoming administration starting January 1. This enables us to examine the media's initial reception of the incoming president's proposed agenda and his cabinet nominees and other appointments. It also provides a comparable twelve-month sample across political institutions, since the new Congress is organized shortly after New Year's Day. (Stories about the outgoing, lame-duck administrations were dropped from the analysis.)

For 1981, 1993, and 2001, we examined government coverage on network evening news shows (ABC's *World News Tonight*, CBS's *Evening News*, and NBC's *Nightly News*), and in all front-page stories of two national newspapers (the *Washington Post* and the *New York Times*) and four highly regarded regional newspapers (the *Austin American-Statesman*, the *Des Moines Register*, the *San Jose Mercury News*, and the *St. Petersburg Times*). Stories were included if they devoted at least one-third of their length to the federal government. For the regional newspapers, we examined staff-written stories about national government but excluded stories originating from the national papers and wire services.

Over the course of the three years we examined in depth, the evening newscasts on ABC, CBS, and NBC aired more than 16,000 stories on the national government, representing more than four hundred hours of airtime—almost eight minutes a night on average for each network. To these we added more than 13,000 front-page newspaper stories, for an overall sample of nearly 30,000 stories during these years.

To fill out this portrait of the modern mediated presidency, we also examined all network newscasts during the first four years of the George W. Bush presidency, the full eight years of Bill Clinton's tenure, and the full four years of George H. W. Bush's service as president. We also included special case studies of key news events such as the Iran-contra scandal, the Clinton-Lewinsky scandal, and America's wars against Iraq in 1991 and 2003. We also provide an extensive analysis of network news coverage of economic matters during recent presidencies.

All told, this research project involves more than one hundred thousand news stories relating to the federal government over the past quarter century, one of the largest collections of analyzed news content in existence. We mined this data to determine whether the quality of coverage has declined over the past quarter century, as many critics have charged (Project for Excellence in Journalism 2004) and research on presidential election news has shown (cf. Farnsworth and Lichter 2003a; Patterson 1994).

In each case, we considered the changing amount of coverage overall and for each branch of government. We examined each story's focus on the job performance, personal character and ethics, political effectiveness, and other qualities of government officials. We analyzed the leading policy issues that were addressed and the sources who were used. We noted the location of all sources within the political environment—the various branches, former officials, think tank experts, and so on—as well as whether they were identified or remained anonymous.

Next, we compared the tone of the coverage of the individuals and institutions that make up the federal government, as well as the foreign and domestic policy issues they debated. Since allegations of partisan media bias are a staple of the political debate, we compared coverage of the sole Democratic administration with its Republican successor and predecessor, the treatment of Congress during periods of Democratic and Republican legislative control, and reporting on individual lawmakers from the two parties.

Our analysis is based primarily on individual statements or sound bites within each story. Although time-consuming and labor-intensive, this allowed us to analyze the building blocks of each story separately, rather than making summary judgments of entire stories. Instead of treating an entire story as "positive" or "negative" toward an individual or institution, we examined each evaluation within the story for its source, topic, object, and tone. A single story might contain several evaluations of various actors; our system captured each one individually. This produced a very detailed picture of the news media's treatment of government.

Evaluations were coded as positive or negative if they conveyed an unambiguous assessment or judgment about an individual, an institution, or an action. Only explicit evaluations were coded, evaluations in which both the target of the evaluation and its direction were clear. An example of a positive evaluation is the comment of a voter quoted on ABC: "I think that Bill Clinton represents the best hope that this nation has for a brighter future" (January 17, 1993). An example of a negative evaluation is this comment from NBC reporter Lisa Myers: "The president already had a reputation on the Hill for making contradictory promises and not keeping commitments. Now House members say even if he tells them the truth, they can't trust the president not to cave later under pressure" (June 10, 1993).

A description of events that reflected well or badly on some political actor was not coded for its tone unless it contained an evaluative comment. For example, an account of the passage of a bill supported by the president would be coded as positive only if a source or reporter explicitly described it as a victory for the White House, a validation of the president's views or efforts on its behalf, and so on.

News coverage of the executive branch has powerful effects on the public's perceptions of government. More favorable treatment of the executive than the legislative branch could create unrealistically high expectations for presidents, leading to presidential overpromising and public disillusionment (cf. Lowi 1985). Emphasis on certain issues and deemphasis of others helps set the public agenda, encouraging the public and its elected representatives to focus on issues that are most prominent in the news, regardless of their importance to the nation (Iyengar and Kinder 1987).

In addition, we look for evidence that bears on charges of media bias made by those on both the left and right (Alterman 2003; B. Goldberg 2002). The comparison of the many media outlets examined here allows for a far more focused assessment of which media outlets, if any, display a distinct partisan tilt and whether any bias is more pronounced in certain areas or at certain points during a president's term.

Of course, every presidency changes over time. The White House gains experience that can help it deal with Congress and the news media, as demonstrated by Bill Clinton's adopting a more centrist image after his health care reform bill was defeated in 1994. This helped him tar the Republican Congress as ideologically extreme during the federal government shutdowns in 1995 and 1996. The reverse can happen as well, as administrations that achieve early legislative victories become arrogant or complacent and myopically blunder into disaster. This pattern was illustrated by the Iran-contra affair during Ronald Reagan's second term (Neustadt 1990). This is why we consider the entire terms of office for these four presidents, insofar as our data permit.

## The Mediated Presidency: An Overview

The comprehensive data set developed for this book provides a systematic portrait of how news coverage has changed from one administration to another over the past quarter century. We consider the coverage of specific issues like the economy and foreign policy, as well as allegations of partisan bias and media negativity. In this opening chapter we have outlined the research project, the questions it is designed to answer, and the current state of our knowledge based on past research.

The second chapter focuses on the struggle between the executive and legislative branches for media attention. Federal judges are not elected and are far less concerned with media attention than other federal officials; their lack of interest is generally returned by journalists. We discuss major trends in presidential coverage since 1981, especially the president's dominance over Congress. Key topics here include the Clinton health care debate of 1993–1994; the congressional shutdown of the U.S. government during the 104th Congress (1995–1996); the "surrogate presidency" of Newt Gingrich's first hundred days as House Speaker in 1995; and the September 11, 2001, al Qaeda terrorist attacks and the subsequent U.S. attacks on Afghanistan and Iraq.

Chapter 2 also outlines the life cycle of relations between the president and the press, including the early "honeymoon" phase, the "hundred days" checkup, the typical midterm disappointments, and the summer distractions. In the cases of Bill Clinton and Ronald Reagan, the only presidents (as of this writing) to have served a full eight years in office since Eisenhower, we compare the coverage of their first and second terms.

Voters mainly evaluate government in general and presidents in particular along two dimensions: the economy and issues of war and peace. Of the two, the economy usually dominates public perceptions and media coverage. This subject, the topic of chapter 3, also dominates the policy agendas of most recent presidential administrations. Key topics analyzed here include Bill Clinton's struggle to pass his 1993 economic plan, George H. W. Bush's "read my lips" reversal on tax increases, Ronald Reagan's tax cuts and subsequent budget deficits, and George W. Bush's efforts to try to talk the country back into higher stock prices and economic prosperity during much of 2002 and 2003.

A key area of presidential responsibility is that of commander in chief. The last several presidents have faced dramatically different foreign policy challenges, which we discuss in chapter 4. Although they all struggled, in one way or another, with the Middle East, recent presidents have also faced various challenges in the Balkans, Northern Ireland, Somalia, Iraq, Afghanistan, and the Soviet Union and its successor nations. This chapter examines media coverage of President George W. Bush in the wake of the September 11, 2001, terrorist attacks, along with the subsequent U.S. invasions of Afghanistan and Iraq. The coverage of the 2001 terrorist attacks and the 2003 Iraqi war (and subsequent occupation) is compared to news reports of the crisis in Kosovo during Bill Clinton's administration and to the Persian Gulf War launched by President George H. W. Bush in 1991 following Iraq's invasion of Kuwait the previous year.

Another significant focus of presidential media coverage is a topic chief executives would rather not talk about: personal scandal. Chapter 5 considers the Clinton administration scandals of Whitewater and the Monica Lewinsky affair, which ended in failed impeachment proceedings. It also discusses coverage of scandals linked to the George W. Bush administration, including controversies surrounding no-bid contracts to rebuild Iraq and President Bush's controversial tenure with the National Guard. These more recent scandals are compared with those from previous presidential administrations, including the Iran-contra affair, which erupted during Ronald Reagan's second term. In chapter 5 we also address "scandals that weren't," such as unproven allegations concerning an extramarital affair between George H. W. Bush and a federal employee.

Chapter 6 compares news coverage of the presidency in different media outlets, including the broadcast networks, national newspapers, and local newspapers. The seventh and final chapter focuses on potential reforms, most notably the future trajectory of media-government relations and the growing opportunities to go beyond the traditional media by using newly available options such as the Internet.

# CHAPTER 2

## PRESIDENTS VERSUS CONGRESS
### The Competition for Media Attention

### Where Do You Stand on Pennsylvania Avenue?

Competition between the White House and Congress for the public's attention and loyalty is built into the U.S. political system. The statesmen who wrote the Constitution believed that a political system where various government officials competed for the public's attentions would make it harder for any part of the government to become oppressive (Carey 1989; Cronin and Genovese 2004; Hamilton et al. 1990, 47). Friction within the political system, in other words, was viewed not as a hindrance to efficient government but as a means to preserve liberty.

In the never-ending competition among government officials for the public's attention and affection, however, the modern presidency has gained the advantage. Research over several decades has shown that young children already view the president in favorable hues, and their early affection develops into positive evaluations of the executive branch in adulthood (T. Clark 2002; Easton and Dennis 1969; Jennings and Niemi 1974, 1981; Lowi 1985). Modern media coverage of government likewise provides an additional boost to the executive branch by focusing on the president (cf. Farnsworth and Lichter 2005; Stuckey 1991; Waterman et al. 1999).

The public's tendency to elevate the president above Congress is a mixed blessing for presidents as they try to respond to public demands (Lowi 1985). The more powerful a president seems to be, the greater the public expectations of the executive branch. But presidents cannot consistently dominate legislators, and the gap between what the public expects and what the president can deliver leads to overpromising and eventual public disappointment (Edwards 1989; Lowi 1985).

This "boom-and-bust" cycle of presidential expectations can create serious problems for the country. They can be seen through Lyndon Johnson's efforts to minimize the economic consequences of the Vietnam War, Richard Nixon's secret plan to end that war, Jimmy Carter's commitment never to lie to the country, and the promises of both Ronald Reagan and George W. Bush that large tax cuts would not lead to massive federal budget deficits (Cronin and Genovese 2004; Lowi 1985; Neustadt 1990; Stevenson 2002; Weisman 2002; Woodward 1999).

Recent research suggests that this public frustration with government has real-world consequences (Craig 1993, 1996; Hibbing and Theiss-Morse 1995). Declining levels of trust in government—a long-term trend in U.S. public opinion dating back to the 1960s—also increases negative evaluations of presidents (Hetherington and Globetti 2003). Suspicion of government makes it more difficult for presidents to convince citizens to accept short-term pain for long-term gain in difficult times like those of war and economic dislocation (Craig 1993, 1996; Farnsworth 2003a).

The president's ability to make policy is limited largely by his success in persuading Congress to go along (Neustadt 1990), sometimes aided by his ability to persuade the public to side with him and thereby pressure Congress from the grass roots (Kernell 1997). In practice, the influence of "going public" tends to be modest, existing largely on the margins of a political system where two branches share lawmaking powers (Cronin and Genovese 2004; Edwards 1989, 2003; C. Jones 1994, 1995).

The growing partisanship on Capitol Hill in recent years has perhaps made it even more difficult for presidents to be successful away from crisis environments such as wartime and the aftermath of terrorist attacks (Baker 2002; Bond et al. 2003; Edwards 1997). Indeed the rising partisanship in Washington has coincided with growing conflict in many policy areas, which makes it difficult for a president to govern from the ideological center, even if he (and someday she) wishes to do so (Dickinson 2003).

Given the strategic difficulties facing a president in the modern constitutional and political environments, news coverage represents the best leverage available for the presidency to muscle ahead of the constitutionally equal legislative branch in setting public policy (Gilbert 1989). Television, with its focus on emotionally laden images, can be particularly effective for rejuvenating public sympathy for the president over the mostly faceless crowd of lawmakers on Capitol Hill (Stuckey 1991; Waterman et al. 1999). Made-for-television spectacles—sometimes called "pseudo-events"—can be managed to inflate a president's popularity through engaging, emotionally charged visuals (cf. Adams et al. 1994; Boorstin 1961, M. Robinson 1976; Waterman et al. 1999).

Foreign policy, where Congress traditionally has been more deferential to presidential preferences, is particularly amenable to the president's use of television (Gilbert 1989). In fact, presidential influence over Congress in foreign policy forms such a sharp contrast with the president's difficulty in securing congressional support for his domestic policy initiatives that scholars have referred to these two areas of responsibility as "two presidencies" (cf. Sullivan 1991; Oldfield and Wildavsky 1989).

## The Executive Branch's Dominance of News Coverage

Debates over news coverage of government usually begin with the broadcast networks, particularly their flagship evening news shows. Although they are less dominant then they once were, the nightly news shows still attract huge audiences—as they have for over forty years (Farnsworth and Lichter 2003a; Pew 2000a, 2000b). They also continue to define and shape political discourse more than any other media genre, as cable news channels and online news sites frequently follow their lead. Network television's unique social and cultural influence was most recently illustrated by its role in bringing the country together through the aftershocks of the 9/11 terrorist attacks. All this makes the networks lightning rods for controversy, especially regarding their political and governmental coverage (Alterman 2003; B. Goldberg 2002).

The most straightforward debate over government news concerns its volume. While the networks pay less attention to government than they once did, the decline has not been steady. Our research found far more stories and airtime devoted to government in both 1981 and 2001 than in 1993, the first year of the Clinton administration. As shown in table 2.1, during Ronald Reagan's first year as president (1981), the three networks provided 7,216 stories on the national government. The coverage shrank to just over half that level (3,848 stories) when Clinton took office in 1993. It then rose again to 5,014 stories during George W. Bush's first year in office. Nonetheless, the 2001 total represents a decline of over 30 percent from 1981.

Moreover, the increase in governmental news in 2001 reflected spe-cial—indeed, unprecedented—circumstances. In fact, the rebound was

| TABLE 2.1 | Network News: Amount of Coverage | | | |
|---|---|---|---|---|
| | 2001 | 1993 | 1981 | Total |
| Number of Stories | 5,014 | 3,848 | 7,216 | 16,078 |
| Number of Hours | 138 | 107 | 178 | 422 |
| Avg. Minutes per Night | 23 | 18 | 29 | 23 |
| Number of Minutes ABC | 2,807 | 2,128 | 3,012 | 7,947 |
| Number of Minutes CBS | 2,110 | 2,065 | 3,931 | 8,106 |
| Number of Minutes NBC | 3,372 | 2,223 | 3,707 | 9,302 |
| | Pre-9/11 | Post-9/11 | | |
| Number of Stories | 2,909 | 2,105 | | |
| Number of Hours | 84 | 54 | | |
| Avg. Minutes per Night | 20 | 29 | | |
| Projected 2001 Totals without 9/11 Coverage Effects | | | | |
| Number of Stories | 4,197 | | | |
| Number of Hours | 121 | | | |
| Avg. Minutes per Night | 20 | | | |

entirely due to the sharp increase in coverage that followed the 9/11 terrorist attacks on the World Trade Center and the Pentagon. After the attacks, airtime devoted to governmental coverage increased almost 50 percent, from a combined average of twenty minutes a night from January 1 through September 10, to twenty-nine minutes a night for the rest of the year—about as high as the average nightly coverage for all of 1981. (Our analysis includes only the regularly rescheduled evening news time slot during the unprecedented four days of continuous coverage that followed the attacks.) If the pre-9/11 coverage had continued at the same rate, the number of stories for 2001 would have been only slightly higher than in 1993. The decline can also be seen in the falling proportion of the news that the networks allocated to government-related stories.

The drop in the amount of government coverage was not simply the result of a shifting news agenda that devoted less attention to government news. It also reflects a decline in the total news hole of the broadcasts—the amount of airtime available once commercials and promotional messages are removed from the half-hour time block. The average daily news hole of these three network news programs dropped from 22 minutes 22 seconds in 1981 to 18 minutes 37 seconds in 2001, a decline of 18 percent or nearly 4 minutes per program (Lichter and Farnsworth 2003) (see table 2.2).

Executive branch coverage has dwarfed that of the other branches, accounting for 76 percent of all government coverage in 1981, 88 percent in 1993, and 82 percent in 2001. But the overall decline in government news means that even the executive is receiving less attention than it once did—a drop of 40 percent from 1981 to 2001. It is especially striking that the downward trend continued in 2001, in view of the unprecedented events that year that stimulated an intense and sustained burst of activity from executive branch officials. Even the deadliest terrorist attack in our history, and the subsequent military intervention in Afghanistan, could not reverse the trend of decreasing coverage of the executive branch.

Despite the overall decline in news about the executive branch, the remaining coverage increasingly revolves around the president (relative to the cabinet, White House staff, and other departments and agencies). In 1981, personal coverage of Ronald Reagan was exceeded by cover-

| TABLE 2.2 | **Network News: Number of Discussions by Branch of Government** | | | |
|---|---|---|---|---|
| | **2001** | **1993** | **1981** | **Total** |
| **Executive** | **3,924** | **4,871** | **6,512** | **15,307** |
| President | 1,212 | 1,395 | 1,789 | 4,396 |
| White House & Cabinet | 850 | 715 | 2,483 | 4,048 |
| Other Executive | 1,862 | 2,761 | 2,240 | 6,863 |
| **Legislative** | **734** | **531** | **1,739** | **3,004** |
| House | 201 | 122 | 636 | 959 |
| Senate | 343 | 273 | 833 | 1,449 |
| Other Congress | 190 | 136 | 270 | 596 |
| **Judicial** | **146** | **156** | **293** | **595** |

*Note:* More than one individual or institution may be featured in one story.

age of the White House and cabinet staffs, as well as the coverage afforded other parts of the executive branch. In 1993, Bill Clinton personally received more coverage than his White House and cabinet staffs. But the remaining parts of the executive branch, including federal agencies, received more than twice his coverage. By contrast, President George W. Bush received more coverage than his White House and cabinet staffs, and the gap between coverage of the president and other parts of the executive branch narrowed in 2001.

The 3,004 discussions of Congress during the three years amounted to less than one-fifth of the executive branch's coverage. In fact, the 535 members of Congress combined for less TV news coverage than the president alone received. As we found with the executive, discussions of Congress dropped sharply from the Reagan to the Clinton presidency before rebounding slightly under Bush. But the amount of congressional coverage in 2001 was less than half that of twenty years earlier. Within the Congress, the upper chamber consistently held the upper hand in getting the media's attention. The Senate attracted about 50 percent more coverage than the House, with substantial leads in all three years. The Senate's coverage frequently stems from the great uncertainty over the chamber's eventual action—the filibuster and other procedural issues make predicting Senate action a highly uncertain science—as well as the fact that many senators are more nationally known figures than the members of the far larger House of Representatives.

The judiciary is sometimes called the invisible branch of government, and this proved to be literally true on network television. The three years that we studied contained only 595 discussions that featured the federal courts, including the Supreme Court, less than one-fifth of Congress's total. The judicial branch, like the other branches of government, suffered a severe reduction in coverage over the years. The coverage in 1981 roughly doubled that of 1993 and 2001, when the networks averaged only about fifty stories apiece on the federal courts. Thus, a viewer who faithfully watched a network newscast every night would have seen a discussion related to the federal courts less than once a week.

## GOVERNMENT COVERAGE FOLLOWING THE 2001 TERRORIST ATTACKS

The competition for media coverage among the branches of the federal government became even more one-sided in the weeks that followed the 9/11 terrorist strikes, as table 2.3 shows. The networks' attention focused almost entirely on the executive branch in the wake of the attacks—88 percent of coverage, compared to 79 percent earlier that year. The 1,327 stories that featured the executive branch after 9/11

| TABLE 2.3 | Network News: Number of Discussions by Branch of Government Before and After 9/11/2001 | | |
|---|---|---|---|
|  | Pre-9/11 | Post-9/11 | 2001 Total |
| **Total Executive** | **2,597** | **1,327** | **3,924** |
| President | 914 | 298 | 1,212 |
| White House & Cabinet | 544 | 306 | 850 |
| Other Executive | 1,139 | 723 | 1,862 |
| **Total Legislative** | **584** | **150** | **734** |
| House | 164 | 37 | 201 |
| Senate | 280 | 63 | 343 |
| Other Congress | 140 | 50 | 190 |
| **Judicial** | **118** | **28** | **146** |

Note: More than one individual or institution may be featured in one story.

represented nearly nine times the coverage provided to the legislative branch. Indeed, President Bush alone received nearly twice the news coverage received by all members of Congress combined during this period. Meanwhile, the judicial branch almost disappeared, only twenty-eight stories (less than two per week) through the end of the year.

During times of crisis, leadership typically becomes more personalized as the positive effects of 9/11 on former New York mayor Rudy Giuliani's public image attest. Indeed, scholars and journalists alike tend to treat this as a given. In light of this, we were surprised to find that the proportion of President Bush's personal coverage actually dropped by almost 30 percent, from 28 to 20 percent of all government news. Indeed, Bush was criticized at the time for not moving more quickly to project a "take-charge" image. (Hence *Time*'s selection of New York City mayor Rudy Giuliani in 2001 rather than Bush as "Person of the Year." Bush did receive the recognition in 2004 after winning reelection.)

This pattern of news coverage likely reflects a leadership style in which the president frequently called upon his subordinates to give a public face to the administration's response. President Bush's managerial style of delegating authority and visibility to his cabinet, the White House staff, and other appointees was reflected in increased airtime for Defense Secretary Donald Rumsfeld and Attorney General John Ashcroft, among others (cf. Kumar 2003a, 2003b).

This finding echoes previous research showing that President Clinton's coverage dropped sharply in 1995 after the Republicans gained control of the House. There were serious discussions in the media as to whether the president had become "irrelevant." During 1995, the spotlight shifted to new House Speaker Newt Gingrich, who soon discovered that the media's glare could burn as well as burnish. Thus, although presidents are usually in the media spotlight, they can also step out of its glare (like George W. Bush after 9/11) or be pushed out (like Clinton in 1995). We discuss Gingrich's "media moment" later in this chapter.

## THE DISAPPEARING HONEYMOON IN PRESIDENTIAL NEWS COVERAGE

New presidents were long thought to enjoy a "honeymoon" when they first entered the White House—a "settling-in" period when neither the press nor the Congress nor the public was particularly hard on the new chief executive. But this has become a thing of the past. In a media environment far more aggressive than that faced by presidents before the television age, and a political environment far more partisan than a generation ago, new presidents now are obligated to "hit the ground running" (Dickinson 2003; Fleisher and Bond 2000a; Pfiffner 1988; Sabato 1993; Sabato et al. 2000; Sinclair 2000). New administrations no longer get many forgiving evaluations during the first few months of on-the-job training.

In 2001, network news coverage of the George W. Bush administration had a very slow start, averaging barely three minutes per night during his first hundred days in office—a little more than 28 percent less than Bill Clinton received in 1993 during his first hundred days as president and 11 percent less than George H. W. Bush in 1989.

Overall, evaluations of President George W. Bush were only 43 percent favorable on network television during his first three months. That was still more positive than that of Bill Clinton, whose own coverage was only 40 percent favorable during the same period in 1993. Both presidents fell far short of the "honeymoon" of 61 percent positive coverage George H. W. Bush received during his first hundred days in office in 1989. (Taking office after eight years as vice president almost certainly reduces the chances for mistakes stemming from inexperience—like the incoming Clinton administration's failed cabinet appointments of Zoë Baird and Kimba Wood [O'Brien 1996].)

## CONGRESSIONAL COVERAGE

For Congress, the high point in coverage was 1981, when 20 percent of network news reports featured the legislative branch. The higher percentages of coverage of Congress in 1981 and 2001 than in 1993 likely reflect the distinctive partisan circumstances: 1981 marked the first Republican majority in the Senate since the 1950s, and 2001 marked the first time the GOP controlled the White House, the House, and the Senate since the mid-1950s. Novelty makes news, and the Republican legislative gains in 1980 and 2000 made the first year of both administrations especially different from what preceded them.

In contrast, the continuation of Democratic control of both chambers of Congress in 1993 drew less attention on the network newscasts. Another reason for the relatively high number of discussions that focused on Congress in 2001 was the brevity of that unified control. GOP dominance lasted only until midyear when Sen. James Jeffords of Vermont left the Republican Party and returned control of the Senate to the Democrats.

## JUDICIAL BRANCH COVERAGE

In all three years, the Supreme Court and the other federal courts were largely absent from the evening network news programs. Coverage of the judicial branch reached a high point, such as it was, in the early part of 2001 when 4 percent of the network news stories on government focused on the judiciary. Even that total fell by half after the terrorist attacks. One reason the federal courts were not the subject of intense network news coverage stems from the issues that they addressed: the leading foreign and domestic policy issues faced by the government in recent decades were largely executive and legislative matters that rarely involved the federal courts. While the effects of court decisions continue to reverberate through the other branches— indirectly setting the agenda for further discussion and legislation—the Supreme Court in recent decades has been less likely to provide transformational decisions along the lines of a generation ago (when *Roe v. Wade* [1973] legalized abortion), or of two generations ago (when *Brown v. Board of Education, Topeka* [1954] ended legally authorized public school segregation) (cf. Domino 1994; Epstein and Kobylka 1992; Lazare 1996; O'Brien 1993). The prohibition of cameras in the Supreme Court and other federal courts, as well as the unwillingness of the justices to hold press conferences discussing their decisions, also place the courts at a coverage disadvantage when compared to more politically oriented parts of the national government (Davis 1994).

## NEWS SOURCES: ANOTHER EXECUTIVE BRANCH ADVANTAGE

As they prepare their stories, reporters most frequently turn to the president's appointees for the information they need to cover the federal government. The president dominates the news, and the president and his appointees dominate what government officials say about the issues of the day. In all three years subject to the most intensive scrutiny in this project, the new administration was the place reporters went most often for information: 45 percent of the sources cited by name or affiliation in government stories aired during 2001 were from the executive branch, as were 35 percent in 1993 and 48 percent in 1981. In addition, reporters were far more likely to use the legislative branch for information than the judicial branch, former federal government officials, or state and local government officials.

Despite this reliance on high officials, the narratives of television news have become more publicly oriented over time. The voices of ordinary Americans outside of government, interest groups, and the circle of pundits were increasingly heard: 13 percent of the sources quoted in government news stories during 2001 and 19 percent of the sources in 1993 came from outside the traditional "inside the Beltway" categories, compared to only 9 percent in 1981.

Conversely, the frequency with which interest group representatives were quoted fell to 5 percent of the stories in 2001 from 8 percent eight years earlier, largely as a result of the more extensive focus on foreign policy matters. Foreign sources were quoted 10 percent of the time in 2001, as compared to 6 percent in 1993 and 7 percent in 1981. Many news reports in late 2001 solicited international perspectives on the terrorist attacks, especially with respect to the U.S. invasion of Afghanistan.

The heavy reliance on administration sources helps explain why the executive gets much more coverage than the legislative branch, as well as why that coverage is often more positive. Lawmakers on Capitol Hill can't "spin" public impressions of current events without getting more coverage. To make matters worse for Congress, the costs to reporters of irritating a single elected official on Capitol Hill with a negative story may be modest; they can always turn to one of the 534 other lawmakers. Offending someone in the more tightly controlled executive branch could have far more serious consequences to a reporter's ability to get the necessary information for a breaking story (Kurtz 1994).

A recurring criticism of government news concerns the audience's inability to identify sources and evaluate their credibility. This criticism gained new force during the 2004 general election when CBS's anonymous source of a forged memo regarding President Bush's National Guard service turned out to be a partisan opponent of the president, whose previous charges had been dismissed by other news organizations. CBS News anchor Dan Rather ultimately apologized for the coverage mistakes and subsequently announced plans to resign in early 2005 (Steinberg and Carter 2004).

Overall, roughly one out every five sources cited was not identified with respect to name, title, or institutional affiliation. However, network news reduced its use of unnamed sources in 2001 to the lowest proportion of the three years. Only one out of seven sources who appeared in network newscasts during 2001 was not identified by name, title, or organizational affiliation compared to one out of five in 1993. We cannot know whether this was an instance of reporters responding to public concern or differences in the media relations strategies of the Bush and Clinton administrations. Nonetheless, the declining use of anonymous sources represents a positive trend.

## Tone of Coverage

Although the judicial branch received far less network news coverage than other parts of the federal government, the courts consistently received the most favorable coverage. As table 2.4 shows, evaluations of federal judges and the courts were 61 percent positive overall, compared to only 37 percent positive executive branch coverage and 29 percent positive treatment of Congress.

However, much of this favorable coverage reflects the praise accorded two successful Supreme Court nominees, one in 1993 and one in 1981. For example, Rep. Eleanor Holmes Norton (D-DC) said of Clinton nominee Ruth Bader Ginsburg, "She was the chief navigator in the journey that took women after more than 100 years into the safe harbor of the United States Constitution" (ABC, July 20, 1993). Two decades earlier, Rep. Morris Udall (D-AZ) was similarly complimentary toward Reagan nominee Sandra Day O'Connor: "She can be tough but she's gentle. She clearly is conservative, but she never has placed partisan political values before justice" (ABC, September 9, 1981). Both these nominees were confirmed easily. If our study had included more

| TABLE 2.4 | Network News: Tone of Coverage (Percent Positive) | | | | | | | |
|---|---|---|---|---|---|---|---|---|
| | 2001 | | 1993 | | 1981 | | Total | |
| Executive Total | 36% | n= 2,509 | 38% | n= 4,658 | 34% | n= 1,606 | 37% | n= 8,773 |
| President | 39 | n = 1,397 | 38 | n = 2,708 | 36 | n = 705 | 38 | n = 4,810 |
| White House & Cabinet | 44 | n = 455 | 53 | n = 739 | 31 | n = 607 | 43 | n = 1,801 |
| Other Executive | 26 | n = 657 | 26 | n = 1,211 | 34 | n = 294 | 27 | n = 2,162 |
| Congress Total | 35% | n = 543 | 28% | N = 562 | 13% | n = 196 | 29% | n = 1,301 |
| House | 37 | n = 244 | 42 | n = 747 | 12 | n = 106 | 33 | n = 497 |
| Senate | 34 | n = 179 | 22 | n = 263 | 18 | n = 60 | 26 | n = 502 |
| Other Congress | 25 | n = 120 | 23 | n = 152 | 3 | n = 30 | 25 | n = 302 |
| Judicial Total | 48% | n = 31 | 70% | N = 66 | 60% | n = 82 | 61% | n = 179 |
| Overall Total | 36% | n = 3,083 | 37% | n = 5,286 | 33% | n = 1,884 | 36% | n = 10,253 |

Note: Based on evaluations made by sources and reporters on the evening news.

controversial Supreme Court nominees—like Robert Bork and Clarence Thomas—the picture would have looked very different.

For these three years examined in depth, the federal judiciary endured by far its most negative treatment during 2001, in the wake of the Supreme Court's controversial 5–4 decision to stop the 2000 presidential election ballot recounts in Florida. Indeed, Sen. Orrin Hatch (R-UT) felt obliged to rebut the criticism as "being way overblown . . . to try and malign the current justices on the Supreme Court" (NBC, September 9, 2001). As shown in table 2.4, the 48 percent positive coverage the courts received in 2001 was still favorable enough to finish first among the three branches.

Coverage of the executive branch was quite similar in tone for all three administrations, ranging from a low of 34 percent positive in tone in 1981 to a high of 38 percent positive in 1993. Personal coverage of the presidents was nearly identical despite their very different media management styles: 39 percent positive evaluations for George W. Bush, 38 percent for Bill Clinton, and 36 percent for Ronald Reagan. Coverage of Congress was most favorable in 2001, rising to 35 percent positive from 28 percent in 1993 and 13 percent in 1981.

Television news coverage during 2001 was a tale of two presidencies, as shown in table 2.5. Before September 11, coverage of the new administration was only 35 percent positive. For example, Sen. Tom Daschle (D-SD) complained in April, "These first 100 days give us real concern about the next 1,360" (CBS, April 29, 2001). President Bush enjoyed a dramatic increase in favorable coverage after 9/11, rising from 36 percent positive evaluations before the tragedy to 63 percent positive afterwards. For example, NBC interviewed a small-town shopkeeper who said, "People come in and they want to tell us they're proud of how President Bush is doing and that they're standing behind him" (September 11, 2001). However, comments directed toward presidential appointees and executive agencies actually became more negative after the attacks, dropping to only 31 percent positive for the rest of 2001.

This is not the paradox it may seem. This period included pointed questioning as to why the nation's intelligence services did not do more to protect the public against the attacks, as well as debate over the Justice Department's secretive and sometimes controversial detention procedures toward suspected terrorists. The administration's strategy of limiting the president's exposure on network news allowed Bush to

| TABLE 2.5 | Network News: Tone of Coverage Before and After 9/11 (Percent Positive) | | | | | |
|---|---|---|---|---|---|---|
| | **Before 9/11** | | **After 9/11** | | **2001 Total** | |
| **Executive Total** | 35% | n = 2,093 | 42% | n = 416 | 36% | n = 2,509 |
| President | 36 | n = 1,267 | 63 | n = 130 | 39 | n = 1,397 |
| White House & Cabinet | 48 | n = 351 | 31 | n = 104 | 44 | n = 455 |
| Other Executive | 23 | n = 475 | 34 | n = 182 | 26 | n = 657 |
| **Congress Total** | 37% | n = 498 | 13% | n = 45 | 35% | n = 543 |
| House | 41 | n = 169 | 10 | n = 10 | 37 | n = 244 |
| Senate | 39 | n = 236 | 0 | n = 8 | 34 | n = 179 |
| Other Congress | 27 | n = 93 | 19 | n = 27 | 25 | n = 120 |

concentrate on executing his commander-in-chief functions, including televised speeches to the nation, a formal address to Congress, and comments made during visits of other heads of state (Gregg and Rozell 2004).

This was also a year of two Congresses on network news, but in the opposite direction, as table 2.5 shows. Coverage of the legislative branch before the attacks was 37 percent positive in tone, falling to only 13 percent positive in their wake. The House and Senate had roughly similar ratings during both periods. The heavy criticism of Congress after 9/11 reversed a long-term trend toward more favorable coverage; the legislative branch received 28 percent positive coverage in 1993, compared to only 13 percent in 1981.

The abrupt change in tone after 9/11 may reflect a redirection of partisan politics away from a newly popular president and his policies and toward the congressional realm, where criticism was less likely to be branded as unpatriotic. Such one-sided coverage makes it difficult, if not impossible, for the legislature to compete with the president on anything approaching a level playing field.

## A PARTISAN BIAS OR NEGATIVISM?

The results shown in tables 2.4 and 2.5 also offer opportunities to evaluate recurring charges of partisan media bias. Conservatives have long complained about receiving biased coverage from the "liberal media." The chorus usually reaches its crescendo during presidential election campaigns. In 2000, Democrats returned the favor by accusing the media of harboring an anti-Gore bias, as a result of either personal antipathy or "bending over backwards" to be fair to Bush.

The scholarly evidence on election news is mixed. Over the past two decades, content analyses of election news have found that Democratic presidential candidates sometimes (in 1984, 1992, and 1996) received more favorable treatment than their GOP opponents; at other times (1980, 1988, and 2000), coverage of the major-party nominees was roughly balanced (cf. Clancey and M. Robinson 1985; Farnsworth and Lichter 2003a; Just et al. 1996; Kerbel 1998). Overall, Democratic primary candidates have received more positive TV news coverage than their Republican counterparts since 1988 (Media Monitor 2004).

However, our data can address the question of whether the media favor one political party over the other after the winners turn from running for office to running the government.

Once in office, were Democratic presidents and legislators treated more favorably on network news than Republicans? To find out, we first compared first-year evaluations of Democrat Bill Clinton with those of Republicans Ronald Reagan and George W. Bush. The personal coverage of Reagan was 36 percent positive, compared to 38 percent positive for Clinton and 39 percent for George W. Bush. For the executive branch as a whole, the comparable figures were 34 percent positive in 1981, 38 percent positive in 1993, and 36 percent positive in 2001. Thus, all three administrations received mainly (and almost equally) negative coverage during their first years (cf. Farnsworth and Lichter 2003a).

Of course, many of the judgments that are rendered toward presidential administrations have little to do with policy issues. They may concern personal traits, ethical questions, political skills, and so on. For example, opinion polls showed quite different responses depending on whether the public was asked how well Bill Clinton was handling his job as president or what they thought of him as a person. To control for the personal factor, we examined only those evaluations that dealt with the policies each administration advocated or executed.

Examining only the issue-based comparisons, we found that network sources who evaluated the policy agendas of the three administrations again produced a roughly two-to-one negative tilt overall—34 percent positive evaluations of all policies combined. The three administrations received virtually identical judgments of their domestic agendas—35 percent positive for Bush, 33 percent positive for Reagan, and 32 percent positive for Clinton. Foreign policy evaluations produced greater, but still slight, differences: positive evaluations of Clinton administration foreign policies exceeded the Reagan administration's by 38 percent to 28 percent. Bolstered by relatively good press for the war on terrorism after September 11, the George W. Bush administration received 35 percent positive comments.

Given this general media negativity, it is easy to see why partisans on both sides would perceive the media as biased against their own party's policies. Among the most heavily debated issues across all three administrations, only Clinton's policies toward Iraq received a majority (56 percent) of favorable evaluations, although his support for the North American Free Trade Agreement (NAFTA) came close with 48 percent positive comments. George W. Bush's first-year issue agenda topped out at 42 percent favorable judgments of his tax cuts. Reagan's best issue-oriented news coverage in 1981 came in the 41 percent positive comments on his tax policies and the sale of Airborne Warning and Control aircraft (AWACs) to Saudi Arabia. At the other end of the spectrum, Bush's defense policies generated 83 percent negative evaluations (i.e., only 17 percent positive), Reagan's handling of the air traffic controllers' strike was criticized by 87 percent of all judgments commentary, and Clinton's tax policies were rejected by 91 percent of on-air opinions.

Congressional coverage showed greater evidence of partisan differences. But the same party was not always favored. The increasingly positive coverage of Congress masks a disparity in the fortunes of the two parties—an upsurge in favorable commentary on Democratic members offset a decline in favorable commentary on their Republican colleagues. Of course, the term "support" is relative, since evaluations of both parties were heavily negative in all three years.

The proportion of positive press for Congressional Democrats increased sixfold, from a low base of only 7 percent positive in 1981 to 42 percent positive in 2001. Simultaneously, evaluations of Republicans slipped from 30 percent positive in 1981 to 20 percent positive in 1993 and then partly rebounded to 26 percent positive in 2001. Democratic members of Congress were favored by a 42 percent positive tone versus 26 percent positive for Republicans in 2001, a margin of 16 percentage points. Democratic legislators also held a 14 percentage point margin in the tone of coverage in 1993, with 34 percent positive comments compared to 20 percent positive for Republicans. But Republican lawmakers in 1981 held a 23 percentage point margin over Democrats. That was partly the result of Democratic disagreements over whether to support some of Reagan's controversial policies. For example, one House Democrat criticized members of his party who voted for President Reagan's tax reform legislation as "a cop-out, a caving in on something we have all campaigned against" (ABC, June 3, 1981).

Finally, many of the sources whose evaluations were broadcast had partisan affiliations, which can affect the extent to which viewers value their opinions. The head of the Republican National Committee, for example, is unlikely to fault a Republican president; the same holds true for Democrats. Comments from nonpartisan sources are more influential since viewers are more likely to discount explicitly partisan evaluations (Page and Shapiro 1992). Therefore, media scholars often base their measures of bias on comments by sources not identified with either party (Robinson and Sheehan 1983).

The results among nonpartisan sources also demonstrated a presidential advantage, though not a partisan one. Ronald Reagan barely edged out Bill Clinton by 30 percent to 29 percent positive evaluations among these sources, while George W. Bush lagged behind with only 24 percent favorable reviews. This finding belies assertions that Reagan's TV news coverage during his first year was unusually positive because it reflected the sympathetic public response that followed his 1981 shooting and subsequent recovery (Lowi 1985).

A more significant change was the increased negativity across the board that resulted from the exclusion of partisan sources. When sources affiliated with either of the parties were excluded, the remaining evaluations dropped from 37 to 26 percent positive for the executive branch, 29 to 23 percent for the legislature, and 61 to 47 percent for the judiciary. For example, NBC interviewed a day care center operator who objected to President Reagan's budget cuts: "Saying he's balancing the budget while cutting bureaucracy, while a lot of people are suffering as a result, just shows where the insensitivity is and how removed he is from the lives of most people" (October 10, 1981).

These declines from already low levels of favorable coverage contradict the assumption that political news is so negative simply because the two parties have become more contentious and less civil in their dealings with each other. The evaluations that the networks chose to put on the air from journalists, experts, interest groups, and ordinary citizens were consistently more critical of governmental actors and actions than were sound bites from the partisan actors themselves.

Critics of network negativism toward government often allege that the steady diet of criticism erodes the public's respect for our political institutions (Cappella and Jamieson 1997). The negative tilt is usually inferred from television's portrayals of individual officeholders; but TV news often characterized governmental institutions directly as well. For example, an ABC reporter summarized surveys as showing that "most Americans support the various law enforcement measures *the government* is taking in the campaign against terrorism" (ABC, November 28, 2001, emphasis added).

To address this issue, we compared the tone of coverage for the institutions of government, on one hand, and individual public figures, on the other. For the executive branch, evaluations of individuals were more positive than those that characterized their subject institutionally, such as "the White House" or "the cabinet." The coverage of executive branch officeholders varied only slightly from one administration to another. In each instance, the figures for individuals were substantially more favorable than those for institutions.

The difference was widest for the Clinton administration at 18 percentage points (42 percent personal versus 24 percent institutional positive comments). For example, CBS's Susan Spencer commented, "When it comes to damage control, *this White House* can sometimes make the bull in the china shop look graceful" (May 21, 1993, emphasis added). The difference shrank to 12 percentage points during the two Republican administrations. But the clearest finding was that the media's overt portrayal of institutions was consistently more negative than that of the individuals who occupied them.

For Congress, personal coverage was also consistently more positive in tone than institutional coverage. In 2001, personal evaluations were 43 percent positive, while evaluations of Congress as an institution were only 22 percent positive. In 1993, the balance of personal to institutional evaluation was 32 percent to 17 percent positive; and in 1981, it was 15 percent to 10 percent positive. For example, Sen. John McCain (R-AZ) told NBC in 2001, "I used to say that Congress was spending money like a drunken sailor. But I've never known a sailor who ever had the imagination that Congress does for spending money" (NBC, April 9, 2001).

For the judicial branch, where there was considerably less coverage, individual evaluations were highly favorable: 81 percent positive in 1993 and 62 percent positive in 1981. These were years marked by presidential nominations and Senate confirmation of justices for the Supreme Court: Sandra Day O'Connor, the first woman to serve on the Court, was nominated and confirmed in 1981, and Ruth Bader

Ginsburg, the second woman to serve on the Court, was nominated and confirmed in 1993.

In a rare instance of institutional criticism, NBC quoted a high school principal who objected to court-mandated desegregation plans: "The federal courts are running our schools and I'm sick and tired of it" (NBC, October 8, 1981). Conversely, there were too few judicial branch evaluations of individuals in 2001—a year without a Supreme Court appointment—to reliably assess institutional differences. In both 1981 and 1993, however, there were too few evaluations of the judiciary as an institution to permit meaningful comparisons with assessments of the individual justices.

These comparisons show the judicial branch's great advantage in favorable coverage. Coverage of the courts for those years with sufficient cases to enable meaningful analysis was 46 percent positive for the institution and 72 percent positive for individuals, compared to a three-year average of 41 percent for the individuals and 26 percent for the institutions of the executive branch. Congress was the lowest in both categories, with 35 percent positive coverage of individuals over the three years and only 18 percent positive coverage of Congress as an institution.

Individuals were far more likely to be the focus of evaluations in the executive and legislative branches, while the judicial branch was more often evaluated on the institutional dimension. In years that featured a Supreme Court nomination, however, coverage of the judicial branch focused more on the nominees. Some scholars argue that the relative anonymity of Supreme Court members orients coverage toward the justice system rather than individual jurists (Biskupic 1995; O'Brien 1993). In contrast, efforts by elected officials to increase their public recognition lead to more individually oriented coverage of the executive and legislative branches (cf. Jacobson 2001). More than two-thirds of the assessments of the executive branch in all three years concerned individuals, as did at least half the assessments of the legislative branch.

## TRIVIAL COVERAGE?

Job performance was also an important part of the legislative and judicial branches' evaluations, as shown in table 2.6. Ethics was more a

| TABLE 2.6 | Network News: Focus of Evaluations (Percent of All Evaluations) | | | | |
|---|---|---|---|---|---|
| | | 2001 | 1993 | 1981 | Total |
| Executive | Job Performance | 83 | 74 | 68 | 76 |
| | Ethics/Character | 2 | 5 | 4 | 4 |
| | Political Conduct | 5 | 13 | 11 | 10 |
| | Political Effectiveness | 2 | * | 4 | 1 |
| | Other | 7 | 8 | 14 | 9 |
| | | 99% | 100% | 101% | 100% |
| Congress | Job Performance | 59 | 62 | 52 | 59 |
| | Ethics/Character | 20 | 20 | 7 | 18 |
| | Political Conduct | 14 | 11 | 28 | 15 |
| | Political Effectiveness | 1 | 1 | 6 | 2 |
| | Other | 6 | 6 | 8 | 6 |
| | | 100% | 100% | 101% | 100% |
| Judicial | Job Performance | 87 | 41 | 34 | 46 |
| | Ethics/Character | 0 | 2 | 1 | 1 |
| | Political Conduct | 3 | 8 | 0 | 4 |
| | Political Effectiveness | 3 | 0 | 0 | 1 |
| | Other | 6 | 50 | 65 | 48 |
| | | 99% | 101% | 100% | 100% |

*Too few evaluations for meaningful analysis.
Percentages do not total 100 due to rounding error.

matter for congressional than executive branch evaluations, at least in the first year of each administration. Even in the Clinton administration, such assessments constituted a mere 5 percent of all executive branch evaluations. (The sex scandals that dominated media coverage of the Clinton White House for more than a year came later [Edwards 2000; Rockman 1996; Sabato et al. 2000].) Once again we saw a strikingly different pattern for the judicial branch in years with and without Supreme Court nominations. Job performance evaluations for the judicial branch made up 87 percent of all evaluations during 2001. However, they were overshadowed by stories relating to the Court nominations in 1993 and 1981.

Although their focus on job performance is to the networks' credit, this offers yet another example of media negativity. For the job performance of the executive branch, the tone of coverage was about two-to-one negative for all three administrations. Two months into George W. Bush's administration, for instance, Philip Clapp of the National Environment Trust told NBC, "Every single one of the decisions this administration has made on the environment has been made to benefit the chemical industry, the oil industry and the timber industry" (March 21, 2001).

By contrast, plaudits were given to the Reagan administration's political effectiveness (63 percent positive) and to George W. Bush's team in 2001 (56 percent positive). Both presidents successfully pushed Congress to adopt major tax-cut programs in their first year in office. The Clinton administration attracted too few evaluations of its political effectiveness to make a meaningful comparison (Woodward 1994).

In all three years, the executive branch's job performance received more positive assessments than that of the legislative branch. This finding is consistent with the argument of scholars that the complicated procedures of Congress make it easy to portray that institution in a negative light (Hibbing and Theiss-Morse 1995). The image of Congress did improve over time, although one might argue that it had no place to go but up.

Network news evaluations of the judiciary's performance were consistently more positive than those of the other two branches: 52 percent positive in 2001, 41 percent positive in 1993, and 56 percent positive in 1981. However, these percentages were based on very little coverage. For every evaluation of the federal courts' job performance, there were nearly a hundred evaluations of the executive branch.

As one would expect, there were few discussions of politics in the wake of the 2001 terrorist attacks. Job performance was virtually the only topic addressed in network television evaluations during the final months of that fateful year. For the executive branch, only 4 of the year's 102 assessments of political conduct aired after the attack, as did 4 of the 50 assessments of political effectiveness (Farnsworth and Lichter 2004b). Thus, the Bush administration was aided not only by favorable coverage of the job it was doing but also by an absence of attention to any other topic after 9/11.

## White House News Coverage after the First Year

Although our most extensive data assess media coverage of the first years in office of Ronald Reagan (1981), Bill Clinton (1993), and

George W. Bush (2001), we can compare those first years to network news coverage of some other presidential years. Our comparison data, which includes only some of the years since 1981, is found in table 2.7.

By far the most positive year for network news coverage of a president examined here was 1989, the first year in office of President George H. W. Bush. The 55 percent positive tone was by far the highest of the eight full years we have analyzed over the past quarter century. The second-most-positive year for the tone of presidential coverage on network news was shared by father and son: George W. Bush received 39 percent positive coverage during 2001, as did George H. W. Bush during 1991—the year before he lost his reelection bid. The Democrat who replaced George H. W. Bush, Bill Clinton, received 38 percent positive coverage in 1993, the highest-ranking Democratic year analyzed here. Thus, all four presidents—except Bush I during 1989—were treated roughly equally negatively. And the elder Bush's coverage soured throughout the rest of his term.

Other than George II. W. Bush's first year, the tone of presidential coverage was remarkably consistent across the years analyzed, with all the other years ranging from 39 percent positive in tone to 36 percent

| TABLE 2.7 | Network News: Tone of Presidential Coverage (Percent Positive) | | |
|---|---|---|---|
| | Percent Positive | Number of Evaluations | Number of Stories Featuring Each President |
| 2003 George W. Bush (May 1 through Oct 31) | 32% | 470 | 715 |
| 2001 George W. Bush | 39 | 1,397 | 1,212 |
| 1995 Bill Clinton | 36 | 1,390 | 1,179 |
| 1994 Bill Clinton | 36 | 2,660 | 1,599 |
| 1993 Bill Clinton | 38 | 2,708 | 1,395 |
| 1991 George H. W. Bush | 39 | 766 | 1,160 |
| 1990 George H. W. Bush | 36 | 461 | 1,005 |
| 1989 George H. W. Bush | 55 | 309 | 642 |
| 1981 Ronald Reagan | 36 | 705 | 1,789 |

Based on evaluations by sources and reporters on the ABC, CBS, and NBC evening news.

positive in tone. Partial-year coverage of George W. Bush during 2003 (May 1–October 31) was only 32 percent positive, but that period of time—which starts when President Bush stood on the deck of an aircraft carrier beneath the notorious "Mission Accomplished" banner—was marked by more negative coverage than that before May 1, when news reports focused on what appeared at first be a relatively painless U.S. military victory over Iraq. (Further discussion of war and postwar news coverage of Iraq is found in chapter 4.)

Overall, these results suggest that network television is consistently hostile to presidents regardless of party, giving them on average positive coverage slightly more than one-third of the time. Further, coverage does not seem dramatically different in tone for presidents across their terms in office. This evidence does not support the claim of a liberal or Democratic media bias, as presidents received almost equally negative coverage over these years—and the one president who received unusually positive coverage over a full year was a Republican.

## THE IRRELEVANT PRESIDENCY OF 1995?

The November 1994 elections were devastating for Democrats in Washington and around the country. Two years after Bill Clinton soundly defeated George H. W. Bush, he saw his party lose majority control of both the House and the Senate. The Republicans were to remain the majority party in both chambers throughout the six remaining years of Clinton's presidency. When Bill Clinton took office in January 1993, Democrats had a 57–43–seat majority in the Senate and a 258–176 majority in the House (not counting Rep. Bernard Sanders, a Vermont independent who usually votes with the Democrats). Two years later, Republicans held a 54–46 majority in the Senate and a 232–202 majority in the House (again, not counting the independent Sanders), severely limiting Clinton's ability to work his legislative will on Capitol Hill. Many observers interpreted the 1994 election as a rebuke to Bill Clinton, who was not on the ballot but nevertheless generated considerable hostility among conservatives and some moderates over a controversial health care reform proposal, as well as questions regarding the president's character (Ceaser and Busch 1997; Hershey 1997; Skocpol 1997).

In early 1995, newly installed House Speaker Newt Gingrich (R-GA) envisioned a revival of congressional dominance in Washington and pushed through a wide-ranging package of legislation known as the Contract with America. Gingrich had risen to lead his party through an aggressive partisanship that appealed to many Republican House members irritated by their decades in the political minority and by the go-along, get-along approach of their party's House leaders during the 1980s (Farrell 2001; Gingrich 1995). The news media were central to Gingrich's vision of a restored legislative branch: during his first months as speaker, Gingrich conducted far more scheduled press briefings than did President Clinton (Groeling and Kernell 2000).

In 1995, Gingrich turned the traditional executive branch domination of network news upside down. Not only was he far more newsworthy than his Democratic predecessor and his Republican counterpart at the other end of the U.S. Capitol, he even made more news than the commander in chief!

During the first four months of the year, President Clinton received only half as much airtime (9.4 hours) as the new Republican Congress (19.2 hours) on the three evening newscasts. During that period, even the O. J. Simpson murder trial eclipsed the president's coverage. House Speaker Gingrich received over four times as much network evening news airtime with 138 network news stories during the four-month period (4.2 hours of airtime)—greatly eclipsing the coverage of Senate Majority Leader Bob Dole (R-KS)—and over ten times as much airtime as Gingrich's predecessor, House Speaker Tom Foley (D-WA), who lost his seat in the 1994 Republican sweep.

During this brief period of congressional dominance of the national media agenda, reporters produced very negative stories about both Clinton and the Republican legislative majorities on Capitol Hill. Although the Republican-majority Congress received 89 percent positive coverage for its attempts at congressional reform, it received far more criticism than praise on all ten policy issues that received substantial media attention during the period: the budget, taxes, welfare reform, the environment, education, crime, legal reform, school lunches, term limits, and the proposed balanced-budget amendment to the Constitution.

In fact, some political observers managed to attack both Clinton and

Gingrich simultaneously. The two men, said commentator Joe Klein, were "very much the same: blabby, preaching, undisciplined and not very dignified" (CBS, December 11, 1994).

Clinton did receive some high marks from the networks during early 1995, most notably 80 percent positive coverage for his handling of terrorism following the deaths of 168 people in the Oklahoma City federal office building bombing on April 19, 1995 (Romano 2004). Clinton also received 71 percent positive coverage for his proposal to offer loan guarantees to Mexico following the peso's collapse in early 1995. But these were exceptionally positive assessments of the embattled president. On many other issues—including the budget, his efforts to increase the minimum wage, and his peace negotiations involving Northern Ireland—network news coverage of the president was far more negative than positive.

Eventually, though, Clinton regained the upper hand, in large measure through Republican overreaching on the budget impasse of 1995–1996 (Ceaser and Busch 1997). There were nearly six hundred federal budget stories on network newscasts during 1995, and over 20 percent of them dealt with the partial federal government shutdowns in November and December. Both sides came in for criticism: coverage of Clinton's handling of the budget crisis was 82 percent negative in tone, but coverage of the congressional Republicans was even worse—92 percent negative. During the stalemate, ABC reporter Jim Wooten called the White House and Congress "one big dysfunctional family" (ABC, December 29, 1995).

The press and, eventually, the public came to see Congress as more to blame than the president for the government shutdowns, and Clinton easily won a second term in 1996 (Ceaser and Busch 1997). The congressional Republicans got even two years later, when Americans learned more than they wanted to know about Clinton's involvement with a young presidential intern named Monica Lewinsky (I. Morris 2002; Sabato et al. 2000). The subsequent Clinton impeachment proceedings, another titanic struggle between Capitol Hill and the White House, will be covered in chapter 5.

## Conclusion

The breadth and depth of this study permitted us to test some widely held assumptions about television news coverage of the federal government. We are not the first to find that TV news coverage of government has decreased in recent years. However, our findings challenge the notion that the focus of this coverage has narrowed as the networks increasingly highlight the president's role as communicator in chief (cf. Kurtz 1994; Waterman et al. 1999).

In the age of television, the president has the most decisive voice in American government, and that public role is heightened during times of crisis (Lowi 1985; Woodward 2002). But presidential media management stories can shift some of the coverage away from the Oval Office toward other parts of the executive branch. In the wake of the 9/11 terrorist attacks, George W. Bush received proportionately less attention than he had earlier in the year, as the administration sought to shift TV news coverage toward Bush's executive branch subordinates.

Thus, there was a mild increase in the proportion of discussions about President Clinton above those of President Reagan, but no further increase in the attention paid to President George W. Bush. Taking into account the declining news coverage of government, the attention given to the president actually fell by nearly one-third from 1981 to 2001.

Media management strategies and leadership styles can be important weapons in the president's battles with Congress and the press. Bush's post-9/11 media strategies are the latest examples of a trend across all three presidencies to direct television news coverage of executive agencies and other administration appointees outside the traditional power centers of the White House and the president's cabinet. Given the negative orientation of much of the executive branch coverage seen here, this deflection can be a very effective strategy for maintaining a president's public prestige by directing public and media criticism toward subordinates.

Declining coverage of the president did not mean increased coverage for other elected officials. Most senators, even party leaders, are far less well known than presidents. Stories involving these less visible figures are more difficult and time-consuming to present than a report that focuses on the president as either commander in chief or legislator in chief (cf. Iyengar 1991). Members of the House are typically even less recognizable and nationally influential than senators, and they receive even less airtime. Given the decentralized nature of Congress, this growing legislative disadvantage is not likely to be reversed in the years ahead.

Because the networks portray the executive branch as the central focus of government, members of a president's administration become major news sources; they were cited more often than any other component of government or any collection of voices outside the government. In 2001 and 1981, executive branch officials were cited twice as often as members of Congress. An unexpected but welcome trend in sourcing was the growing tendency to identify sources in news stories. The percentage of unnamed sources used on network television fell by one-third from 1993 to 2001.

The "rally round the flag" effect is normally used to explain increases in public support for the president during crises (Adams et al. 1994; Nincic 1997). We found a similar tendency on network news. During the final sixteen weeks of 2001 (after September 11), George W. Bush was portrayed far more positively than he was before the terrorist attacks, while coverage of the cabinet and the White House staff actually became more negative. Favorable congressional coverage fell more sharply than that of the president's staff, further evidence of the great media advantages that Bush and the executive branch had over the legislative branch in late 2001.

In other words, on television the legislative branch is losing the battle for the "hearts and minds" of citizens to the executive branch—and losing it by increasing margins. Future legislatures may be even more deferential to presidents, unless news coverage reverses the anti-Congress trends seen in recent decades. Of course the increasingly large number of gerrymandered "safe seats" for lawmakers makes many House members largely immune to presidential influences regardless of the news coverage. (This gerrymandering also makes lawmakers more immune to citizen influences—hardly a desirable development from the perspective of responsible and responsive legislating.)

Our findings on the tone of TV news coverage belie overarching generalizations about partisan bias. The two Republican presidents, Ronald Reagan and George W. Bush, received roughly as much negative coverage during their first year in office as their Democratic counterpart Bill Clinton. Overall, the Clinton administration received slightly better coverage than did its GOP counterparts on some measures. But the most favorable coverage of an incoming president went to George H. W. Bush in 1989.

The results for Congress were more mixed. When evaluations of individual Democratic and Republican members of Congress were aggregated, Democratic legislators fared considerably better than Republicans overall, and by substantial margins under both Bill Clinton and George W. Bush. But Republicans fared better during Ronald Reagan's presidency. We can't know whether the two parties' shifting fortunes on TV news represent a long-term trend or circumstances peculiar to the first years of these particular administrations.

A confounding factor that makes it difficult to assess partisan balance is the pervasive negativism of television news coverage. Here the picture is much clearer, as we found a predominantly negative cast to political news. Coverage of the first year of these three presidencies was nearly two-to-one negative in tone, and evaluations of Congress during those years were even more critical, as much as seven-to-one negative in 1981. It is no wonder that supporters of each new administration see the media as uniquely biased against them. But it would be more accurate to say that the networks were about equally "biased" against both parties.

Even these totals understate the negative perspective of television news reports. When the partisan sources were excluded from our totals, the remaining comments were roughly three-to-one negative toward both the executive and legislative branches. Thus, network news negativism cannot be dismissed as an accurate reflection of the partisan rhetoric inside the Beltway. The expert voices chosen by journalists to supplement the partisan to-and-fro increase the negative images the public receives of government.

Television news is often derided for focusing on trivial or ephemeral matters like personal foibles and gaffes or political strategy and tactics rather than policy issues (cf. Farnsworth and Lichter 2003a; Patterson 1994). But we found more coverage of the policy stands and job performance of government officials on network television than we expected, particularly in light of the networks' performance in covering recent presidential elections. The vast majority of evaluations of both the executive and legislative branches dealt with "the issues"—matters of substance—during all three years covered most extensively by our study.

# CHAPTER 3

## PRESIDENTS IN GOOD TIMES AND BAD
### Covering the Economy

For a quarter century, incumbent presidents of both parties have worried about becoming the next Jimmy Carter. Carter was defeated in his 1980 reelection bid largely because of voter concerns about the faltering economy and the hostage crisis in Iran.

Ronald Reagan, the victor in the 1980 presidential election, had a particular gift for plain speech. And nowhere did it serve him better than in his closing remarks at the October 28, 1980, presidential debate. Voters, the former California governor said, should ask themselves a few questions before they cast a ballot:

> Next Tuesday all of you will go to the polls, will stand there in the polling place and make a decision. I think when you make that decision, it might be well if you would ask yourself, are you better off than you were four years ago? Is it easier for you to go and buy things in the stores than it was four years ago? Is there more or less unemployment in the country than there was four years ago? (quoted in Abramson et al. 1982:45)

Those questions, together with Reagan's confident presentation, helped make Carter a one-term president (Hunt 1981). Voters focused intensely on economic matters in 1980, as they had in 1976 when Carter narrowly defeated President Gerald Ford (whose own election campaign was stymied by economic troubles and his controversial pardon of his predecessor, Richard Nixon, for Watergate crimes). Economic issues had been more significant in those two elections than they had been for a generation. In both years, more than three-quarters of those surveyed identified either inflation or unemployment as the country's top problem (Schneider 1981).

As the 1980 election neared, voters expressed considerable disappointment with Carter's economic policies. Economic problems were cited as the country's top issue by more than 60 percent of those surveyed in CBS News/New York Times polls during every month of the fall campaign (Schneider 1981). In all these polls, fewer than one in five respondents mentioned either the hostage crisis in Iran or relations with the Soviet Union (which was fighting a war in neighboring Afghanistan) as the top problem for the United States. Asked on the eve of the election which candidate would do a better job on the economy, those surveyed favored the Republican challenger by a nearly two-to-one margin (Schneider 1981).

Reagan offered an effective strategy for future challengers hoping to defeat an incumbent president: pound away at his economic failures. Challengers should encourage what is known as retrospective voting: selecting a candidate based on how well or how poorly the incumbent party has done on key governmental responsibilities, such as managing the economy (Abramson et al. 2002; Fiorina 1981; Key 1966). Challengers can also encourage news coverage of this matter by frequently drawing public attention to the incumbent's shortcomings, as Reagan did in 1980 (Schneider 1981; Hunt 1981).

The candidate who learned Reagan's lesson best, of course, was Bill Clinton, who defeated incumbent president George H. W. Bush in 1992 by focusing intensely on economic matters (Glad 1995). Whereas Reagan saved his devastating question for the end of a close campaign struggle, Clinton concentrated his message in a single slogan at the outset: "It's the economy, stupid." During his first term, Clinton also worked effectively to make sure that he could not be portrayed as the next Carter (or, if you prefer, the next George H. W. Bush) by taking substantial political risks to pass his economic plan in 1993 (Renshon

1995; Woodward 1994). Clinton trumpeted his economic successes at every opportunity during the 1996 campaign, urging voters to look at his past record in this area to predict where he would take the country in the future. By presenting himself as someone who had delivered good times and painting his rival as possessing only risky and untried schemes, he left Republican nominee Bob Dole with virtually nothing to say on this key topic (Farnsworth and Lichter 2003a; Pomper 1997).

Four years later, the 2000 presidential election featured relatively little debate over economic matters, as Vice President Al Gore, the Democratic nominee, tried not to tie himself too closely to Bill Clinton's scandal-plagued presidency. Though economic matters were not decisive in the 2000 election, George W. Bush made no secret of his intention to avoid the mistakes of his father (and Carter before him) in this area. So Bush sought to imitate Clinton's aggressive early implementation of new economic policies—in Bush's case, with tax cuts (Edwards 2004). This economic program did not generate economic improvement in time for the 2002 midterm elections. Fortunately for the Republicans, however, voters did not consider economic matters as significant as foreign policy matters so soon after the 2001 terrorist attacks (Mucciaroni and Quirk 2004). The health of the national economy had begun to recover in time for Bush's reelection campaign, but throughout 2004 unemployment remained high in the industrial midwestern heartland, a battleground region key to both parties' plans for securing an Electoral College majority (Weisman and Henderson 2004). Fortunately for Bush, however, large numbers of citizens were concerned over terrorism, the war in Iraq, and moral values issues like abortion and gay marriage, while a relatively small number of voters cast ballots in 2004 over economic matters (Pew 2004c).

## Research on Economics and Elections

Like the elected officials they study, political scientists attach great importance to the economy's performance for explaining presidential approval. Many economic-based predictive models have done quite well in predicting increases and declines in public assessments of the presi-

dent as well as the results of presidential elections (Abramson et al.
2002; Nickelsburg and Norpoth 2000; Erikson et al. 2000).

The mass media play a crucial role in this process by placing economic matters on the public agenda and framing the way people examine economic conditions. It is a truism that presidents receive more
credit than they deserve for good economic times and more blame than
they deserve for bad economic times (Bowles 2003; Edwards and
Wayne 2003). Television news, which amplifies conventional wisdom
through heavy use of establishment sources, frequently repeats this
message of presidential responsibility (Iyengar and Kinder 1987). It is
also a truism that bad news is covered more extensively than good
(Niven 2001). The arguably unfair approach of assigning so much responsibility to the president for economic outcomes (intensified by the
media's focus on the negative) makes such assessments of economic
conditions no less real for politicians.

> So many factors that affect the economy and impact on the society lie
> beyond the president's control. Yet presidents are held responsible for
> the state of economic affairs during their presidency and have been since
> Franklin Roosevelt's administration. Carter's defeat in 1980 and, espe-
> cially, Bush's defeat in 1992 can be attributed to their perceived failure
> as economic policy makers, while Reagan's victory in 1984 and Clin-
> ton's victory in 1996 can be attributed to their successful policies. (Ed-
> wards and Wayne 2003:462)

It is important to appreciate the magnitude of citizens' economic
demands upon government and to recognize the difficulties presidents
face in trying to satisfy them. Public economic priorities include income
growth, increased employment, less inflation, lower interest rates for
home loans, and an improving stock market. Although they are at the
center of the public's expectations concerning governmental performance, presidents nevertheless are limited by law in what they can do
without securing the support of Congress or the tacit assistance of the
independent Federal Reserve Board.

> The president has neither the constitutional authority nor resources of
> another sort to bend the economy to his will. It is hard to think of any
> step the president could take to affect the state of the economy that
> would not require prior Congressional approval. All tax and spending

proposals fall under the watchful scrutiny of Congress and matters of interest rates and the money supply are removed from direct manipulation by either branch of government. (Nickelsburg and Norpoth 2000:315–16)

## INFLATION, DEFICITS, AND THE FEDERAL RESERVE BOARD

To make matters worse, some of these economic factors work at cross-purposes. For example, while workers welcome larger paychecks, rapid income growth can lead to inflation. This will reduce the purchasing power of that paycheck and will eventually lead the Federal Reserve Board to increase interest rates. A higher interest rate makes it more difficult to borrow money; a higher rate also slows business growth (Cochran et al. 2003). Fed governors are appointed to fourteen-year terms, making them relatively immune from political pressure. While the Fed's actions can slow the economic growth so desired by the public (and therefore by presidents seeking reelection and/or public approval), the central bankers will act as they see fit. However desperately the president may want the Fed to lower interest rates, there is little he can do to assure such an outcome. Thus, Ronald Reagan had to suffer through a period of deep unpopularity while the Fed brought inflation under control at the cost of creating a severe recession in 1981–1982.

Moreover, some of the things a chief executive can promote to bring good economic times in the short run can hurt the country's overall economic health in the long run. Citizens like tax cuts, but they also like tax-supported government programs; so, in practice, tax cuts are rarely accompanied by corresponding reductions in government spending. This was the case for the Reagan tax cut in 1981 and the George W. Bush tax cuts of 2001 and 2003. As a result, the federal budget deficit expanded in all three instances. The economic growth during the Clinton years created the first balanced budgets in a generation, but George W. Bush's tax cuts, coupled with the massive unanticipated Iraq war expenses, led to renewed—indeed, record—federal budget deficits (Mucciaroni and Quirk 2004).

By themselves, large federal budget deficits represent threats to long-term economic growth. They can rattle the stock market and can lead an inflation-wary Fed to raise interest rates (Suskind 2004; Woodward

2000). Since both steps can depress consumer confidence, some long-term effects of tax cuts (e.g., escalating deficits) can undermine the economic good times that the president sought to bring about in the first place (Suskind 2004; Woodward 2000). Presidents concerned about reelection often place the short-term benefits ahead of long-term costs, and administration officials who express doubts about such a strategy—like Paul O'Neill, who served as George W. Bush's first treasury secretary—risk being sacked if they raise such concerns publicly (Suskind 2004).

But others have a different perspective. For example, adherents of supply-side economics argue that the effects of tax cuts and spending reductions can fuel an economic boom. So far, however, those who favor the supply-side approach have been far more effective in cutting taxes than in cutting programs, which has led to increased government interest payments on an expanded federal debt (Woodward 2000). Supply-siders argue that fears about current deficits are overstated and that reduced taxation now will lead to future economic growth, which will in turn increase tax revenues. This is a minority position among economists, but it is highly influential within the Republican Party.

But not all news is bad for presidential policymakers. On the bright side, new presidents are often given considerable public deference when it comes to their economic policies, particularly if the previous president's approach to the economy was seen as less than successful. This public latitude clearly benefited both Reagan and Clinton, two presidents who came to office largely as a result of public frustration with the economy under their predecessors (cf. Abramson et al. 1982, 2002).

> The new administration can count on a substantial credit of goodwill from the public. That is remarkable since that new regime has an utterly unproven record in dealing with the economy. To render this plausible it is worth pointing out that the instances of partisan advantage in the White House follow on the heels of bad economic times. At such moments, with the economy in dire straits, the public votes for a change in the White House and is flush with optimism about the future and the new regime. (Nickelsburg and Norpoth 2000:321)

## PREDICTING PRESIDENTIAL ELECTIONS THROUGH ECONOMIC PERFORMANCE

Many of the most effective economics and elections models include these same key government measures that are of great concern to poli-

cymakers, including gross domestic product (GDP), which is the overall measure of all the goods and services produced in the nation,
unemployment, per capita income, and inflation (Abrams 1980; J.
Campbell 1992; Erikson et al. 2000; Fair 1982; Kiewiet 1983; Lewis-
Beck and Rice 1992). While many citizens are not highly sophisticated
about the intricacies of the economy's performance—few could cite the
unemployment rate or the inflation rate off the top of their heads—past
research has shown that people do receive useful cues about economic
conditions and other political matters through the mass media and from
political elites, as well as their own personal economic experiences
(Erikson et al. 2000; Fiorina 1981; Granato and Krause 2000; Popkin
1991). In other words, citizens use news reports about the national
economic conditions, combined with their own personal experiences,
to help make an assessment of the economy's condition. They then use
that assessment—together with other factors, including their partisan
identification—to determine whether to reward or punish the party that
controls the White House.

While these economic variables have been quite effective in predicting the winners of presidential elections over the past century, the models are not flawless. In 2000, the average forecast for an Al Gore victory
among the seven most popular academic models predicted Gore would
get 56.2 percent of the two-party vote; in actuality the vice president
received 50.2 percent of the votes cast either for himself or for George
W. Bush. Political scientists have tended to blame Gore's campaign
blunders, not the mathematical models themselves, for the poor predictions in 2000 (J. Campbell 2001; Lewis-Beck and Tien 2001; Wlezien
2001). In other words, the economically based predictions might have
worked in 2000 if Gore had focused more intensely on the strong economic growth the United States enjoyed during the Clinton/Gore years,
rather than worrying that any reference to Clinton would link Gore to
the former president's personal misconduct.

There is a certain element of sour grapes about this argument, since
the point of such models is to predict voting behavior on the basis of
underlying conditions regardless of a candidate's behavior. It seems
ungracious, if not unscientific, for theorists to blame practice for failing
to match theory. Nevertheless, some evidence suggests that Gore
should have drawn more attention to the economic gains of the Clinton/
Gore years.

A survey conducted shortly before each presidential election asks voters if their family's financial situation is better, the same as, or worse than a year earlier. In 1996, Bill Clinton received 66 percent of the two-party vote of those who said conditions had improved. In 2000, Al Gore received only 56 percent of the two-party vote of those who agreed with that statement (Abramson et al. 2002). That 10 percentage point gap between the people who made the link between good economic times and the incumbent party in 2000 and 1996 may have been quite significant. Had Gore (together with Clinton) been more persuasive about the economy's improved condition—and had they done more in the campaign to convince journalists and voters that the Democrats deserved the credit for the strong economy—the decision over who would become the forty-third president might never have gotten to the Supreme Court.

Personal impressions can be an important part of the public's assessments of economic conditions in other ways as well. Some scholars believe one of Ronald Reagan's public relations accomplishments as president was to blame the era's economic difficulties on poor performance by the U.S. government, thereby giving people an alternative to blaming themselves for their hard times (Alford 1988). This claim—that the fault lay in one's stars and not in oneself—is, of course, something that many people would prefer to believe under any circumstances. Particularly when contrasted to Carter's depiction of an America in the grip of a malaise, Reagan's arguments improved the public's self-image and helped restore consumer confidence battered by the economic problems of the 1970s (Alford 1988).

## Television's Coverage of Economics

Just as economic issues can be a key factor in public evaluations of presidents, they can dominate network news coverage of presidencies. As table 3.1 demonstrates, stories on economic and business news were the second leading topic on network evening newscasts during the 1990s. The more than 10,000 stories on economic news that appeared throughout the decade represent an average of about one story every night on each network, year after year, as the news agenda zigzagged through short-term saturation coverage of wars, crises, scandals, and elections.

| TABLE 3.1 | **Top Network News Topics** | |
|---|---|---|
| **2000–2004** | **31,339 Total Stories** | **Years as Top Story** |
| Iraq | 6,628 | 2003, 2004 |
| Economy/Business | 5,970 | |
| Terrorism | 5,635 | 2001, 2002 |
| Crime | 5,241 | |
| Health Issues | 4,140 | |
| Disaster/Weather | 2,845 | |
| Campaign '00 | 2,420 | 2000 |
| Israel/Palestine | 2,377 | |
| Sports | 1,737 | |
| Campaign '04 | 1,688 | |
| Accidents | 876 | |
| Russia | 233 | |
| **1990–1999** | **135,449 Total Stories** | **Years as Top Story** |
| Crime | 14,289 | 1993, 1994, 1995, 1997 |
| Economy/Business | 10,488 | |
| Health Issues | 8,817 | |
| USSR/Russia | 5,550 | |
| Disaster/Weather | 5,516 | |
| Yugoslavia/Serbia/Bosnia | 5,412 | 1999 |
| Persian Gulf Crisis/War | 4,869 | 1990, 1991 |
| Sports | 4,487 | |
| Israel/Palestine | 3,244 | |
| Accidents | 2,801 | |
| Clinton Scandals/Impeachment | 2,358 | 1998 |
| Iraq | 2,507 | |
| Campaign '92 | 2,477 | 1992 |
| Campaign '96 | 1,865 | 1996 |

Note: Number of stories on ABC, CBS, and NBC evening newscasts as recorded by the Center for Media and Public Affairs. The number of stories per year fell during the more recent period because the networks produced fewer very short stories and because of the increasing frequency of preemptions for sports programming.

Although some of these stories focused on particular industries and individual businesses, the bulk of them focused on government policies or at least made reference to the government's industrial and trade policies that affected the industry or business being profiled. In addition, many of the stories that focused on the presidential campaigns of 1996 and (especially) 1992 contained considerable economic content.

Economic coverage was exceeded only by crime news, which generated over fourteen thousand stories during the 1990s. Some of this
coverage was relevant to presidential policymaking, such as debates
over sentencing laws and gun control that were influenced by sensationalistic coverage of some criminal acts. But much of it bore little
relation to public expectations and evaluations of a president—the un-
solved killings of Jon-Benet Ramsey and Chandra Levy, the O. J. Simpson murder trial, and many now forgotten cases that briefly made
headlines and then receded from view. Since the bulk of crime news
focuses on particular criminal rampages and trials in particular states, it
is not surprising that this heavy coverage does not make crime salient
to presidential approval. The only exception is terrorism, which is addressed at length in the next chapter. (All references to crime here
do not involve the 9/11 bombings and the anthrax attacks, which are
calculated separately from general crime news.)

Thus, economic news is a kind of default option for the networks,
an ongoing topic always relevant to viewers, which leads the agenda
until it gives way to some major story that shoves it aside. George
W. Bush's administration shows how economic coverage rises and falls
according to competition from major crises. Economic matters were
covered in 11 percent of the network news stories from January 1
through September 10, 2001, but only 7 percent from September 11
through the end of the year. Economic news increased to 10 percent of
the news hole in 2002 but dropped back to 7 percent during 2003—the
year of the American-led invasion and occupation of Iraq.

## Tone of Presidential Economic News Coverage

One clear pattern of economic coverage is that bad news drives out
good news. Bad times are covered extensively, as demonstrated by the
intense media focus on budget, tax, and other economic policies during
the first year of both the Ronald Reagan and Bill Clinton presidencies.
These administrations were primed to focus on economic matters, following the emphasis on those themes in media coverage of the presidential elections of 1992 and 1980 (Abramson et al. 2002).

Table 3.2 shows about equally negative evaluations of all three presi-

| TABLE 3.2 | Tone of Network News Evaluations by Policy Area (Percent Positive) | | | |
| --- | --- | --- | --- | --- |
| | All Evaluations | Foreign Policy | Domestic Policy | Non-Issue Specific |
| **2001** | | | | |
| George W. Bush (n) | 35% (2,197) | 35% (732) | 35% (1,348) | 32% (117) |
| **1993** | | | | |
| Bill Clinton (n) | 34% (3,567) | 38% (740) | 32% (2,680) | 33% (147) |
| **1981** | | | | |
| Ronald Reagan (n) | 33% (1,093) | 28% (330) | 33% (653) | 45% (110) |

dencies. Overall, policy evaluations of the first year of each administration were negative roughly two-thirds of the time: 33 percent positive for Reagan, 34 percent positive for Clinton, and 35 percent positive for George W. Bush. There were more substantial differences from one issue to another. Clinton had the most positive foreign policy coverage, Bush had the highest assessments in domestic policy coverage, and Reagan's evaluations were highest in the non-issue-specific areas, that is, general expressions of support for his policies without naming them.

This pattern does not fit general impressions that scholars and journalists have of the first years of the Clinton and George W. Bush presidencies. Clinton is often seen as more successful in the domestic than in the international arena, as passage of his economic plan was balanced by a disastrous military mission to Somalia, which became the basis for the movie *Black Hawk Down* (Jacobs and Shapiro 1995; Woodward 1994). George W. Bush was widely praised for his response to the terrorist attacks of September 11, but his handling of domestic matters—particularly his tax bill and the partisan defection of U.S. Sen. James Jeffords of Vermont, which cost the Republicans control of the Senate—was more frequently panned (Edwards 2004; Woodward 2002).

Table 3.3 compares the tone of network news coverage on tax policy and in general economic news for the first year in office of these three presidents. The Reagan team's handling of tax policy received the most positive network news coverage of the three administrations, with 45 percent positive coverage. George W. Bush's performance in dealing

| TABLE 3.3 | Tone of Network News Coverage by Domestic Policy Area (Percent Positive) | | | | | |
|---|---|---|---|---|---|---|
| | **2001** | | **1993** | | **1981** | |
| | **Percent** | **Number** | **Percent** | **Number** | **Percent** | **Number** |
| Taxes | 41% | 280 | 20% | 147 | 45% | 51 |
| Economy in General | 44 | 39 | 41 | 205 | 35 | 92 |
| Health Care | 28 | 99 | 34 | 253 | — | — |
| Labor/Air Traffic Controllers' Strike | — | — | — | — | 17 | 59 |

with the economy in general and tax policy in particular during 2001 received almost as much support, with 44 and 41 percent positive coverage, respectively. Coverage of general economic news under Clinton was 41 percent positive in tone, while Reagan's economic coverage was 35 percent positive.

These figures may seem like faint praise, but they are more balanced than the highly negative coverage that presidents can expect many of their policies to receive, as the overall figures indicate. One example is the four-to-one negative ratio (20 percent positive) that greeted Bill Clinton's tax increase, more than twice as negative as the coverage of the tax policies of the other two presidents. Moreover, much of the positive coverage came from administration sources themselves defending their policies.

Table 3.3 also includes a leading noneconomic domestic policy issues for purposes of comparison. Health care was a key issue in the first terms of the two most recent presidents, and Clinton received higher marks than Bush for health care, 34 percent versus 28 percent positive. Reagan received the most negative score on a major domestic issue: the meager 17 percent positive assessment of his decision to fire striking air traffic controllers.

OTHER ECONOMIC NEWS COVERAGE DURING THE
GEORGE W. BUSH YEARS

Even bad economic news can be overshadowed by wars and national defense crises. The Iraq war and its aftermath pushed aside discussion of economic issues during 2003, even though the economic conditions through most of Bush's first term were consistently more challenging than they had been during the Clinton years. During 2003, the network evening newscasts carried four times as many stories on Iraq as on economic and business matters. That represents a drop of almost 30 percent in economic policy news from the previous years, which helps explain why the president's popularity ratings did not suffer from that year's feeble economic growth.

The reduced coverage was no less negative than that seen at other times and for other presidents. Coverage of the Bush's administration's tax policies—the centerpiece of the administration's plan for managing the economy—was only 25 percent positive during 2003, while coverage of other economic policy matters was a mere 16 percent positive in tone.

But all domestic policy issues took a backseat in 2003 and early 2004 to the Iraqi war and the turbulent occupation that followed. The relative lack of attention paid to economic matters during 2003 and early 2004 proved a mixed blessing for the president. The shortage of economic news during this period kept citizens from focusing intensely on economic matters when conditions were disappointing. But that same shortage obscured the fact that overall economic conditions started improving as the 2004 presidential election drew closer.

## ECONOMIC NEWS COVERAGE DURING THE CLINTON ERA

In nonelection years, economic coverage tends to be inversely related to the economy's performance—the better conditions are, the less newsworthy they become. For example, after Bill Clinton won office with his campaign slogan "It's the economy, stupid," TV news coverage on the economy dropped by more than 50 percent, from 1,457 stories in 1993 to 1,192 stories in 1994 to only 710 stories in 1995. It's not as if there was less economic news to report. The record rise of over 1,200 points in the Dow Jones Industrial Average was featured in only 28 stories during 1995 (not counting the "headline" summaries of the Dow's daily movement). In contrast, the networks aired 39 "market crash" stories in only two days after the Dow endured a 500-point drop in October 1987. The networks shouted the bad news but whispered the good news.

The focus of economic coverage during 1993 shifted from Main Street to Pennsylvania Avenue as the new president convinced Congress to pass his budget and tax plans. The debate over the Clinton economic agenda was the top economic issue story of they year, and discussion of international trade matters—including NAFTA (the North American Free Trade Agreement) and GATT (the General Agreement on Tariffs and Trade)—ranked second among economic news stories. The focus on government economic policies meant fewer anecdotes of hard times, stories that had been a key factor in George H. W. Bush's electoral defeat in 1992. The biggest downturn came in the area of unemployment news, down 40 percent from 1992 totals.

But these overall results for Clinton's first twelve months in office obscure important differences in coverage over the course of the year. Coverage of Clinton's economic plan was particularly intense during the first quarter of 1993, which coincided with his crucial "first hundred days" in office. From January through March 1993, the three broadcast networks devoted over five hundred stories and fourteen hours of airtime to the national economy, an increase of 80 percent from the fourth quarter of 1992. The Clinton administration's stated intentions to raise taxes made tax-related issues the most frequently discussed economic topic of early 1993. Various types of taxes were mentioned in one out of every three economic stories, while unemployment and job concerns, the leading economic topic of 1992, dropped to second place. President Clinton's February 17, 1993, State of the Union address generated expanded media coverage of the federal deficit and the need to reduce government spending, the third- and fourth-most-frequent news topics.

The upsurge in coverage of these economic topics after Clinton's inauguration followed an upturn in the tone of economic coverage. During the preceding two years, network news tone of coverage was consistently—and sometimes overwhelmingly—negative. (Our measure derives from clearly positive or negative evaluations of economic health, not inferences about economic statistics.) At least 90 percent of all economic evaluations on network television were negative during thirteen of the twenty-four months from October 1990 through September 1992. During April 1991, not a single positive view was expressed out of sixty-two on-air economic assessments. Audiences were hearing a seemingly endless stream of pessimism, such as a worker's comments that CBS aired on April 15, 1991: "We're in a depression. . . . There's no work. There's no jobs." Throughout the third quarter of 1992 (July–September), 97 percent of all sources offered negative assessments of economic conditions.

The media's gloom lifted during the fourth quarter of 1992, which was punctuated by the presidential election. Positive assessments on economic matters jumped from 3 percent in the third quarter to 50 percent in the fourth quarter. From Election Day, November 3, 1992, through the end of the year, over 60 percent of all evaluations of the economy were favorable—by far the best two-month period of economic news coverage during the Bush administration. The second-most-positive period was the 34 percent positive coverage aired during May 1992. In other words, George H. W. Bush started getting more positive news coverage on the economy only after it was too late to do him any good at the polls.

The glow faded somewhat during Clinton's first quarter in office, but the proportion of positive comments stayed well above previous levels of favorable economic news. Paradoxically, the frequency of economic evaluations that were voiced in TV news stories dropped sharply during the first quarter of 1993, even as overall economic coverage soared. Fewer sources evaluated the economy in those three months than in December 1992 alone. This partly reflects the principle that good news is no news—the better the economic news, the less newsworthy it is deemed. But it also reflects a shift in the national economic debate from whether the economy is broken to how it can be fixed. This trend reflects the considerable difference between covering a presidential campaign and covering the winner once he takes office.

Opinions expressed on network news about the Clinton economic package were balanced during the first quarter of 1993, with a slight majority of sources (54 percent) quoted on network newscasts endorsing the president's plan. Typically, evaluations split along partisan lines: 64 percent of the Democratic sources supported the plan and 91 percent of Republican sources opposed it. This is the unending battle of the sound bites to which politicians devote considerable time and effort. For example, U.S. Rep. Gerald Solomon (R-NY) made the *NBC Nightly News* on March 19, 1993 with this less-than-bon mot: "This bill is a squealer. . . . Oink! Oink! Oink!" Most importantly, nonpartisan sources, such as reporters, experts, and ordinary citizens, voiced approval of Clinton's plan 75 percent of the time. For example, an Amtrak traveler told NBC on February 18, 1993, "I think [Clinton's] concepts are good, the ideas are good, and I'm willing to give it a shot." Such statements from apparently neutral corners have higher "source credibility" with viewers than a partisan politician's barnyard imitations.

Although the general outlines of the plan were well received, some implications were viewed with more skepticism than others. The greatest debate surrounded the prospect of higher taxes, which were rejected by 62 percent of sources during the first quarter of 1993. A California resident told CBS, "I don't like it. All the taxes we've increased, it don't seem like it's helping nothing" (January 25, 1993). Supporters of what nervous politicians sometimes call "revenue enhancements" usually spoke up for particular types of taxes. An environmental activist, for example, expressed support for an energy tax: "You're making the American economy more efficient. You're saving money. You're improving the environment" (ABC, February 18, 1993).

Sources quoted on network news were far more likely to favor cuts in government spending. Over three out of four opinions (77 percent) expressed on network news during the first quarter of 1993 supported this approach. Less spending was usually advocated as either an alternative or a precondition to new taxes. U.S. Rep. Sam Johnson (R-TX) even invoked Clinton's campaign slogan: "It's spending, stupid! The administration should reduce spending before they even talk about tax increases" (ABC, February 16, 1993).

## ECONOMIC NEWS IN PRESIDENTIAL ELECTIONS

During the heat of a presidential campaign, when voters are particularly primed to assess a president's economic performance, economic matters can get short shrift in the news. Television coverage of presidential campaigns often focuses on the "horse race," the question of who is ahead in the latest polls, and the strategies employed by the campaigns to cross the finish line first (Farnsworth and Lichter 2003a; Patterson 1994). In the 2000 election—when many political scientists predicted that Al Gore would win on the basis of the strong economic performance of the country under eight years of Democratic leadership—the broadcast networks said little about economic policies. During the general election, network evening news stories about the Gore and Bush campaign strategies outnumbered stories about their economic policies by a three-to-one margin. The tone of the coverage of economic matters was particularly negative—72 percent of the assessments of Bush's economic plan were negative, as were 64 percent of the assessments of Gore's economic program.

Reporters also ignored the public's concerns over economic matters in the 1996 presidential election, when Bob Dole sought to unseat Bill Clinton. Between Labor Day and Election Day, the tactics and tone of the campaign attracted two hundred stories on the evening news, compared to only fifty-two stories on the candidates' policies on taxes and the economy. Without an effective economic claim to make against Clinton, Dole found it difficult to gain traction with voters. As a result, economic reporting played a more significant role in presidential politics before and during the 1992 elections.

For President George H. W. Bush, the economy was the subject of sustained network news attention when conditions were the worst. During a two-year period starting in October 1990 and ending in September 1992 (a time when the presidential campaign was well under way), the three broadcast networks aired over 2,500 stories totaling 63 hours and 36 minutes of airtime to economic matters. Economic coverage more than doubled in the second half of this period. The coverage peaked with 276 stories in January 1992, driven by Bush's Asian trade trip, the New Hampshire primary, and the analysis of the holiday shopping season. The negative coverage of Bush helped propel television commentator Pat Buchanan—a fierce critic of Bush economic and trade policies—to a strong second-place finish in the New Hampshire primary that year.

Buchanan, who had never held elective office, challenged a sitting president on unemployment, and the intensely negative portrayal of the economy on network television helped fuel his renegade movement. Unemployment was the most newsworthy economic topic for eleven straight months, from October 1991 through August 1992, before being edged out by trade issues in September 1992. This drumbeat of negative economic news triggered worries among even the employed that they might also lose their jobs and helped frame the George H. W. Bush presidency as one of economic underperformance.

After surviving Buchanan's primary challenge, the politically weakened president then faced Clinton and independent billionaire Ross Perot, who joined in hammering away on the consequences of Bush's economic policies. Perot particularly objected to Bush's trade policies, saying they would result in even greater U.S. job losses. Media coverage of the economy helped Bush's two general-election challengers immensely, lending considerable credibility to their criticisms of Bush's economic stewardship. From October 1990 through September 1992, over 90 percent of all network news evaluations of economic conditions were negative. Thus, both Clinton and Perot enjoyed a strong tailwind from the news media during the year, while Bush sailed into a punishing headwind as he campaigned for a second term.

Even as Bush promised that conditions would soon improve, most sources quoted by reporters said otherwise. Three out of five sources (60 percent) quoted during this two-year period predicted more hard times ahead, with the greatest pessimism coming during the 1992 campaign, and 97 percent depicted the coming recovery as weak or slow to develop. As one unemployed man said on the June 5, 1992, edition of ABC's *World News Tonight*, "This recovery is a crock. This is not a real recovery." More than two-thirds of the ordinary citizens profiled on the networks during this period were victims of hard times.

After having some time to reflect on his 1992 defeat, George H. W. Bush lamented the fact that he did not have the communications skills of his predecessor, who so swiftly disposed of both Jimmy Carter in 1980 and Walter Mondale in 1984 (Gold 1994). In particular, Bush observed that reporters were somewhat "behind the curve" in recognizing improving economic conditions in the final months before the 1992 election.

> The reality was that the recession had bottomed out in 1991, and the economy had grown not just by the 2.7 percent [annual rate] I claimed for the third quarter, but by 3.4 percent. And in the fourth quarter it grew at a very robust 5.8 percent [annual rate]—not exactly a recession. The last two quarters of 1992 were better than what the economy had done under President Clinton, but I failed as a communicator. (Bush, quoted in Gold 1994)

WHAT ABOUT HEALTH CARE?

Although health care rivals economics on the news agenda, coverage of health care policy is far more volatile than that of economic policy. While health care issues may affect presidential popularity in particular elections and other periods, they are few and far between. Nineteen ninety-four was such a year, as U.S. Rep. Newt Gingrich (R-GA) helped lead the Republican Party to majority status in both the House and Senate by opposing Bill Clinton's health care reform plan (Skocpol 1997). One could probably add 1993 to the list, as the Clinton administration sought to turn public dissatisfaction with rising medical costs into support for comprehensive reform. But one would be hard-pressed to make the case that health care issues were highly significant during the other six years of the Clinton presidency, much less during recent Republican administrations.

The media's relative inattention to health care policy may change in the future as growing numbers of baby boomers retire and dramatically expand the demands placed upon Medicare—the system of government-supported health care for senior citizens. This pattern may also change if a future president proposes health care changes as sweeping as those proposed by Bill Clinton more than a decade ago. Major changes in the number of people who are uninsured or in the amount of coverage offered insured citizens might increase public attention to health care matters. But for now, the economy takes precedence over health care in political news unless a president makes a concerted effort to change the perspective of reporters.

## Conclusion

This chapter has shown that bad economic news trumps good news, particularly around the time of presidential elections. Incumbent presidents typically face economic news reports that portray the bleak fortunes of ordinary workers, insofar as conditions warrant. The exception to this pattern occurs when other issues pull media and public attention away from the central question of what the economy has done for us lately. By reporting anecdotal stories of suffering individual citizens, news reporters encourage citizens to blame presidents, directly or indirectly, for the country's subpar economic performance (cf. Iyengar 1991; Iyengar and Kinder 1987). These episodic reports rarely provide sufficient context. Reporters do not often talk about how difficult it is for a president to influence the nation's overall economic fortunes and whether the worker being profiled bears some responsibility for his or her plight. To make matters worse for a president, when the economic news is good, some other topic arises to dominate news coverage. Thus, network news gives presidents more blame for economic performance than is appropriate, given the nation's constitutional system of limited government.

The often harsh, negative treatment of the president's performance on economic matters, coupled with the president-centered news coverage of government, helps inflate public perceptions of the president's capacity. When citizens see presidents falling short of unreasonable standards, citizen discontent with the status quo can grow. But how much can one reasonably expect from a president in our political system where power is shared widely?

But the news is not all bad for presidents. Although incoming presidents do not get much of a media honeymoon anymore, economic news appears to be an exception. For example, even though the economy did not pick up immediately after Bill Clinton took office in 1993, the economic coverage nevertheless was far more positive than that which plagued his predecessor. But, even when the economy was improving, Clinton's coverage was not universally upbeat. Discussion of his proposed tax increases—a part of his 1993 plan to reduce a budget deficit that had grown rapidly during the Reagan and George H. W. Bush presidencies—was almost universally negative.

Finally, the evidence once again does not support claims of partisan bias on the part of network television. In chapter 2 we learned that overall network news coverage was almost equally negative toward presidents, regardless of political party. The same holds true for the crucial issue of economic policy, and for domestic policy more generally. Among heavily covered issue areas, the greatest difference in tone appeared on tax policy, on which Democrat Bill Clinton fared far worse than Republicans Ronald Reagan and George W. Bush. If there is any evidence of bias in these economic news data, it is that presidents get better press for lowering taxes than for raising them.

# CHAPTER 4

## PRESIDENTS IN WAR AND PEACE
### Covering Military and Foreign Policy

I can hear you," President George W. Bush said to rescue and salvage workers gathered around a wrecked fire truck that, a few days earlier, had rushed to the crumbling World Trade Center. "The rest of the world hears you. And the people who knocked these buildings down will hear all of us soon" (Frum 2003:140).

Bush was not speaking only to those within earshot of his bullhorn. His true megaphone was the mass media, which sent his vow—and the roars of the crowd shouting, "USA! USA!"—around the world in an instant. Even the new president's most devoted supporters admitted that Bush had struggled in the first few days after that terrible morning, but atop that mangled fire truck the president found his voice—and set in motion a plan designed to remove the continuing threat posed by Osama bin Laden, the terrorist network al Qaeda, and the Taliban government of Afghanistan (Frum 2003).

The terrorist attacks altered the political environment with a suddenness rarely seen in Washington (cf. Pfiffner 2004a). On September 10, 2001, George W. Bush had relatively low public approval ratings: 51 percent in the Gallup survey conducted September 7–10, 2001. He faced a combative Congress, emboldened since May when Bush lost a

Republican Senate majority because of his mishandling of Sen. James Jeffords of Vermont, who left the party to become an independent (Jeffords 2003; Tenpas and Hess 2002). In addition, significant numbers of citizens considered him an illegitimate president put in place by rigged vote-counting in Florida and a partisan Supreme Court that had handed him the presidency on a 5–4 vote (Dimock 2004; Nelson 2004; Pfiffner 2004a).

But all that changed in an instant. Bush's approval ratings shot up to 86 percent in the next Gallup poll (September 14–15, 2001), and Congress quickly approved the aggressive anti-terrorism measures Bush requested, including the Patriot Act and a bailout of the airline industry (Nelson 2004). Virtually all talk of the president's alleged political illegitimacy vanished overnight (Dimock 2004; Pfiffner 2004a). For more than a year after the attacks, Bush continued to possess significant political advantages in Washington, including high approval ratings largely caused by the foreign policy situation (Hetherington and Nelson 2003). A still largely docile Congress in late 2002 allowed Bush to wage war in Iraq, even though that country's links to bin Laden and its alleged weapons of mass destruction programs were doubted in some parts of the national security community (Clarke 2004; Fisher 2004; Gaines 2002; Pollack 2004; Suskind 2004).

What bin Laden and his associates had wrought during George W. Bush's first year as president was nothing short of remarkable. Even a critical news media turned largely compliant. While Americans have frequently rallied around their president in times of crisis, the magnitude of the transformation post-9/11 was extraordinary. Four decades earlier, the Cuban missile crisis of October 1962—the closest the United States and the USSR ever came to nuclear war—triggered only a 12 percentage point jump in President Kennedy's approval ratings (Pfiffner 2004a). And the peace treaty that ended U.S. military involvement in South Vietnam and allowed for the return home of prisoners of war held by the North Vietnamese gave Richard Nixon a 16 percentage point bounce, roughly half the 35 points George W. Bush gained in public approval in the immediate aftermath of the terrorist attack (Pfiffner 2004b).

September 11, 2001, marked the deadliest day on American soil since the Japanese attack at Pearl Harbor—a fact frequently mentioned in the first days of news coverage of the terrorist attacks. Had an earlier generation of pollsters conducted comparable presidential approval surveys sixty years ago, we still might not have seen as large a jump in the poll ratings, since in December 1941 Franklin Delano Roosevelt was already a highly popular figure (Beschloss 2002; Burns and Dunn 2001), and the attack took place far from the U.S. mainland in the days before television brought war up close and personal.

This chapter examines network news coverage of the most powerful policy aspect of the presidency: the conduct of military and foreign policy. It represents a sharp contrast from news coverage of economic matters, an area where the president receives far less deference—and has far less authority to act unilaterally. In chapter 2 we compared news coverage of government before and after the 2001 terrorist attacks. In this chapter we analyze the coverage of leading foreign and military policy matters across recent presidencies. We first discuss some of the leading research in this area, which helps place our findings in context. We then describe network news coverage of specific foreign policy events during George W. Bush's first term. These include the 2003 Iraq war, the early phase of the occupation of Iraq, the war in Afghanistan, and the immediate aftermath of the 2001 terrorist attacks on the Twin Towers and the Pentagon. We compare these portions of the George W. Bush presidency with news coverage of Bill Clinton's air strikes in Kosovo and the 1991 Gulf War, led by President George H. W. Bush. (The controversies over the torture of prisoners in Iraq and whether Bush and others in his administration told the truth about what they knew regarding weapons of mass destruction in Iraq and alleged links between Saddam Hussein and bin Laden are examined in chapter 5, which focuses on presidential scandals.)

## Presidential Messages in Military and Foreign Policy

### THE TWO PRESIDENCIES THESIS

Traditionally, presidents have had far more success in shaping defense and foreign policy than domestic policy. The differences are so stark that scholars often speak of "two presidencies"—one foreign and one domestic. The president exercises greater latitude in foreign policy for three reasons: he has greater constitutional authority in that area, the executive branch can act more quickly in a crisis, and the president traditionally has taken the leading U.S. role in international matters (Edwards and Wayne 2003; Oldfield and Wildavsky 1989; Sullivan 1991; Wildavsky 1966).

Congress, which is frequently preoccupied with domestic matters, does not simply accept all executive branch approaches to foreign policy crises indefinitely. Presidential overreaching and deceit in Vietnam, coupled with Richard Nixon's trampling of legislative prerogatives, led to the War Powers Resolution of 1974, which was designed to strengthen Congress's authority in foreign policy matters (Edwards and Wayne 2003). While presidents continue to exercise great control over foreign policy decision making, many recent presidents (but not George W. Bush) have granted Congress additional influence in this sphere (Carter 1986; Fisher 2004).

The two presidencies thesis has had powerful public effects as well. Numerous political scientists have long argued that citizens rally to the president during an international crisis, particularly one that is unexpected and highly threatening (Mueller 1973). Presidents may take on the role of a national "father" during such times (cf. Easton and Dennis 1969). If there is no substantial vocal opposition to the president's handling of an unfolding crisis, the chief executive's poll numbers usually improve, often for an extended period of time (Brody 1991; Hetherington and Nelson 2003; Nincic 1997). The president is less likely to see greater public support in the face of vocal opposition. Even if such a rally effect occurs despite such criticism, it will likely not last long (Hetherington and Nelson 2003).

The combative partisan politics of the past decade may mark the end of the "two presidencies" theories in practice. Researchers argue that—at least apart from the 9/11 period—the profound partisan divisions seen in Washington in recent years have greatly reduced the traditional legislative branch dictum that "politics stops at the water's edge" (cf. Fleisher and Bond 2000a, 2000b). Indeed, the modern presidency could be defined as the "polarized presidency"—a time of ideologically opposed congressional parties and divided party government that affects the conduct of both domestic and foreign policy (Cameron 2002).

Presidential appeals to build public support may be increasingly difficult for the polarized presidency—even in foreign policy—because most voters and elected officials already have made up their minds about the nation's chief executive. The president's adversaries, armed with research studies, think-tank expertise, and other independent sources of information, are far more able to challenge the president's perspective than in the past (Pious 2002). "In sum, presidents will increasingly be tempted to use Theodore's Roosevelt's 'bully pulpit,' only to find that it has become little more than a noisy corner in Hyde Park" (Cameron 2002:658). "Going public," in other words, may not be what it used to be.

The demands of modern life are great, and many busy people use the news media as a labor-saving device. By watching television news, citizens attempt to learn which issues are most important and what the latest developments are on these high-priority topics. The shape of news coverage, in other words, encourages people to think more about certain issues and to think about those issues in certain ways (Iyengar 1991; Iyengar and Kinder 1987). The first process is called agenda-setting; the second is called framing.

> Frames serve multiple functions for different actors. Political leaders can respond to events and communicate political priorities simply and effectively by adopting predominant culture frames to streamline and simplify their message ("I condemn all such acts of terrorism"). Reporters can "tell it like it is" within 60 seconds, or with brief newspaper headlines, rapidly sorting key events from surrounding trivia. And the public can use frames to sort out and make sense of complex and unfamiliar events, peoples and leaders. (Norris et al. 2003:11)

Consistent with the agenda-setting function of the mass media, Americans are particularly likely to use foreign policy matters in their evaluations of a president during and immediately following an international crisis (Krosnick and Brannon 1993; Soroka 2003). However, past research on media coverage and public opinion during the 1991 Persian Gulf War found that the effect on the public was limited to the crisis itself. Increased media attention to the war increased public use of that issue—but not other foreign policy topics—in evaluations of George H. W. Bush. The rapid ejection of Iraqi forces from Kuwait, coupled with the relatively small numbers of U.S. casualties, helped boost Bush's approval in early 1991 beyond what it would have been had his public assessment been based more on economic conditions (Krosnick and Brannon 1993). When the fighting stopped, voters again focused on the economy, and the first President Bush's approval numbers fell dramatically (Edwards et al. 1995:120).

The same pattern was found for President Reagan in the immediate aftermath of the Iran-contra affair disclosures of 1986. When the news agenda shifted to the scandal, more citizens incorporated that issue into their evaluations of the president (Krosnick and Kinder 1990). But the news media's focus is not always decisive. President Clinton retained high approval numbers throughout his impeachment because many people cared more about the economy than they did about Monica Lewinsky, even though that scandal generated massive news coverage (I. Morris 2002).

Overall, researchers have found that citizens evaluate presidents roughly equally on economic and foreign policy matters most of the time (J. Cohen 2002a, 2002b; Edwards et al. 1995; Nickelsburg and Norpoth 2000). Quarterly and monthly presidential approval measures demonstrate the importance that both domestic and international matters play in public assessments of the president. But the two issues vary greatly in influence from month to month and from year to year, depending on which issue dominates public discussion.

The range of debate in Washington, particularly on foreign policy, is often limited by the range of opinions expressed by government officials (Bennett 2005; Iyengar and Kinder 1987). When considerable disagreement exists among policymakers in Washington, it is also reflected in news reports. Foreign policy news published before the 1991 Persian Gulf War rarely made reference to congressional war powers, unless Congress itself was challenging executive power (D. Lewis and Rose 2002). The relative paucity of such discussion can leave readers and viewers with an erroneous impression that these military policy decisions are solely executive branch matters (D. Lewis and Rose 2002; Lowi 1985). It also raises the possibility that some people may equate legislative disagreement with disloyalty—a link the president's advocates sometimes try to encourage (cf. Fisher 2004; Lindsay 2003).

## THE GEORGE W. BUSH PRESIDENCY: NEW RESEARCH QUESTIONS AND ANSWERS

The 2001 terrorist attacks dramatically affected the legislative branch's approach to foreign policy. During the 1990s, President Clinton faced a Congress that sought to block his international initiatives and frequently succeeded. Bush's post-9/11 presidency has been marked by considerable legislative branch deference on matters that otherwise would have been very controversial—most notably the Iraq Resolution of 2002 and the Patriot Act of 2001 (Baker 2002; Kassop 2003; Lindsay 2003). The antiterrorism measures in particular have helped the executive branch regain presidential prerogatives that had been undermined after Watergate and during the Clinton impeachment period (Baker 2002).

Wars usually expand executive branch power, and the authority claimed by George W. Bush is at least on par with that claimed by previous wartime presidents (Fisher 2004; Lindsay 2003). The United States has been in an effective state of emergency throughout nearly all of his administration. In the wake of the terrorist attacks, Bush established a military tribunal system, convinced Congress to approve virtually open-ended authorizations for the use of force in both Afghanistan and Iraq, denied some U.S. citizens constitutional protections (including prompt access to a lawyer), rejected effective congressional oversight of military expenditures, and unilaterally exempted certain military detainees from the prisoner-of-war protections of the Geneva Convention (Baker 2002; C. Brown 2003; Fisher 2004). As we see in this chapter, few objections were raised to these policies at the outset, either in Congress or in the media.

> The change that September 11 caused in executive-legislative relations was extreme but not unprecedented. The pendulum of power on foreign policy has shifted back and forth between Congress and the president many times over the course of American history. The reason for this ebb and flow does not lie in the Constitution. Its formal allocation of foreign policy powers, which gives important authorities to both Congress and the president, has not changed since it was drafted. Rather, the answer lies in politics. How aggressively Congress exercises its foreign policy powers turns on the critical questions of whether the country sees itself as threatened or secure and whether the president's policies are succeeding or failing. (Lindsay 2003:531)

Times of national emergency draw considerable public and media attention to the president, giving the White House an even more dominant position in the tug-of-war within official Washington over how to frame news events. George W. Bush has been particularly effective since 9/11 in the use of a frame that minimizes public disagreement over how to interpret foreign policy events (Norris et al. 2003). If citizens or lawmakers criticize presidential policies during wartime, they face being portrayed as disloyal by a president who holds the world's loudest bullhorn (Kellner 2003). When Bush said in the wake of the terrorist attacks, "You are either with us or with the terrorists," he reduced the amount of criticism he would receive from Democrats—at least in the short term. Under such conditions the judicial branch—the part of the political system designed to be least susceptible to public opinion—may become the most effective check on the executive.

Despite Bush's post-9/11 domination of Congress, there were some efforts on Capitol Hill to impose limits on the president's antiterrorism powers. Even though Congress passed the Patriot Act, for example, lawmakers of both parties pushed for "sunset" provisions in the law to ensure that the act's most controversial provisions would not remain in force after 2005 without further congressional action (Lindsay 2003).

Congress was far less deferential in the domestic policy realm. Democrats blocked Bush's economic stimulus plan and his proposal to drill for oil in the Arctic Wildlife Refuge, and they filibustered many of his more controversial judicial nominees (Lindsay 2003). In addition, some foreign policy issues received more scrutiny as time passed. When word surfaced in early 2003 of draft legislation for a "Patriot Act II," lawmakers rushed to criticize the proposal (Lane 2003).

Discontent with the Bush presidency among the general public also grew stronger as the months passed. The president's critics became increasingly vocal—and increasingly visible on television—as 9/11 receded into the past, as more critical information emerged concerning the Bush administration's justification for the Iraq war, and as the 2004 presidential election grew nearer. Likewise, the president's poll numbers returned to pre-9/11 levels as the 2004 election season approached and the Iraq controversies captured greater media attention (Clarke 2004; Suskind 2004; Pew 2004b).

In deciding to go to war in Iraq, President Bush took a strategic gamble of potentially historic proportions. He vowed not just to unseat a ruthless dictator and destroy his weapons of mass destruction but also to bring democracy to the Iraqi people and to the Middle East. Should the military occupation of Iraq begin to look like the U.S. peace-keeping mission in Lebanon in 1983, the political winds could quickly reverse. In that event, Bush would discover what Lyndon Johnson learned more than three decades ago—the fact that members of Congress defer to the White House when his foreign policy takes off does not mean they will be deferential when it crashes. (Lindsay 2003:545)

## THE CNN EFFECT?

For more than a decade, academics have debated the "CNN effect," noting that the growing pervasiveness of news forces politicians to become increasingly sensitive to the content of news reports being beamed around the world (cf. P. Robinson 2002). The international media makes it more difficult, as well, for individuals—even presidents—to shape media coverage of international matters to their liking, particularly during armed conflicts (R. Brown 2003; Hall 2001).

The new media environment is marked by a vast increase in the flow of information from and to war zones via news organizations, NGOs and individuals. . . . As information flows out of the battle space more quickly, it becomes more feasible for external groups to exert influence through their political response to events. These external groups may be the American public, governments sympathetic or opposed to the cause, allied publics and the Arab street. Reports are events in their own right. (R. Brown 2003:47)

The effects of this new media environment are not limited to military matters. Once images of humanitarian crises—whether of widespread starvation in Ethiopia, concentration camps in Serbia, or flooding in Bangladesh—are aired worldwide on television, government officials in western democracies may come under pressure to respond to public outrage (Entman 2000). While Western nations sometimes intervene (as in Kosovo), they often take insufficient measures (as in the genocides in Rwanda in 1994 and in Sudan a decade later). Thus, political leaders do not always face a domestic public outcry associated with the CNN effect theory (Kristof 2004; Power 2002).

In addition, some research suggests that the pattern is actually the opposite. Officials may use the media to build up public pressure for intervention, rather than responding to the "bottom up" pressure proposed by the CNN effect theory. In the case of Somalia in 1992, for example, government officials made considerable efforts to draw media and public attention to the civil unrest before the television networks turned their attention to the troubled country (Mermin 1997). Still other findings suggest that this effect is most pronounced when policymakers are divided over a course of action and the debate spurs greater news coverage (P. Robinson 2002).

## POLITICAL PSYCHOLOGY AND THE FOREIGN POLICY PRESIDENCY

Presidential scholars who examine presidential–public relations in the area of foreign policy sometimes turn to the field of political psychology for guidance. Research regarding Ronald Reagan, in particular, often turns to psychological theories to explain the enduring appeal of the fortieth president. Reagan, who became president during a time of unusual stress in the international political environment, may have been particularly appealing to many citizens because of his frequent references to traditional American values—in particular the long-time desire for renewed independence from international entanglements (Alford 1988).

Reagan's aggressive support for space-based weapons systems (dubbed by critics at the time as "Star Wars") was a particularly appealing vision that created the possibility of restoring the pre–World War II perspective of U.S. invulnerability to potentially hostile nations. People who felt vulnerable because of the "mutually assured destruction" of the Cold War, the aggressiveness of the Soviet Union, and the U.S. economic dislocations of the 1970s could latch onto an appealing nostalgic vision of a more secure past, according to some scholars (Alford 1988).

Taking a page from Ronald Reagan, George W. Bush also has tried to make emotion-invoking appeals based on cultural values. By calling for bin Laden to be captured "dead or alive," Bush drew upon traditional images of the frontier sheriff in the days of the Wild West. Bush's frequent references to religious imagery in his speeches likewise offer comfort to those familiar with the biblical language employed (Gregg 2004). The president's plan to use the Iraqi transfer of power to create another beachhead for democracy in the region also draws upon widely accepted values in the United States (Linsday 2003). In other cases, though, his comments can rankle. Muslims from around the world were not pleased with Bush's original use of the word "crusade" to refer to U.S. Middle East policies, as that word recalls past Christian-Muslim religious wars (Kellner 2003). In fairness, it should be noted that conservatives have attacked such psychopolitical critiques as attempts to explain away the appeal of some Republican presidents as irrational, when the same sorts of emotional appeals could be applied to any successful exercise of presidential leadership (Frum 2003; Gregg 2004).

Groupthink—the tendency of several people to reach consensus during discussion of a particular issue—is a major source of miscalculation in presidential administrations (Janis 1982). Too often presidents reward members of their administration who say what the president wants to hear, creating a powerful incentive for even high-ranking administration officials to go along with what they perceive as the president's preferences (Burke and Greenstein 1989). The media sometimes reflect this group consensus, narrowing the range of "acceptable" public debate (Bennett 2005; Gitlin 1980). The pressure for groupthink may be particularly powerful in foreign policy, since only limited information from a small number of sources may be available. But that is where groupthink may have the most dangerous consequences (Burke and Greenstein 1989; Janis 1982; Lowi 1985). During wartime, even the lawmakers from the opposing party may accept the president's pronouncements on foreign and military policy (Fisher 2004).

## Foreign Policy News Coverage Trends

### FOREIGN POLICY COVERAGE ACROSS PRESIDENCIES

Much like Pearl Harbor sixty years earlier, the al Qaeda attacks on the World Trade Center and the Pentagon triggered disbelief among Americans, not only over the massive loss of life, but also over the magnitude of change in the public's worldview. No longer could the

United States stand on the sidelines as other parts of the world raged with extremist violence. The "Pax Americana" thought to have descended on these shores after the collapse of the Soviet Union had proved fleeting.

For network news as well, the terrorist attacks signaled the need for greater attention to international matters. Network news budget cuts and the end of the Cold War had led to substantial declines in the number of expensive foreign news bureaus operated by the networks and the share of newscasts devoted to foreign news. Coverage of foreign topics had fallen by more than a third from the 34 percent of the nightly news reports that focused on foreign topics in 1991, dropping to as low as 20 percent of the newscasts in 1996 and 1997.

As shown in table 4.1, foreign news coverage during that part of 2001 before September 11 stood at 21 percent of total news coverage

| TABLE 4.1 | Proportion of Foreign News on Network Evening Newscasts |
|---|---|
| **George W. Bush** | |
| 2003 | 43% (19% without Iraq) |
| 2002 | 27% |
| 2001* (full year) | 27% |
|   (post–September 11) | 36% |
|   (pre–September 11) | 21% |
| **Bill Clinton** | |
| 2000 | 22% |
| 1999 | 21% |
| 1998 | 24% |
| 1997 | 20% |
| 1996 | 20% |
| 1995 | 27% |
| 1994 | 30% |
| 1993* | 26% |
| **George H. W. Bush** | |
| 1992 | 29% |
| 1991 | 34% |
| 1990 | 33% |

*Note:* Based on ABC, CBS, and NBC evening newscasts. All percentages above are for full calendar years unless otherwise noted.
*Presidents do not take office until January 20.

in 2001, rising to 36 percent of coverage after the terrorist attacks. But the increase triggered by the terrorist attacks and the subsequent war in Afghanistan was only temporary. In 2002—a year when Bush pressured Congress to authorize an invasion of Iraq, the U.S. government frequently issued warnings of impending terrorist attacks, and Osama bin Laden remained at large—foreign news dropped to 27 percent of all coverage, comparable to the amount of foreign news coverage that the networks aired during the early 1990s.

## The Iraq War and Occupation of 2003

All this changed with the invasion of Iraq. That single country in 2003 was the subject of one-quarter of all news stories aired on the broadcast network evening news shows, and 43 percent of all news stories focused on foreign news—by far the highest percentage of foreign news since the Center for Media and Public Affairs (CMPA) started calculating these annual percentages in 1990.

The 3,433 stories on Iraq represent over ten times the amount devoted to the foreign country that ranked second in U.S. news—Israel, the subject of 337 stories during the year. North Korea ranked third with 152 stories, and fourth-place Afghanistan—so recently the center of public attention—attracted only 98 stories.

There were 810 stories on Iraq before the war started on March 18; 1,052 stories during the period between March 19 and May 1, when President Bush declared an end to major hostilities; and another 1,571 during the final eight months of the year. During this period the United States occupied Iraq, pursued and eventually captured Saddam Hussein, and searched for the "weapons of mass destruction" that had been the Bush administration's key stated justification for the war.

When George W. Bush decided to wage war in Iraq, both media and public attention turned away from the occupation of Afghanistan and the hunt for al Qaeda. Only 132 stories in 2003 focused on the ongoing efforts to capture or kill Osama bin Laden and otherwise combat al Qaeda, further evidence of the short attention span of television news. This paucity of coverage suggests that citizens need not worry so much about al Qaeda and should not evaluate the Bush administration on whether or not it was able to succeed in capturing bin Laden "dead or alive."

Throughout his presidency, George W. Bush's coverage on the network evening news programs has oscillated between very positive and very negative periods. He received 63 percent positive coverage in 2001 after the terrorist attacks of September 11, in contrast to the 36 percent positive coverage he received during the first two-thirds of the year. During 2002, Bush's coverage was 38 percent positive in tone.

Embedded reporters and military successes early in 2003 sparked another period of relatively even-handed coverage—49 percent positive in tone during the actual war. Once the occupation and reconstruction activities began in Iraq, reporters turned increasingly to questions that did not place the Bush administration in a favorable light: Where were the weapons of mass destruction? Why is there continued armed resistance, particularly since the administration had promised the U.S. troops would be greeted as liberators? Thus his coverage was only 32 percent positive during the six months after May 1, 2003, when the president declared major combat operations had concluded.

Partisan sources from May 1 through October 31 generally were predictable in their assessments during the early phase of the occupation of Baghdad. Only 3 percent of foreign policy assessments of Bush from people identified on-air as Democrats were positive, as compared to 82 percent positive assessments from people identified as Republicans. Sources who were not identified with either party (therefore less likely to be discounted by voters) were generally negative: only 31 percent of nonpartisan comments expressed support for Bush's policies.

The intense Democratic criticism during this period may have reflected bad feelings growing out the 2002 midterm elections (Nelson 2004). In addition, the rise of insurgent Democratic presidential candidate Howard Dean, the former governor of Vermont, may have increased pressure on the other candidates to join Dean's harsh denunciations of Bush's foreign and domestic policies. For example, U.S. Rep. (and presidential candidate) Dick Gephardt (D-MO), complained on NBC on May 2, 2003, "He's really asking now to do more of what's already failed. It makes no sense."

On-air assessments of other institutions and individuals associated with the Iraq policy faced particularly harsh treatment on the evening news programs during this six-month period. The Defense Department was the subject of coverage that was 26 percent positive in tone, and Secretary Donald Rumsfeld—who had been something of a media darling earlier in the administration—was treated favorably only 22 percent of the time. CIA Director George Tenet was treated a bit more positively than was his agency (27 percent positive personal coverage versus 23 percent positive institutional coverage), but again the coverage was quite negative in both instances. The State Department (33 percent positive) and Secretary of State Colin Powell (31 percent positive), who put his credibility on the line with a prewar speech at the United Nations on Iraq's alleged weapons of mass destruction programs, were also treated quite negatively.

The low spot, though, was "the administration" itself, which received coverage that was only 16 percent positive in tone. U.S. Sen. Joseph Lieberman (D-CT)—a Democratic presidential candidate who supported the invasion of Iraq—told CBS on July 15, 2003, "This administration, when it comes to Iraq, is in the process of giving a bad name to a just cause."

The administration faced heavy criticism for a whole host of international news topics in the wake of Bush's declaration that major combat operations had ceased. Coverage of the administration's handling of international terrorism issues generally—once the key to this president's popularity and positive media treatment—was only 20 percent positive in tone between May 1 and October 31, 2003. News reports of general defense matters were only 21 percent positive, and even news reports on the administration's policy regarding the 9/11 attacks were only 28 percent positive in tone.

The negativity expressed toward the Bush administration during mid-2003 was sometimes quite harsh and a sharp departure from the post-9/11 assessments. As nonpartisan military analyst William Arkin told NBC on September 26, 2003, "What the Bush administration still has not come to grips with is that in fact the Iraqis were not in possession of chemical and biological weapons, and therefore pre-emptive use of force was not justified."

The rally 'round the president effect has been a consistent part of network coverage during recent international military crises, regardless of the president's party. Table 4.2 demonstrates that generally positive

| TABLE 4.2 | Tone of Network News Coverage of Presidents in Wartime (Percent Positive) |
|---|---|

**George W. Bush (2003 Iraq, early occupation phase)**

| All Networks | 32% |
|---|---|
| ABC | 33% |
| CBS | 23% |
| NBC | 38% |

**George W. Bush (2003 Iraq, combat phase)**

| All Networks | 49% |
|---|---|
| ABC | 39% |
| CBS | 55% |
| NBC | 56% |

**George W. Bush (2001 Terrorist Attack)**

| All Networks | 64% |
|---|---|
| ABC | 64% |
| CBS | 65% |
| NBC | 69% |

**Bill Clinton (1999 Kosovo Crisis)**

| All Networks | 62% |
|---|---|
| ABC | 62% |
| CBS | 70% |
| NBC | 57% |

**George H. W. Bush (1991 Persian Gulf War)**

| All Networks | 56% |
|---|---|
| ABC | 44% |
| CBS | 63% |
| NBC | 58% |

*Note:* The 2003 Iraq early occupation phase data are from evening newscasts from May 1 through October 31; the 2003 Iraq combat phase data are from March 19 through April 30; the 2001 data are from evening newscasts from September 11 through November 19; the 1999 data are from evening newscasts from March 24 through May 25; and the 1991 data are from evening newscasts from January 17 through February 27.

coverage and allows us to compare the coverage of the George W. Bush presidency with that of earlier military crises like Kosovo in 1999 and the 1991 Persian Gulf War. Coverage of President Bush in the immediate aftermath of September 11, 2001, stood at 64 percent positive in tone, slightly higher than the 62 percent positive coverage Bill Clinton received during the Kosovo crisis of 1999, and the highest of all military crises examined here. George H. W. Bush received 56 percent positive coverage on network television during the 1991 Gulf War, slightly better than his son received during the combat phase of the 2003 Iraq war, when coverage was 49 percent positive in tone. The 2003 war in Iraq marked the most negative wartime coverage during these four wartime periods.

But once a war ends—or once the president claims it has ended—coverage of the president routinely becomes far more negative, regardless of the war's eventual outcome. Coverage of the first six months of the occupation of Iraq was far more negative than any of the combat periods examined in table 4.2. The coverage was about as negative as that for presidents generally (see table 2.7).

## THE IMAGES OF EMBEDDED JOURNALISM

There were some important differences in network news coverage of the combat phase of the 2003 Iraq war and the 1991 Gulf War. There were, on average, forty-one stories a day on the three networks during the 1991 war, as compared to thirty-two stories an evening on average during the 2003 war—a 22 percent drop.

At the same time, technological improvements in news gathering, together with the Pentagon "embedding" program of placing journalists with individual military units, led to an increased volume of combat footage: over one in three stories in the 2003 Iraq war (35 percent)

| TABLE 4.3 | Tone of Network News Coverage by Foreign Policy Area (Percent Positive) | | | | | |
|---|---|---|---|---|---|---|
| | **2001** | | **1993** | | **1981** | |
| | **Percent** | **Number** | **Percent** | **Number** | **Percent** | **Number** |
| **Terrorism** | 43% | 175 | — | — | — | — |
| **China–Spy Plane** | 34% | 202 | — | — | — | — |
| **Somalia** | — | — | 34% | 113 | — | — |
| **Bosnia** | — | — | 28% | 159 | — | — |
| **AWACS** | — | — | — | — | 37% | 101 |

contained combat footage, compared to only one in five (20 percent) reports on the 1991 Gulf War. The embedding program offers the potential for compromised journalism on the part of even conscientious reporters who must rely on the U.S. military for their personal safety before and after the news reports are filed (cf. Graber 2003). After all, making enemies of one's protectors in such a dangerous environment may be reckless, if not foolhardy.

Even so, traveling with U.S. military units allowed reporters to provide powerful pictures illustrating some of the humanitarian consequences of war. For example, images of civilian casualties were shown in 18 percent of stories during the 2003 combat period, as compared to only 3 percent of the 1991 reports. Images of military casualties from allied forces (U.S. and British), in contrast, declined from 12 percent of the stories in 1991 to 2 percent of the stories in 2003.

## THE 2003 IRAQ WAR ON THE FOX NEWS CHANNEL AND THE NETWORKS

The 2003 Iraq war provides a particularly effective opportunity to compare network news coverage with that of an upstart rival, the Fox News Channel. (Financial limitations prevented our including PBS and CNN in this comparison.) Although the audience for Fox News is far smaller than that for network television, the distinctive approach of Rupert Murdoch's network offers an important point of comparison for viewers and journalists alike—and surveys show that Fox is particularly appealing to conservative viewers (Pew 2004a).

From the first missile attacks of March 19 through the fall of Tikrit on April 14, Fox News Channel's *Special Report with Brit Hume* provided more than twice as much coverage of the war as the big three networks on average (14 hours 39 minutes versus 7 hours 17 minutes). *Special Report* lasts an hour, compared to the thirty-minute evening newscasts on ABC, CBS, and NBC, and the expanded program helps explain the greater volume of coverage. But Fox also offered the most focused coverage of the war on its evening newscast: Iraq accounted for 95 percent of all its stories during the twenty-six-day period of intense combat, as compared to 88 percent of the coverage on ABC, 85 percent on NBC, and 77 percent on CBS.

Even in normal times, the most controversial aspect of media coverage is tone. And wars pose unique issues for the media. Some critics argue that reporters have a patriotic duty to abandon objectivity at such moments and support the war effort. Others argue that this is precisely the time that the country needs an independent perspective from journalism.

Fox promotes itself as "fair and balanced" in its handling of news in contrast to the traditional "liberal media," while its critics see it as a conservative cheerleader for Republican policies. We found Fox to be pro-war overall. But it was neither the most pro-war network nor the least. In fact, the war you saw on television depended greatly on the network you watched.

In order to provide a comprehensive comparison, we examined the tone of coverage on three dimensions—the Bush administration's Iraq policies, the U.S. military's performance, and the debate over going to war. We then combined these three measures to create an overall news coverage index of pro- versus antiwar tone during the twenty-six days of full-scale combat. Overall, sources on the three broadcast networks were evenly balanced: 50 percent of the sentiments that expressed a clear opinion were pro-war, and 50 percent were antiwar. But the overall figures mask very stark differences. ABC, with 34 percent pro-war versus 66 percent antiwar coverage, and CBS, with 74 percent pro-war versus 26 percent antiwar coverage, offered very different presentations of Iraq war news, and both differed from the more evenhanded NBC, with 53 percent pro-war coverage. While Fox's 60 percent pro-war coverage was more hawkish than the network average by 10 percentage points during this period, it was still 14 percentage points behind CBS, the most hawkish network.

Even the late-night comics noticed that the media offered very different descriptions of the war. On April 7, 2003, *Tonight Show* host Jay Leno joked: "I had something strange happen to me yesterday. I'm coming to work, I turn on the radio in the morning. It seems the war is going very badly. We weren't in control. The enemy was escaping, the people of Iraq hated us. Then I'm driving home, we're winning every battle, we're racing towards Baghdad, we're being cheered on by the Iraqi people. And then I realized what happened. On the way in I was listening to National Public Radio. On the way home, I was listening to Fox!"

But of course the stark differences in war coverage represent more than fodder for late-night comics. The quantitative evidence from this twenty-six-day period of intense combat presented here raises important questions about the quality of news coverage. First, one would expect media outlets—particularly the big three networks which are competing for the same general viewership and are covering the same events—to offer relatively similar perspectives of the same news events. What accounts for the differences? Second, one can question how well informed viewers were about this war if the perspective they received differed so profoundly depending on the network they watched.

## The Kosovo Crisis of 1999

As president, Bill Clinton never waged a war anywhere near the magnitude of the invasion of Iraq. The military policies of his presidency were much smaller in scale—usually humanitarian interventions in response to civil wars or repressive governments, including Somalia, Bosnia, Kosovo, bombing runs against Osama bin Laden and Saddam Hussein, and military action against the ruling junta in Haiti (L. Berman and Goldman 1996; Goldman and L. Berman 2000). Kosovo involved by the far the largest military response of the Clinton years—a thirty-three-thousand sortie bombing campaign of Serbia by the United States and its NATO partners that did not involve the death of a single U.S. aviator (W. Berman 2001). Serbia's brutal domination of the Kosovo region triggered U.S. pressure for a negotiated settlement between Serbian president Slobodan Milosevic and the Kosovo Liberation Army in the months before the NATO attacks, but negotiators consistently failed to make progress (W. Berman 2001). The bombing campaign began in March, in the wake of a Serbian campaign that expelled 850,000 ethnic Albanians from Kosovo. In June, Kosovo became, in effect, a NATO protectorate, as Serbians agreed to withdraw from the province (W. Berman 2001).

As a result of his aggressive media management efforts, and the absence of U.S. casualties, President Clinton received mostly favorable on-air assessments for his handling of the crisis. Six out of every ten comments on the evening news supported his administration's efforts, though nearly half of those comments came from the president himself as he defended NATO and U.S. policy. Clinton's aggressive personal media strategy provides another clear example of how presidents can shape the tone of media coverage by a strategy of being very visible, and very vocal, in front of reporters.

Much of the criticism of Clinton's Kosovo policies came from foreign sources. For example, a Serbian man said on ABC's *World News Tonight* on March 29, "Not even Hitler did what Clinton is doing to us." But there was some domestic criticism as well. U.S. Sen. John McCain (R-AZ), a leading congressional voice on military matters, said on the NBC *Nightly News* on May 3, "Publicly and repeatedly ruling out ground troops may be smart politics according to the president's pollster, but it is inexcusable and irresponsible leadership."

McCain's criticism was one of the few voices urging that the president leave open the option of sending U.S. ground forces into the region. During this period, 72 percent of the on-air sources used in these evening newscasts opposed the use of ground troops in the Kosovo crisis. As the Cato Institute's Ted Galen said on the March 31, 1999, edition of ABC's *World News Tonight*, "Somalia should certainly be an object lesson for anyone who suggests sending ground troops to Kosovo. That was a very bitter experience."

The limitations on U.S. involvement prevented Kosovo from taking over the news agenda. In fact, war in this violent corner of Europe barely edged out crime at home in network news coverage of 1999. Coverage of ethnic unrest in Kosovo appeared in 1,615 stories in network evening news programs during the year, accounting for about one-fifth of total evening news airtime. Crime—including the Columbine, Colorado, high school shootings on April 20—was the subject of 1,613 stories.

## Comparing Presidential First Years

News coverage during George W. Bush's first year focused on foreign policy matters (particularly terrorism), while the early coverage of Bill Clinton focused on domestic matters and Reagan's coverage was roughly evenly divided between the two areas. But these presidents faced very different foreign policy issues during their first years in office—a sharp contrast to the domestic arena where economic matters and tax policy usually dominate. And the two Republican presidents fared better than the Democrat on leading foreign policy issues, even though Clinton's foreign policy coverage was the most positive overall (38 percent positive for Clinton, as compared to 35 percent positive for Bush and 28 percent positive for Ronald Reagan). Of the five leading foreign policy issues during these three first years, George W. Bush received the most positive reports—43 percent positive coverage over terrorism during 2001. The second-most-positive tone was found in President Reagan's coverage regarding the controversial sale of AWACs radar warning planes to Saudi Arabia. Coverage of that story in 1981 was 37 percent positive on the network evening news programs.

Finishing in a tie for third place (with coverage that was 34 percent positive in tone) were the reports of Bush's performance regarding the Chinese spy plane incident, where a U.S. surveillance plane was forced in the spring of 2001 to make an emergency landing on Chinese territory after being damaged in a midair collision with a Chinese military plane. After a tense standoff, the U.S. military personnel were returned, though the Chinese continued to study the plane and its high-tech equipment. Clinton's coverage regarding the 1993 crisis in Somalia also received 34 percent positive coverage. The lowest score was also held by Clinton, who received 28 percent positive coverage for his treatment of the Bosnia crisis.

Coverage of these leading foreign policy matters was consistently negative, regardless of the president or the circumstances. Even in the wake of the devastating terrorist attacks of 9/11, coverage of the administration's response was not treated positively half the time.

## Israel versus the Palestinians: A Frequent Presidential Priority

U.S. presidents frequently have turned their attention to the volatile Middle East, in particular the often-violent conflict between Israelis and Palestinians. Presidential efforts to resolve this impasse often are an important news topic, though not every year. For example, the Israeli/

Palestinian situation was the seventh heavily covered significant story on national news in 2000 (365 stories), the fifth most important story in 2001 (523 stories), the fourth most important news story in 2002 (913 stories), and the seventh most important story of 2003 (344 stories).

To understand the coverage dynamics of the flashpoints in this long-running story, we analyzed network evening news coverage during the three-month period following a March 27, 2002, suicide bombing in Netanya that killed twenty-nine people and prompted "Operation Defensive Shield"—a major Israeli military assault against the West Bank and Gaza. During this period, Israeli soldiers stormed the Palestinian Authority headquarters and surrounded the compound of Palestinian leader Yasser Arafat. We selected this period for detailed analysis because it was a time of heightened tensions in the region and because it occurred between the U.S. attacks on Afghanistan (2001) and Iraq (2003), thereby receiving greater media attention than when U.S. military operations push other international news off the evening news.

There were 525 stories on this regional powder keg during this three-month period, nearly 6 per night on average. No matter what the story, or the angle, or the network, the coverage was overwhelmingly negative—92 percent negative toward the Palestinians, 78 percent negative toward the Israelis, and 79 percent negative toward the Bush administration. Assessments of individuals were likewise harsh: 92 percent of the assessments of Palestinian leader Yasser Arafat were negative, as were 78 percent of the assessments of Israeli prime minister Ariel Sharon and 72 percent of the assessments of President George W. Bush's handling of the Israeli-Palestinian situation. Even Secretary of State Colin Powell, who enjoyed unusually favorable treatment from U.S. reporters covering the Bush administration, received a majority (55 percent) of negative coverage.

Bush's policies on the region were under attack from all sides. Hardly anyone supported President Bush's efforts during this period to persuade the parties to get back to the negotiating table. As James Zogby of the Arab-American Institute told NBC on April 3, 2002, "The response of the administration publicly up until now has been both achingly inadequate and has been perceived both in Israel and in the Arab world as giving Ariel Sharon a green light." On the opposite side, prominent Republican William Bennett, who served as education secretary and "drug czar" in previous administrations, said President George W. Bush is "taking a posture or moral equivalence in the Middle East between a friend, an ally, a democracy—Israel—and a sponsor of terrorism, Mr. Arafat" (NBC, April 12, 2002).

In his final year in office, President Clinton focused intensely on the Israeli-Palestinian conflict, hoping to reach a peace agreement. Media coverage increased accordingly, and coverage swung from peace talks to conflict as the year progressed. Coverage of fighting that began in September totaled 160 reports, while reports on various peace initiatives and summits accounted for 163 stories. During 2000, the Israeli-Palestinian struggle was the second-most-heavily-covered international news story—behind the Florida saga of refugee Elian Gonzalez, a six-year-old Cuban boy at the center of an international custody struggle.

As both President Clinton's failed peacemaking efforts and as Bush's more one-sided approach demonstrate, presidents are unlikely to make much progress with their media images when they wade into the Israeli-Palestinian morass. In fact, if presidents listened to the media more, they might abandon efforts to try to defuse this bloody international crisis—with potentially catastrophic results.

## Conclusion

The journalists who covered the collapse of the World Trade Center and the attack on the Pentagon faced challenges to the goal of journalistic detachment of a magnitude that few reporters ever face. Even reporters weaned on the dispiriting violence of "cop shop" crime news or the bloody world of battlefield reporting found it difficult to comprehend and discuss the enormity of the violence visited upon New York City and Washington, DC, that day. In addition to an attack upon their hometowns, this was also an assault upon America and its values, particularly those of a free society that has at its core a profound commitment to a free press. How neutral can we realistically expect reporters to be about tragedies that cut so close to home, particularly while these tragedies were unfolding?

Much of mainstream media reporting was carefully contained within a narrow discourse. The events of September 11 personally affected many journalists. It was hard for many media people to keep a professional distance from a story that seemed also to be an attack on their own way of life. (This sense was inflamed when anthrax spores were sent to news organizations, harming employees who came into contact with it.) . . . For those sent to Afghanistan to cover the war there, journalists saw the U.S. government's enemy as their own when they too began to be targeted. Journalists were as frightened and infuriated as all Americans. It is tough to maintain a sense of professional detachment in such a climate. (Schechter 2003:xlii–xliii)

Human beings have strong emotional reactions during such times. This was illustrated vividly by Dan Rather's tearful admission on a late-night talk show that he was behind President Bush in the wake of September 11. If anything, reporters should be commended for keeping the tone of coverage in the immediate aftermath of September 11 roughly comparable to that of earlier crises, like Kosovo, when U.S. citizens were not directly threatened—nor were the reporters themselves. Although our analysis covers only the half-hour regular newscasts, the networks also deserve recognition for covering the immediate aftermath of the 2001 terrorist attacks without commercial interruptions for hours on end—providing far more information and analysis in those early days than can be captured by our content analysis. It was a terribly expensive, and terribly important, public service in those dark days.

What is particularly notable about foreign policy coverage in recent years is how the news media has been transformed into a vehicle of wartime communication for both sides. While propaganda has long been an important instrument of military policy, the growing internationalization and diversification of media outlets make it possible for the reclusive and elusive Osama bin Laden and his violent band of followers to wage a media campaign against the United States.

Both America and its enemies possess greater opportunities than ever before to disseminate their message, using the Internet and foreign media outlets based in the Middle East. News footage that appears today on al Jazeera may find its way into U.S. living rooms tomorrow. U.S. government officials likewise have the opportunity to use such international networks to disseminate the American message, even though they have not been as quick to appreciate this potential as they might have been (Jasperson and el-Kikhia 2003).

With embedded reporters the U.S. government likewise has an increased opportunity to tell its story. It is difficult to compare effectively the news coverage of the various military events of the last three presidents. Both the 1991 Persian Gulf War and the 2003 Iraqi war involved hundreds of thousands of ground troops, while the terrorist attacks of 2001 involved massive loss of U.S. civilian life and the subsequent war in Afghanistan required few U.S. ground troops. The 1999 Kosovo air war involved even fewer U.S. military personnel than did Afghanistan and was waged by the United States almost entirely through a bombing campaign. Finally, the 2003 Iraq war was launched on the basis of some administration propositions that (as of this writing) remain largely unsupported and took place in the face of greater opposition from within the Western alliance than has been seen since the dark days of Vietnam (Hertsgaard 2003; Nye 2002; Pew 2003a, 2003b).

Despite these distinctions and caveats, it is striking how similar the tone was of network news coverage of the 1991 Persian Gulf War, the 1999 Kosovo crisis, and the 2001 terrorist attacks. Three different presidents, three different political circumstances, and three different military objectives, and yet the tone of the coverage was extremely consistent—ranging from 56 percent positive to 64 percent positive on the big three broadcast networks. The overall coverage was more negative for the combat phase of the Iraqi war of 2003 (49 percent positive), largely because of ABC's coverage, which was far more negative in tone than were CBS and NBC. In fact, both CBS and NBC were more positive than ABC in their coverage of the 1991 Gulf War as well. The difference in 2003 was that the pro-war coverage of the Fox News Channel counterbalanced the more antiwar perspective shown on ABC.

While the tone of coverage of the early occupation phase of the 2003 Iraq war on network television was more negative than the news from the combat periods examined here, the tone was consistent with the coverage of presidents during other noncombat periods. Even though far more U.S. lives were lost in the first year of the occupation of Iraq than during the twenty-six days of full-scale combat, Bush had declared on May 1, 2003, that major combat operations were over in a televised speech from atop an aircraft carrier off the coast of California.

In retrospect, that declaration might have opened the door to the return of media negativity (and increased partisan combat) found in the noncombat periods of all the presidencies examined here. In other words, with that television-friendly moment Bush might have declared the start of a political hunting season—on himself! Another possible reason for why coverage of the occupation was more negative in tone than that of the combat phase was that the latter period might have been more problem-filled than citizens and reporters had been led to expect after Saddam Hussein was deposed (Wright 2004).

The greater worldwide reporting capacities through improvements in satellite news links and the Internet have made it easier than ever before for foreign critics of the United States—including fugitives like bin Laden—to be seen and heard worldwide at will. The all-seeing embedded journalism program also seems to have some downside risks from the perspective of presidential news management, but in practice the coverage from the field of even a highly controversial war like Iraq was quite positive. Although one might expect the wider media information net to serve as something of an antidote to groupthink within a presidential administration, the positive coverage that emerges in practice does little to raise questions in the early stages of an international crisis. Indeed, given their heavy reliance on establishment sources, the networks may do more to enhance groupthink than to undermine it.

For presidents, the key lesson of this chapter is clear: while commanders in chief continue to dominate the network newscasts, opposing political figures have ever-greater access to the global media net. (Sometimes that newfound access can create absurdities, like the then-Iraqi information minister describing how U.S. troops were being routed—even though his own government office building had been burned to the ground and U.S. tanks were advancing behind him.) The new global media environment suggests the need to go public globally in a way that previous presidents have not found necessary—and to do so with greater frequency. Bill Clinton's aggressive effort to provide the Kosovo campaign with good press is a clear example of how media-savvy presidents can use a "going public" strategy to frame the debate to their advantage. President Bush's more detached approach to the public aspects of his presidency may undermine the positive press a military campaign can receive when the commander in chief (not a cabinet secretary) dominates the administration's media message efforts.

The two presidencies thesis—the idea that presidents have greater control over foreign policy matters—may have a renewed life in the modern media environment, at least for as long as memories of 9/11 remain fresh. While critics of administration policies can get airtime, they cannot compete with a president and his administration for sheer volume of coverage, particularly in the early stages of an international crisis. (This may explain the tendency of many partisan critics to fall in line behind President Bush on foreign policy matters following the 9/11 attacks.) The battle for the framing of an international crisis is particularly ill-matched when one side of the debate is represented by the U.S. commander in chief, the other by international critics of the United States. Neither bin Laden, nor Saddam Hussein, nor even French president Jacques Chirac has a chance.

Even so, presidents might be wise to be particularly careful about what message is being sent—a single use of what for some is an emotionally laden word like "crusade" can speak volumes. As much as stepping onto the deck of aircraft in a flight suit may seem like good public relations at the time, future events may make mockeries of such categorical presidential pronouncements. Nowhere are the problems of presidential language and actions clearer than in chapter 5, where we turn our attention to presidential scandals—and the often unsuccessful efforts by presidents to try to talk their way out of them.

# CHAPTER 5

## "CAN'T WE TALK ABOUT SOMETHING ELSE?"
### Covering Presidential Scandals

I did not have sexual relations with that woman, Miss Lewinsky," an apparently earnest President Bill Clinton said as he wagged his finger before a worldwide television audience tuned in to the biggest White House soap opera of the twentieth century. A year later, by the time the House of Representatives impeached the president and the Senate failed to convict him, Americans had spent months considering such unlikely questions as whether sexual relations included oral sex, and what the meaning of the word "is" is.

The immediate political casualties from this controversy were largely on the Republican side, as the GOP lost two House speakers and the sexual infidelities of House Judiciary Committee Chairman Henry Hyde (R-IL) became public (I. Morris 2002). The Republicans also lost five House seats in the 1998 elections, which marked the first time since 1934 that the president's party gained seats in a midterm election (Spitzer 1999). Monica Lewinsky and her onetime confidante Linda Tripp were parodied on *Saturday Night Live* and frequently ridiculed on late-night television talk shows.

Special counsel Kenneth Starr's exhaustive and practically pornographic report on Clinton's sexual behavior and deceits—the product of a four-year, $40 million taxpayer-financed investigation that started with the Whitewater real estate investment scheme—became the most downloaded publication in cyberspace (Seib 2001). The country's persuader in chief, the subject of a yearlong media circus of deceit, sex scandals, and impeachment, emerged with his high public job approval ratings—but not his personal reputation—intact (Andolina and Wilcox 2000; J. Cohen 2002b; I. Morris 2002). And America learned of a new cyberspace gossip columnist, Matt Drudge, whose rapid-fire online reporting helped set the tone for the unfiltered and sometimes inaccurate news found online (Kovach and Rosenstiel 1999; Maltese 2000; Powers 1998; Sabato et al. 2000; Seib 2001).

## The Mass Media and Scandals (Both Potential and Actual)

The combative U.S. press of the past generation has an early pedigree, as the intensely partisan press of the early 1800s delighted in personal attacks on political figures, including allegations that Thomas Jefferson attempted to seduce a neighbor's wife and kept a slave as a concubine (Sabato 1993). But these two periods were separated by more than a century when nearly all personal behavior—even if it had policy consequences—was hidden from the public.

Mental and physical health issues were among the topics rarely broached by yesterday's reporters, who concentrated on following political developments in the nation's capital (Sabato 1993; R. Smith 2001). The most celebrated example of this unwillingness to cover personal matters was the generation of reporters and photographers who hid the nature of Franklin Delano Roosevelt's physical disability during his presidency.

> There was an unspoken code of honor on the part of White House photographers that the president was never to be photographed looking crippled. In twelve years, not a single picture was ever printed of the president in his wheelchair. No newsreel had ever captured him being lifted into or out of his car. When he was shown in public, he appeared either standing behind a podium, seated in an ordinary chair, or leaning on the arm of a colleague. If, as occasionally happened, one of the members of the press corps sought to violate the code by sneaking a

picture of the president looking helpless, one of the older photographers would "accidentally" block the shot or gently knock the camera
to the ground. But such incidents were rare; by and large, the "veil
of silence" about the extent of Roosevelt's handicap was accepted by
everyone—Roosevelt, the press, and the American people. (Goodwin
1994:586–87)

Political scientist Larry Sabato (1993) describes the relative absence
of coverage of nonofficial matters as "lapdog journalism." Such reporting kept the private foibles of public officials off the air and out of the
newspapers well into the 1960s. A case could certainly be made that
the press went too far to protect politicians and not far enough to in-
form the public in those days. John F. Kennedy's reckless presidential
dalliances—ranging from Hollywood starlets to the girlfriend of an organized crime boss—were kept from the public despite the serious risks
of blackmail and the extensive use of public funds, facilities, and personnel to facilitate his liaisons (Pfiffner 2004a, 2004b; Sabato 1993).
Other scholars point to earlier media cover-ups—including Abraham
Lincoln's apparent bout of smallpox in 1863, Woodrow Wilson's mental incapacity following a 1919 stroke, and Warren G. Harding's frequent philandering in the White House during the early 1920s—as
evidence that this pattern of media silence on personal matters was
in place for at least half the nation's history (R. Smith 2001; Pfiffner
2000).

On a more elevated plane, America has a rich tradition of watchdog
journalism that exposes abuses by the rich and powerful. Exposés of
political and financial wrongdoing during the Progressive Era of the
early twentieth century helped reformers break up corporate monopo-
lies, pass laws to reduce the influence of money in politics, and increase
government regulation of food and drugs. But this was also the era of
"yellow journalism," in which tabloid newspapers built circulation with
sensationalistic exposés and editorial crusades that sometimes bore little
relation to the facts. Even so, personal lives of public figures often were
treated gingerly, if at all.

All that indulgent media treatment of politicians' personal behavior
changed in the wake of Vietnam and Watergate, when the political failures of Lyndon Johnson and Richard Nixon were traced in significant
measure to their character flaws (Barber 1992; Pfiffner 2004a). By failing to report on personal matters that illuminate character and judg-

ment, reporters may have failed to give voters the information they needed to assess political candidates effectively. In the wake of those twin scandals, many news organizations resolved that political figures would not be treated so gently in the future.

Recent elections have been filled with psychological assessments of presidential candidates. A few of them—most notably U.S. Sen. Gary Hart (D-CO)—were driven from presidential politics because of extra-marital affairs and other scandals (Sabato 1993). More recently, Howard Dean's televised and retelevised loudly shouted exhortations to his supporters after his third-place finish in the 2004 Iowa caucus were thought by some to illustrate a temperament that made him unsuitable for the high-pressure job he sought—even though Dean claims the media created an inaccurate image because of the noise-canceling microphone used onstage (Eggerton 2004). That moment, dubbed by wags as Dean's "I have a scream" speech, spoke volumes about the new media environment. The tape quickly popped up all over the Internet, and the clip was played hundreds of times on cable television during the following week (Eggerton 2004). As the summer 2004 attacks on John Kerry by the "Swift Boat Veterans for Truth" and the renewed controversy over George W. Bush's National Guard service demonstrate, the new media seem to be even more powerful echo chambers than the old.

While it is clear that scandal coverage has become more pervasive and more negative, scholars disagree about how today's press coverage of personal matters affects public evaluations of presidents once they are in office (Langman 2002). Clinton's public approval numbers, for example, demonstrate the complexity of the link between scandal coverage and public approval ratings. In December 1997, the month before the scandal broke, the public's rating of Clinton's performance as president stood at a relatively strong 61 percent approval. By January 1999, the month he was acquitted by the Senate, Clinton's approval rating stood even higher—at 69 percent (J. Cohen 2002b).

It turned out that many people distinguished between Clinton's public and private roles in their evaluations. When asked about his character, or what they thought of him as a person, most expressed disapproval. But they kept these feelings separate from their judgments of his job performance. Scholars who have examined public opinion during this time say that Clinton was able to survive the scandal for two main reasons: (1) the economy's strong performance during 1998, and (2) his success in portraying himself as an ideological moderate—and his opponents as extremists—in the years since the Republican electoral victories of 1994 (cf. J. Cohen 2002b; Newman 2002; Wayne 2000; Zaller 1998). On the first point, it may be risky to banish a president who has been in office during economic good times. On the second, public perceptions of Clinton and his opponents helped the president to portray himself as the victim of fanatical opponents bent on using the scandal to exact revenge.

The media's behavior during the Clinton scandals led critics to renew arguments that relentlessly negative press treatment of political figures can discourage high-quality candidates from running for office. But others noted that scandal coverage can serve a genuine public service, helping citizens evaluate a candidate's fitness for office.

> Scandal coverage also can have positive effects on the political process. Intense scrutiny by the press and political opponents can drive away scalawags, increase public accountability and foster realistic attitudes about the fallibility of elected leaders. But the costs of today's politics by scandal outweigh any remedial effects. While public trust in politicians is near all-time lows, confidence in the media is no higher, and participants on both sides say the emphasis on scandal is reducing voter turnout, distracting from important policy debates and discouraging the best politicians and the best journalists. (Sabato et al. 2000:xvi)

The saturation coverage of the Clinton sex-and-impeachment saga may have discouraged reporters from examining as quickly and as effectively the potential scandals of his successor. Likewise, the events of 9/11 and the way that pursuing Clinton backfired on the Republicans in 1998 may have discouraged Democrats from aggressively attacking Bush the way the GOP had savaged Clinton. As we discuss in this chapter, there are a number of policy areas where George W. Bush might have been subject to more prompt and thorough investigation by reporters—including more-aggressive pursuit of evidence that would support or refute Bush's claims regarding links between Iraqi president Saddam Hussein and al Qaeda, Iraq's alleged weapons of mass destruction program, and the treatment of prisoners held in Iraq and at a U.S.

military base in Cuba. (Coverage of these topics increased as the 2004 presidential election drew closer, but those reports came too late to affect the debate over whether the United States should attack Iraq.)

This chapter focuses on the two leading scandals of the Clinton years—impeachment and the Monica Lewinsky scandal that helped trigger it, and the Whitewater controversy, which led to the independent counsel's investigation of Clinton in the first place. We also examine the Iran-contra affair, which was the biggest political scandal of the 1980s, and the twin election 2004 issues of what John Kerry and George W. Bush did and did not do during the Vietnam conflict. Finally, we examine the leading first-term G. W. Bush scandal—the president's credibility on Iraq.

## The Clinton-Lewinsky Saga

The Clinton-Lewinsky story had its origins in 1995, when Monica Lewinsky began her White House internship. During the subsequent months, Lewinsky and Clinton shared a number of intimate sexual encounters at the White House. In mid-1996, concerned administration staffers transferred the young woman, now a government employee, to a public relations position at the Pentagon (I. Morris 2002). By mid-1997 (after Clinton had broken off the affair) Lewinsky began confiding to Linda Tripp, a Pentagon coworker, about her encounters with the president. Tripp secretly began taping their conversations, and those tapes came to the attention of independent counsel Kenneth Starr, who was investigating the president over Whitewater (I. Morris 2002). Michael Isikoff, a *Newsweek* reporter who had long followed the Clinton scandals, wanted to listen to those Tripp tapes (Isikoff 2000). Clinton's critics saw to it that Isikoff soon got his wish. On January 17, 1998, *Newsweek* postponed publication of a report about Clinton's intimate liaisons with Ms. Lewinsky in order to do more reporting to confirm the allegations. But the Drudge Report reported the next day that *Newsweek* was sitting on the blockbuster story (Isikoff 2000). Hours later, conservative pundit Bill Kristol mentioned the Drudge Report item on ABC's Sunday morning news program *This Week*, and the yearlong media feeding frenzy began (Isikoff 2000; Powers 1998).

Some might say the Clinton-Lewinsky story had its origins even earlier—Clinton believes this saga has its roots in his difficult childhood (Clinton 2004). Others might start with Gennifer Flowers, whose claim that she and Clinton had had an extramarital affair while he was governor of Arkansas rocked the 1992 presidential nomination campaign (Ceaser and Busch 1993). Or one might start with the story of Paula Jones, a onetime Arkansas state employee who charged that then governor Clinton had crudely propositioned her in a Little Rock motel room. Jones subsequently sued Clinton for sexual harassment; the case was settled in November 1998, when Clinton agreed to pay Jones $850,000 (Isikoff 2000).

Regardless of where one starts, these past allegations had conditioned the media—and the public—to imagine the worst about the politician opponents had nicknamed "Slick Willie." As a result of the disclosures and the developments throughout the year, the Clinton-Lewinsky saga was by far the leading story of 1998. In all, the network evening news shows devoted one-seventh of their airtime that year to this single story (1,636 broadcast reports in all). The Clinton scandals received more attention than the standoff with Iraq, the bombing of U.S. embassies in Africa, the fighting in the Serbian province of Kosovo, the Israeli-Palestinian conflict, nuclear weapons tests in Pakistan and India, and major financial crises in Asia and in Russia *combined*.

The Clinton-Lewinsky scandal coverage also swamped coverage of the 1998 midterm elections. During the fall campaign season (Labor Day, September 7, through Election Day, November 2) there were six times as many stories on the scandal as on the elections. The Texas governor's race, won by future president George W. Bush, was the subject of only three network news reports.

The subsequent impeachment of the president and its aftermath generated over four hundred more stories in 1999, most of them in the first three months of the year, when the media wrapped up the coverage of the scandal after the Senate's failure to convict the president on charges brought by the House.

EARLY SCANDAL COVERAGE

Allegations of an improper relationship between Bill Clinton and Monica Lewinsky were first reported widely on January 21, 1998, fueling a media feeding frenzy unlike any in recent memory. There were 305 network evening news stories on the scandal during the first month, including 183 in the first ten days alone.

This first month of coverage involved far more extensive media attention than previous scandals involving Bill Clinton. Charges that then-governor Clinton had an affair with Gennifer Flowers garnered only twenty-nine network news stories in a comparable time period during early 1992, at a time when many journalists felt that this story should have been left to the tabloids. Likewise, Paula Jones's sexual harassment suit was discussed in only thirteen network news stories when it was filed in May 1994. In March 1994 the three broadcast networks aired 126 reports on the Clintons' involvement in the Whitewater land development scheme—far more than many other scandals, but less than half the number devoted to the Clinton-Lewinsky controversy in the month after it became public.

The White House fought off the allegations through public denials and efforts to "spin" the story as being a personal vendetta against the president. Foremost among the president's defenders was First Lady Hillary Clinton, who spoke on *The Today Show* on NBC on January 27, 1998, to defend her husband and attack his accusers.

> This is the great story here, for anybody willing to find it and write about it and explain it, is this vast right-wing conspiracy that has been conspiring against my husband since the day he announced for president. . . . Having seen so many of these accusations come and go, having seen people profit, you know, like Jerry Falwell, with videos, accusing my husband of committing murder, of drug running, seeing some of the things that are written and said about him, my attitude is, you know, we've been there before and we have seen this before. (Hillary Clinton, quoted in Blaney and Benoit 2001:109)

Despite the frequently salacious tone of these accusations and the tabloid-like atmosphere they created, few reporters rushed to judgment on the network evening news programs. As shown in table 5.1, less than one-fourth of the stories (24 percent) implied probable guilt on the part of the president. Nearly three times as many (71 percent) presented the charges in a balanced or neutral fashion, and another 5 percent indicated the president's likely innocence. Early on, all three

| TABLE 5.1 Presenting the Allegations against Clinton on Network News | | | |
|---|---|---|---|
| | Imply Clinton Innocence | Balanced/ Neutral | Imply Clinton Guilt |
| Total | 5% | 71% | 24% |
| **By Network** | | | |
| ABC | 4% | 68% | 28% |
| CBS | 8% | 73% | 19% |
| NBC | 3% | 71% | 26% |
| **By Charge*** | | | |
| Sex with Lewinsky | 3% | 58% | 39% |
| Lying about Sex | 5% | 79% | 16% |
| Asking Lewinsky to Lie | 5% | 65% | 30% |
| General/Other Cover-up | 7% | 80% | 13% |
| **By Month** | | | |
| Jan. 21–31 | 7% | 67% | 26% |
| Feb. 1–20 | 1% | 79% | 20% |

*More than one charge may have been discussed in a story.
*Note:* The 1998 data are based on evaluations aired on network newscasts from January 21 through February 20 (*Media Monitor*, March/April 1998).

networks provided coverage that was neutral on the question of the president's innocence or guilt at least two-thirds of the time. The early coverage did convey the image of a deeply troubled presidency. Indeed, it revived some of the "war room" imagery of Clinton's successful presidential campaign six years earlier. "Back in '92, they were fighting to get into the White House," Forrest Sawyer reported on ABC on January 25, 1998. "Today, they are fighting to stay there."

The 1992 presidential election was won in part by inducing journalists to train their fire on Clinton's adversaries, short-circuiting further critical coverage of Clinton himself (Ceaser and Busch 1993). A similar pattern occurred in the first weeks of the Clinton-Lewinsky scandal. During the first ten days after the story broke, the president was featured in nearly all (93 percent) of the scandal stories. That figure dropped to 70 percent in the following three weeks, even as the percentage focusing on Monica Lewinsky increased from 47 to 59 percent and the share featuring independent counsel Kenneth Starr also rose from 30 to 41 percent. The growing focus on Lewinsky and Starr in media coverage is a measure of the effectiveness of the Clinton team's approach—increasing the media emphasis on the accusers.

## THE SCANDAL RIPENS

There was no need for a new scandal to fill the summer doldrums in 1998, as Republican calls for the president's impeachment brought the media frenzy to a fever pitch. Between July 27, when speculation over Clinton's grand jury testimony began, and September 20, the night before Congress released the tape of his testimony, there were over five hundred more stories on the scandal.

As table 5.2 illustrates, Clinton's coverage was two-to-one negative in tone during this period. The combination of heavy debate and negative tone meant that over one thousand sources criticized Clinton on the evening news shows in a period of less than two months. A fairly typical example came from a voter quoted on ABC's *World News Tonight* (September 17): "He should do the right thing, and that would be to resign, and let somebody in there that's got morals and wants to run our country and not play around with a bunch of women."

Throughout this period, the only consistent on-air support for Clinton came from the White House and the president's lawyers. Even this group, though, found it necessary to reference the president's admission of improper personal conduct in order to argue that he had done nothing to warrant impeachment, such as lying under oath or encouraging others to do so. As a result, even many sound bites from the Clinton team were negative. In fact, a slight majority (52 percent) of the sound bites from the president himself were positive, as he repeatedly admitted to an inappropriate relationship with Monica Lewinsky. "Indeed, I did have a relationship with Ms. Lewinsky that was not appropriate," Clinton said in a CBS *Evening News* report on September 9. In our age of sophisticated presidential spin, a president has rarely evaluated himself as negatively in his public comments as Clinton did during the second half of 1998.

But the strategy of using offense as the best defense continued to bear fruit. Table 5.3 illustrates the effectiveness of Clinton's aggressive efforts to reframe the scandal story by attacking his opponents through-

| TABLE 5.2 | Tone of Network News Coverage of Bill Clinton during the Summer of 1998 (Percent Positive Press) |
|---|---|

**Overall (July 27–September 20)**

| All Networks | 34% |
|---|---|
| ABC | 37% |
| CBS | 36% |
| NBC | 30% |

**After Release of Starr Report (September 11–September 20)**

| All Networks | 30% |
|---|---|
| ABC | 35% |
| CBS | 27% |
| NBC | 28% |

**After Speech (August 17–September 10)**

| All Networks | 31% |
|---|---|
| ABC | 32% |
| CBS | 34% |
| NBC | 27% |

**Before Speech (July 27–August 16)**

| All Networks | 50% |
|---|---|
| ABC | 54% |
| CBS | 57% |
| NBC | 41% |

*Note:* The data are from evening newscasts from July 27 through September 20, 1998 (*Media Monitor*, September/October 1998c).

out 1998. Although the tone of the coverage of Clinton was about two-to-one negative during two periods of peak coverage examined here (the first month of the scandal and the two-month period in the summer of 1998), coverage of Kenneth Starr, Monica Lewinsky, and other scandal figures were about six-to-one negative. (By way of comparison, network news coverage of Serbian president Slobodan Milosevic, as of this writing being tried by the United Nations for war crimes, was five-to-one percent negative in tone during the weeks of U.S. and NATO bombings designed to force him from power in 1999.)

Public opinion was also an important part of the media discussion of the scandal and what should be done with the president. Ordinary citizens quoted in these newscasts were roughly balanced (48 percent

| TABLE 5.3 | Network News Evaluations of Clinton Scandal Figures (Percent Positive Press) |
|-----------|-------------------------------------------------------------------------------|

**Winter 1998 (January 21–February 20)**

| | |
|---|---|
| Bill Clinton | 48% |
| Hillary Rodham Clinton | 71% |
| Vernon Jordan | 58% |
| Kenneth Starr | 23% |
| Monica Lewinsky | 25% |
| Linda Tripp | 30% |

**Summer 1998 (July 27–September 20)**

| | |
|---|---|
| Bill Clinton | 37% |
| Hillary Rodham Clinton | 96% |
| Clinton's Team | 37% |
| Kenneth Starr and His Team | 13% |
| Monica Lewinsky | 14% |
| Congressional Democrats | 44% |
| Congressional Republicans | 28% |

*Note:* The Winter 1998 data are based on news reports from January 21 through February 20. The Summer 1998 data are based on evaluations aired on network newscasts from July 27 through September 20 (*Media Monitor*, March/April 1998a and September/October 1998c).

positive) in their evaluations of the president. One citizen said on CBS on August 17, "What he does with his personal life is his business, but when he lies to the public, that's our business." A minister attending a White House prayer breakfast during the scandal observed on ABC on September 13, "I think he had a genuine sense of sorrow for what he did, and he has said that, and it came across as genuine."

"WAGGING THE DOG?"

Presidents facing trouble in Washington—whether from scandal, legislative setbacks, or other unpleasantness—often turn to the international arena. Whether or not they do so to distract the media and the public, presidential performances on the world stage often overshadow other issues, particularly long-running scandals. Even during the Clinton-Lewinsky scandal, an international trip served to drive down the volume of scandal coverage. The three networks broadcast fifty-eight stories on the president's trip to China and his policies toward the Asian superpower from June 24 through July 4, 1998, compared to only nineteen stories on the Clinton-Lewinsky scandal. Coverage of the president likewise was more positive, as four out of five sources quoted on the newscasts evaluated his China policies favorably. Many of the positive assessments came from inside the administration and from the president's Chinese hosts, and the White House reveled in its ability to set the news agenda once again.

## THE DYNAMICS OF IMPEACHMENT COVERAGE

Two weeks after the 1998 midterm elections, the lame-duck U.S. House Judiciary Committee began holding hearings on whether to impeach President Clinton. During the three weeks of coverage (November 19 through December 12, 1998), the networks aired 108 stories that focused on the hearings. True to form, evaluations of Clinton were mainly (62 percent) negative, while on-air assessments of independent counsel Ken Starr were even more negative (69 percent), and congressional Republicans fared worst of all (77 percent negative).

Context can be decisive for a president's fortunes, as coverage of this scandal illustrates. If Republicans had succeeded in their efforts to frame the Clinton-Lewinsky scandal as a criminal matter of perjury—that is, the felony of lying under oath—they might have been able to drive the president from office. Instead, the media frame was largely that the president's alleged lies were of a more personal nature, the foibles of a philandering husband trying to avoid embarrassing himself and his family. That alternative perspective, presented aggressively by Clinton's defenders through 1998, was adopted by many citizens, making it difficult for the House Republicans to turn public opinion against the president (Bennett 2005; Blaney and Benoit 2001; Klein 2002; Owen 2000; Sabato et al. 2000).

Administration efforts to portray the scandal as a mudslinging contest also worked to the president's advantage. Independent counsel Starr could not defend himself effectively while his investigation was continuing. Holding press conferences to rebut attacks by Hillary Clinton and others would only damage his credibility further. In addition,

Starr's GOP allies on Capitol Hill could not win the battle for the airwaves against the White House. The media frames of this story were largely along the lines sketched by the executive branch, as is so often the case. The president may not be able to convince reporters to cover something else, but he retains considerable ability to shape the way the story is discussed, even when the topic is a sex scandal.

## Whitewater

The impeachment saga was far from the only major scandal of the Clinton presidency. Near the end of Clinton's first year in office, ABC and NBC aired charges from two former Arkansas State Police officers that then-governor Clinton used his security detail to facilitate extramarital liaisons. The next day, all three networks reported that former Clinton attorney Vincent Foster's files on the Whitewater Development Corporation had not reached federal investigators for more than five months after his suicide. These reports set off a new round of media inquiries into the ethical practices of the First Family and their associates, a range of questions known collectively as Whitewater.

From those first reports on December 20, 1993, through the first three months of 1994, the network evening news shows aired 193 Whitewater stories with over six hours of airtime. Clinton loyalists frequently attached negative motives to those questioning the First Family. Among the most frequent explanations: partisan politics (including opposition to health care reform, and anti–Hillary Clinton and antiwomen sentiment), self-interest (including jealousy, spite, and financial motivations), and a culture of "negativism" that has made political life and the press more mean-spirited. On ABC on January 7, 1994, David Gergen, a communications staffer for Presidents Clinton, Reagan, Ford, and Nixon, blamed "the cannibalism which is loose in our society in which public figures, such as the Clintons . . . get hammered even though they are trying to do the right thing." Only one source in seven (14 percent) suggested the Clintons' accusers were motivated by genuine concern over possible wrongdoing.

Overall, Whitewater evaluations of the Clinton administration were nearly evenly balanced, as news sources offering 48 percent positive and 52 percent negative comments. Evaluations of Bill Clinton and Hillary Rodham Clinton on network news during this period were each 54 percent positive in tone. Much of the criticism concerned not their personal ethics but the administration's inept handling of the scandal. "After a week of serious White House efforts to manage the story," ABC's Jim Wooten reported on January 7, 1994, "the new damage control team may have done more damage than it's controlled."

The Clinton media strategies during the Whitewater controversy often involved a combination of offense and defense, as would be employed during the Clinton-Lewinsky scandal several years later. Partisan political sources favorable to the Clintons were aggressive in making the Clintons' case in the media. Supportive comments from administration sources outnumbered negative remarks from congressional Republicans by a margin of nearly three to one. Nevertheless, coverage during this period frequently portrayed the president as politically wounded by the Whitewater affair. Nearly nine out of ten sources suggested the president was suffering from the scandal, and over 90 percent diagnosed trouble for the First Lady. But early assessments suggested that the damage could be contained. CBS White House correspondent Bill Plante, for example, observed three months into the scandal (March 6, 1994): "Mr. Nixon was almost impeached for high crimes and misdemeanors. I don't see that coming yet for President Clinton."

## WHITEWATER VERSUS IRAN CONTRA AND WATERGATE

For more than three decades, official Washington has kept watch for the next Watergate, the megascandal from 1972 to 1974 that ended the presidency of Richard M. Nixon. In their early days new White House scandals are often given nicknames that end in "-gate," wishful thinking, perhaps, on the part of a president's political opponents. But most do not live up to the original billing. In its early days, the Whitewater affair elicited only occasional on-air comparisons with the Watergate scandal. During news coverage of the scandal between December 20, 1993, and April 1, 1994—a key period of scandal coverage—only twelve stories, or about one in fifteen, included Watergate comparisons. In comparison, Watergate references were nearly twice as frequent during the early weeks of the Iran-contra matter, the leading Reagan-era scandal (and one examined later in this chapter).

Overall, media attention to Whitewater in its first months paled in comparison to the two earlier feeding frenzies over major presidential scandals. The March 1994 average of four nightly Whitewater stories was less than one-third as much as the networks' Watergate coverage (an average of 13.4 stories a night) in April and May 1973, following reports that linked Richard Nixon to a cover-up. Whitewater coverage was also about one-third as heavy as the average of 12.9 network news stories a night devoted to the Iran-contra scandal during November and December 1986.

The Whitewater scandal largely fizzled out in the years that followed. Kenneth Starr eventually moved on to possible obstruction of justice charges over the Clinton-Lewinsky matter. His final report did not allege impeachable offenses by President Clinton over Whitewater (Blaney and Benoit 2001).

## George W. Bush's Credibility on Iraq

The central scandal of George W. Bush's first term, like that of Bill Clinton's, was primarily self-inflicted. Although President Bush had brief periods of very positive news media coverage—particularly in the wake of 9/11 and during the invasion of Iraq—he has also endured periods of very negative coverage. Bush faced several smaller problems that point to a single issue: the president's credibility. And nowhere was that issue more significant than in the case of the march to war in Iraq.

"The problem the administration has is that the predicates it laid down for the war have not played out," said Warren Rudman, a former Republican U.S. senator from New Hampshire and an expert in intelligence matters. "That could spell political trouble for the president, no question" (quoted in Stevenson 2004).

Only time will tell how much trouble faces the United States in Iraq. But conditions in 2004 were severe enough to threaten the president's reelection campaign. A *New York Times*/CBS News public opinion poll taken in June 2004 found that only 18 percent of those surveyed said they believe Bush was being entirely truthful when talking about Iraq, while 59 percent thought he was "mostly telling the truth but is hiding something," and another 20 percent thought he was "mostly lying." Only 15 percent thought the Bush team had told the entire truth regarding torture at Iraq's Abu Ghraib prison (Nagourney and Elder 2004).

By mid-2004, Bush's job approval rating fell to a low of 42 percent, the lowest of his first term, but somewhat better than the 34 percent approval rating that his father had at that point in his own reelection campaign twelve years earlier (Nagourney and Elder 2004). The younger Bush's approval numbers began rising in the late summer of 2004 after the Republican convention focused on the war on terror and the president's allies pummeled Sen. John Kerry for his Vietnam-era activities and his arguably inconsistent statements on Iraq. Questions over the president's credibility were not silenced by Bush's reelection on November 2, 2004.

## SADDAM HUSSEIN, AL QAEDA, AND WEAPONS OF MASS DESTRUCTION

Before the Iraq war, both President Bush and Vice President Cheney sought to convince a wary Congress and public that Saddam Hussein was linked to al Qaeda, frequently implying that the former Iraqi leader was connected to the September 11, 2001, hijackers (none of whom were Iraqi citizens). That claim was questioned before the Iraq war in a few news stories that indicated some government intelligence analysts felt pressured to provide evidence that supported the administration's allegations (Massing 2004). UN weapons inspectors who served in Iraq also expressed doubts regarding the administration's claims (Massing 2004).

After Saddam Hussein was deposed and the occupation began, some former Bush administration officials—including Treasury Secretary Paul O'Neill and counterterrorism chief Richard Clarke—argued publicly that the new president's desire to drive Saddam Hussein from power blinded him to the lack of solid evidence linking the dictator to an international terror network (Clarke 2004; Suskind 2004). Wesley Clark, a former NATO commander and a candidate for the 2004 Democratic presidential nomination, argued that Bush's fixation on Iraq distracted the administration from the more important problem of the worldwide threat posed by al Qaeda (W. Clark 2003).

By June 2004, the Bush team faced attacks on its credibility from many sources. On June 16, roughly two weeks before the United States transferred power to a new provisional Iraqi government, a preliminary report from the bipartisan U.S. commission investigating the 9/11 terrorist attacks found no justification for the administration's claims that there were substantial ties between Saddam Hussein and al Qaeda (Stevenson 2004). Bush and Cheney responded to the commission's assertion by continuing to argue that there were links between Hussein and the bin Laden organization (Stevenson 2004).

The Bush administration's insistent claim that there was a bin Laden / Saddam Hussein link appears to have helped convince a significant portion of the public that Saddam Hussein did have something to do with the attacks on the Twin Towers and the Pentagon. In a *New York Times* / CBS News poll conducted roughly a week after the 9/11 investigating committee's preliminary report was made public, 41 percent of those surveyed said they believed "Saddam Hussein was personally involved in the September 11, 2001 terrorist attacks" (Nagourney and Elder 2004). In a September 2002 poll taken shortly before Congress authorized an invasion of Iraq, 51 percent said they thought Saddam Hussein had a hand in the attacks.

Before the 2003 Iraq war began, Bush administration officials argued strenuously that Saddam Hussein possessed weapons of mass destruction and was prepared to use them on the West or turn them over to terrorists (Stevenson 2003). "If we know that Saddam Hussein has dangerous weapons today—and we do—does it make any sense in the world to wait to confront him as he grows stronger and develops even more dangerous weapons?" Bush asked in Cincinnati in October 2002 (quoted in Stevenson 2003). Even though UN inspectors were unable to find evidence of such weapons during their inspections, the Bush administration successfully persuaded Congress that month to authorize military force to remove Hussein from power (Fisher 2004).

When the predicted weapons did not materialize during the first several months of the post-Saddam occupation, Bush continued to insist the weapons of mass destruction would be found eventually (Stevenson 2003). The Bush administration has also emphasized other aspects of Hussein's rule—mass executions, the use of chemical weapons in Kurdish villages, and even the 1990 invasion of Kuwait—to justify U.S. action (Stevenson 2003). The shifting after-the-fact justifications for the Iraqi war kept the administration's critics off-balance at first, but criticism grew as the number of casualties in Iraq increased. The news media also second-guessed the generally supportive coverage of Bush's rationale for going to war received during the months before the start of the Iraqi war (cf. Mooney 2004; Orkent 2004).

## THE TORTURE SCANDAL

When the horrible pictures of the abuse suffered by Iraqi prisoners in the Abu Ghraib prison scandal first emerged, Bush administration officials stressed that the criminal misconduct was the work of a few rogue soldiers. Subsequently, however, government whistle-blowers leaked an August 2002 Justice Department legal memo that authorized severe interrogation techniques against the captives held at Guantanamo Bay, Cuba, bringing the scandal inside the White House (M. Allen and Schmidt 2004).

In order to quell a growing international and congressional furor over the prison abuse scandal, the Bush administration denied in June 2004 that it authorized torture against prisoners in Cuba and released hundreds of pages of documents detailing aggressive interrogation techniques (M. Allen and Schmidt 2004; Milbank 2004b). These disclosures helped confirm critics' allegations that high-level White House and Pentagon officials gave the green light to questionable interrogation techniques (M. Allen and Schmidt 2004). The documents dealt with the handling of prisoners on the U.S. military base in Cuba, not with the regulations governing the treatment of Iraqi prisoners in Abu Ghraib— the story that launched the controversy. These disclosures failed to stop the scandal coverage.

"The president's directive in February 2002 that ordered U.S. forces to treat al Qaeda and Taliban detainees humanely and consistent with the Geneva Convention does contain a loophole phrase 'to the extent appropriate and consistent with military necessity,'" according to the *Washington Post* (Priest and Graham 2004:A6). The dispute over whether the government's actions constituted torture, and what other government records should be released, continued as this book went to press (M. Allen and Schmidt 2004).

In this negative media environment, it should come as no surprise that the Bush administration tried, as did Clinton's, to start playing offense rather than remaining on defense (cf. Milbank 2004b). Once Sen. John Kerry (D-MA) secured the 2004 Democratic presidential nomination, Bush's reelection campaign tried to portray Kerry as weak on defense, a tax-and-spend liberal, and a flip-flopper on many issues— charges the Democrat denied (Milbank and VandeHei 2004).

## The Scandals of the 2004 Presidential Election (or Was That 1972?)

During the summer and fall of 2004, Democratic presidential nominee John Kerry of Massachusetts and President George W. Bush both faced renewed questions concerning what they did and did not do more than three decades earlier, when both were young men staring into the void that was Vietnam (Seelye 2004; Wilgoren 2004). Kerry, a naval officer, had been awarded several medals for bravery and for being wounded while patrolling the waterways of Vietnam. After Kerry locked up the Democratic nomination, a group of Kerry opponents began raising money to pay for advertisements that argued the senator did not deserve his medals and that he impugned his fellow veterans when he later described war crimes allegedly committed by U.S. soldiers in Vietnam and led a liberal group called Vietnam Veterans Against the War (Bumiller 2004; Rutenberg 2004b; Zernike and Rutenberg 2004).

The controversy reopened old wounds endured by the Vietnam-era generation, a time that split the nation like few others in American history (Egan 2004). Although media investigations did not validate the group's allegations that Kerry did not deserve his medals, the news media gave the organization's claims extensive coverage. The Kerry campaign's failure to respond promptly and effectively to the charges by an organization called the Swift Boat Veterans for Truth cost him considerable support among veterans and probably contributed to his eventual defeat (Easton et al. 2004; Nagourney 2004; Wilgoren 2004).

Network news carried eighty-nine sound bites on Kerry's military records between June 2 and September 2—when the Kerry controversies were prominent in the news—and 54 percent of them were positive in tone, in part because a number of Kerry's former naval comrades rose to his defense. One fellow veteran, Jim Rasmussen, even traveled with the Kerry campaign to tell audiences how the once-young naval officer risked his life to pull him out of a river under enemy fire (Rasmussen 2004). There were fewer than ten sound bites regarding Bush's military record during that three-month period, too few to measure tone effectively.

But Bush received his turn for a Vietnam-era scandal as the election drew closer. Critics argued that Bush used family connections to secure a place in the National Guard (Rimer et al. 2004). Once in the Texas Air National Guard, the *New York Times* reported that Bush failed to undergo a required physical or show up for required training for at least five months when he transferred to an Alabama guard unit (Rimer et al. 2004; Seelye and Blumenthal 2004). The spotty records that have survived—and have been released—show that Bush left the guard with an honorable discharge (Rimer et al. 2004).

During the election-year controversy, no one came forward to vouch publicly that Bush served his time as required in Alabama. But, in the end, the Bush campaign did not need to produce character witnesses from the Alabama base. Questions over his activities in 1972 and 1973 were eclipsed by a larger controversy—an erroneous report on the CBS News program *60 Minutes II* that used documents later revealed to be forgeries to question Bush's guard service (Rutenberg 2004a; Rutenberg and Zernike 2004). The documents, which allegedly came from the personnel files of one of Bush's commanders in Texas, claimed that high-ranking officers wanted Bush's immediate supervisors to "sugarcoat" the young man's record (Rutenberg 2004a).

Internet bloggers quickly pounced on the memos used by CBS, claiming they were fakes because of the font used—which suggested they were not produced on a 1970s-era typewriter—and because of the abbreviations used—which did not conform to standard military practice (Rutenberg and Zernike 2004). After nearly two weeks of withering controversy, the network retracted the story, and Dan Rather and CBS News apologized (Rutenberg and Zernkie 2004).

In January 2005, after a lengthy independent investigation, CBS

News fired three top executives, including the producer of the September article. The investigators also concluded that Dan Rather exercised bad judgment in pursuing the story as aggressively as he did and in defending it after legitimate questions about its authenticity were raised (Kurtz 2005).

The big three network evening news programs aired a total of forty-seven sound bites on Bush's military record between September 7 (the day before the story broke on *60 Minutes II*) and November 1 (the night before the election). The coverage was 81 percent negative in tone, far more negative than the coverage of Kerry's war record. (Like Kerry, Bush did not vigorously defend his Vietnam-era record during the peak of this controversy.) During the two-month period before the election, there were fewer than ten evaluations of Kerry's wartime service, too few to make a valid of assessment of tone during that period.

To some of the network's critics, what some wags have dubbed "Rather-gate" demonstrated the liberal bias long thought to exist at CBS News (cf. B. Goldberg 2002). To other critics, the incident demonstrates the declining standards of mainstream news organizations that cut corners in the rush to be first with an explosive investigative report. To still other media observers, the success of bloggers in monitoring network television suggests that reporters may be less reckless in the future. But because the media environment is in a great flux, the long-term consequences of the changing media environment illustrated by "Rather-gate" remain to be seen.


## Ronald Reagan and Iran-contra

On November 4, 1986, ABC's *World News Tonight* broke (to U.S. audiences, that is, as the story had already appeared in a Middle East publication) one of the biggest political scandals since Watergate: that the United States had, with the president's knowledge, sold arms to Iran, a longtime U.S. enemy. Since Ronald Reagan had come to office in 1980 promising not to negotiate with terrorists, these arms sales to a nation that had held Americans hostage for more than a year during 1979–1981 seemed like a broken presidential promise and a betrayal. In addition, while the sales were not illegal, they seemed unwise, as such payments could both reward existing hostage-takers and encourage others to do the same.

On November 25, the other shoe dropped. Attorney General Edwin Meese revealed that, allegedly without the president's knowledge, some of the proceeds of those sales had been diverted by the National Security Council staff to support the anticommunist contras in Nicaragua—an action that did appear to be illegal. These two revelations severely damaged Reagan's public standing. In the month after these disclosures, Reagan's public approval rating fell from 67 percent to 46 percent, and his approval rating hovered in the 50 percent range for the next several months (Ceaser 1988).

During the first month of this scandal, the three broadcast networks provided 297 stories on their twenty-three weekday evening newscasts. That averages out to about thirteen stories a day, or just over four per network. The stories ran for a total of nine and a half hours, or about 38 percent of the news time available. The scandal was the lead story on three out of every four newscasts during the period. The coverage became particularly intense after the attorney general's news conference broadened the scope of the improper activity.

Among all the major topics covered in this first round of coverage, three stood out: policy issues concerning the Iran arms sales, legal questions raised by the various disclosures, and problems of leadership within the Reagan administration. All three received roughly equal treatment and together account for a majority of all Iran-contra coverage during this period. In other words, the story was at first framed in equal measure by questions of policy, legality, and leadership. This is a sharp contrast from the horse-race-oriented presidential campaign coverage that offers little news relating to matters of substance (cf. Farnsworth and Lichter 2003a).

As we saw in the Clinton and Bush efforts to start playing offense while on the defensive, President Reagan also emerged as his own staunchest supporter on network television, with forty-three separate defenses of administration policy and no criticism during this period. (While Clinton found it in his interest to criticize his own behavior as improper some of the time, the president and his allies trained their most withering fire on Clinton's critics.)

Before long, Reagan's biggest scandal arrived on Capitol Hill. Congressional hearings into the Iran-contra matter triggered a summer-long feeding frenzy, with 462 news stories on the network news programs between May 5 and August 3, 1987. Ironically, two key subjects of the inquiry—President Reagan and White House aide Oliver North—both received a majority of positive coverage (55 percent and 54 percent positive, respectively).

Congress fared worse, with 67 percent negative assessments of the legislative branch and the hearings themselves. This is an important finding, for it offers a key insight into why congressional Democrats did not pursue Reagan more aggressively despite the fact that the Iran-contra affair demonstrated either presidential deceit (Reagan's claims that he didn't know what was going on) or incompetence (failing to supervise his subordinates properly or even failing to realize what was going on in his own administration).

Nonetheless, Iran-contra marred the final two years of the Reagan presidency, lowering Reagan's approval numbers and sapping the aging administration of its strength. The controversy did not die with the end of the Reagan administration, though, as reporters and investigators continued to ask questions about then vice president George H. W. Bush's role. Independent counsel Lawrence Walsh continued to investigate the matter through the George H. W. Bush presidency. The Iran-contra matter dogged Bush even during his 1992 reelection campaign— six years after the scandal first became public (Woodward 2000). Caspar Weinberger, Reagan's defense secretary, was indicted by Walsh shortly before the 1992 election, and on December 24, 1992—less than a month before he left office—President G. H. W. Bush pardoned Weinberger, former national security adviser Robert (Bud) MacFarlane, and others for possible crimes committed during Iran-contra (Woodward 2000). Walsh attacked Bush for the pardons, saying they were "the last card in the cover-up" to prevent prosecutors from getting to the president (Woodward 2000:215). For his part, Bush said he always told the truth on Iran-contra but had been pursued anyway by an overzealous investigator (Woodward 2000:222).

## Scandals That Weren't

Given the time, energy, and attention that politicians and the media devote to presidential scandals, the best way for a president to deal with them may be to learn how to avoid them—or at least minimize their ability to deter the administration from pursuing its policies. While that is easier said than done, an examination of controversies that have not exploded into full-scale scandals (at least, not so far) may offer insight into how to contain those damaging and distracting presidential scandals.

## GEORGE W. BUSH AND CORPORATE CRIME

George W. Bush ran for president in 2000 partly as a businessman, arguing that America could use an MBA as CEO. Although that was an effective campaign approach in 2000, the stars of leading corporate figures dimmed greatly in the first few years of the twenty-first century, as the stock market "bubble" burst and corporate crime scandals captured the headlines. Between the first public rumblings of trouble at Enron that appeared on the network news on November 28, 2001, and the collapse of WorldCom at the end of July 2002, evening news shows on the three television networks broadcast more than fifteen hours of corporate financial scandal reports, mainly focusing on the alleged wrongdoing and the impact of these scandals on the larger economy.

In his rise to the White House, no company helped George W. Bush more than Enron. Throughout his political career, the president received aid from the Texas energy company and its top executives— and before that the top executives helped George H. W. Bush— providing the Bush family with hundreds of thousands of dollars in political contributions during the 1990s (C. Lewis 2004; M. Peterson 2004). As a whole, the oil and gas industry gave more than $25 million in hard and soft money contributions to Republican organizations and candidates during the 1990s—seven times the amount given to Democrats—and G. W. Bush received more of that money than any other Republican, including his father (M. Peterson 2004). After he took office, George W. Bush sought to return the favor, supporting further deregulation of the energy business, even in the wake of the California electrical crisis of 2001—a crisis some critics charged was triggered by corporate plans to create and then profit from West Coast energy shortages (J. Peterson and Wotopka 2004).

Despite these powerful connections—and the questions over deregulated energy policies—the Enron scandal did not envelop George W.

Bush in the way the Whitewater scandal triggered a media frenzy surrounding President Clinton (M. Peterson 2004). Corporate connections to the White House were the subject of only 188 discussions
during this eight-month period, slightly fewer than the discussions of
corporate connections to Congress (195 discussions). And those discussions include references to Vice President Cheney, who developed
the Bush administration energy plan after consultation with Enron executives. (Before becoming vice president, Cheney had been CEO of
Halliburton, another Texas company facing accusations of accounting
irregularities and other misconduct.) There were only thirty-one explicit assessments of George W. Bush's role in the unfolding scandals
during more than seven months of peak network news coverage of the
scandals (471 stories from January 1 to July 31, 2002). That works out
to less than two evaluations of the president a month per network on
corporate crime matters.

So why did this potential scandal not take flight? Part of the explana-
tion for this story's sudden death was the result of the intrusion of other
events. During the fall of 2002, the Bush administration began its efforts
to convince Congress to pass a resolution authorizing military force to
remove Saddam Hussein from power in Iraq. The war and occupation
of Iraq then followed. In addition, this was not a story that could be
told as easily—and as visually—as Clinton's finger-wagging denial of a
sexual relationship with a former White House intern.

But, perhaps most importantly, there simply was not enough evidence on the public record for this story to gain traction. Critics never
produced a smoking gun that clearly linked Bush to corporate crime—
and when the desperate Enron executives asked for a U.S. government
bailout of their failing company, the Bush administration refused to
save the firm from financial collapse.

## GEORGE H. W. BUSH'S OWN JENNIFER SCANDAL

In June 1992, several months after America first learned of Clinton
paramour Gennifer Flowers, President G. H. W. Bush had to face his
own Jennifer scandal—or, more accurately, mini-scandal—as the story
came and went relatively quickly. The *New York Post* reported without
supporting evidence that Bush, then vice president, may have spent a

romantic night together with an aide in a Swiss villa in 1984 (Loth 1992). The story quickly spread through the country when a CNN reporter asked Bush about the story during a news conference being carried live by CNN (McDonald 1992). The president immediately branded the accusation a lie, but the story still made a brief appearance on network news and on the inside pages of a number of leading newspapers (Loth 1992; Kurtz 1992). In an effort to extinguish the story quickly, the following day First Lady Barbara Bush told a leading Texas paper, the *Houston Chronicle*, that the story was "a lie" and complained that "the mainline press has sunk to an all-time low, and CNN gets the top of my list" (Hines 1992).

This scandal failed to take flight because of a lack of evidence. The Bush-Fitzgerald story evaporated quickly, as there was no Matt Drudge or Kenneth Starr to keep the controversy alive and—most importantly—no admission from anyone and no other evidence demonstrating there had been an extramarital affair. In addition, there were no pictures published of Bush and the woman together, a sharp contrast from the campaign-ending photo of Donna Rice—the Monica Lewinsky of the 1980s—sitting on the lap of a leading presidential candidate of the era, Sen. Gary Hart (D-CO). In contrast to the Bush nonscandal, the Clinton-Lewinsky story took on a life of its own, and the controversy nearly brought down a president. Although the stories have many differences, they have one important similarity: a quick, apparently persuasive denial from the president, followed up with a harsh attack of the president's critics by the First Lady. In the same way that Hillary Clinton tried to turn attention to Kenneth Starr, Barbara Bush blamed the media outlets pursuing the story.

"The gloves are off," Barbara Bush warned the mass media. "I would be ashamed if I were the press" (Hines 1992).

Shame, however, is not something found in abundance in newsrooms.

## Comic Relief: All Clinton All the Time

Unlike some of the other topics we have covered thus far in our study of network television's coverage of government, presidential scandals sometimes become markers of an era, and a man. The Lewinsky sex scandal was a popular theme for late-night television comics as well as for journalists. These late-night comedy shows have become a barometer for public opinion of young adults, many of whom use these talk shows as an alternative way to obtain political information (Pew 2000a, 2000d). President Clinton was the subject of more than 1,712 jokes in 1998, more than in any other year of his presidency. In fact, that year's total set a record for the number of jokes about any individual since the Center for Media and Public Affairs began annual tallies of late-night humor in 1989. Clinton had also been the number-one topic of the late-night comics the previous year, but in 1998 comics more than doubled the previous year's high-water mark of 810 jokes about the president. Others who were a part of the scandal also were the butt of the late-night humor: Monica Lewinsky was the subject of 332 jokes, followed by scandal investigator Kenneth Starr (139 jokes), First Lady Hillary Clinton (100 jokes), Lewinsky confidante Linda Tripp (90 jokes), and Paula Jones, who had accused the president of sexual harassment when he was governor of Arkansas (88 jokes). In all, late-night comedians told 2,461 jokes about the Clinton-Lewinsky affair.

As table 5.4 illustrates, Bill Clinton was the top target of the late-night comics for six of his eight years as president, "losing" only to George W. Bush in 2000 and to Bob Dole in 1996. Clinton retained the first-place position in 2001, the only former president ever to defeat an incumbent president in this category. As of the end of 2003, Clinton has been first or second on the joke list for twelve consecutive years— ever since he first ran for president in 1992.

George W. Bush won the gold medal for being the subject of the most late-night jokes in two of his first three years as president and in 2000, when he was the Republican nominee. The one year he did not receive the award was for 2001, when Clinton's reluctant departure from the national stage (together with the relative absence of jokes about George W. Bush after 9/11) reduced the number of jokes told about the new chief executive. In all, Bush has placed first or second in number of jokes told for four consecutive years (2000–2003), a record that already exceeds that of his father. George H. W. Bush, another frequent target of the comics, finished first in 1989 and 1992, second in 1990, and third in 1991.

| TABLE 5.4 | Political Humor of Late-Night Television Comedians | | |
|---|---|---|---|
| **Top Joke Targets by Year** | **First** | **Second** | **Third** |
| **George W. Bush** | | | |
| 2003 | G. W. Bush 374 | Bill Clinton 241 | Schwarzenegger 153 |
| 2002 | G. W. Bush 311 | Bill Clinton 190 | Martha Stewart 91 |
| 2001* | Bill Clinton 657 | G. W. Bush 546 | Gary Condit 227 |
| **Bill Clinton** | | | |
| 2000 | G. W. Bush 910 | Bill Clinton 806 | Al Gore 530 |
| 1999 | Bill Clinton 1319 | Lewinsky 344 | Hillary Clinton 293 |
| 1998 | Bill Clinton 1712 | Lewinsky 332 | Kenneth Starr 139 |
| 1997 | Bill Clinton 810 | O. J. Simpson 260 | Al Gore 103 |
| 1996 | Bob Dole 838 | Bill Clinton 655 | O. J. Simpson 376 |
| 1995 | Bill Clinton 338 | O. J. Simpson 145 | Newt Gingrich 103 |
| 1994 | Bill Clinton 556 | Ted Kennedy 87 | Dan Quayle 5 |
| 1993* | Bill Clinton 761 | Ross Perot 100 | Al Gore 97 |
| **George H. W. Bush** | | | |
| 1992 | G. H. W. Bush 608 | Bill Clinton 423 | Dan Quayle 357 |
| 1991 | Saddam Hussein 160 | Dan Quayle 150 | G. H. W. Bush 11 |
| 1990 | Dan Quayle162 | G. H. W. Bush147 | Saddam Hussein 137 |
| 1989* | G. H. W. Bush 143 | Dan Quayle 135 | Ronald Reagan 79 |

*Presidents do not take office until January 20.
Note: The data include the jokes about public affairs and public figures from the monologues of the late-night television programs *Late Night* with David Letterman, *The Tonight Show* hosted by Johnny Carson and Jay Leno, and (from 1993 on) *Conan O'Brien*. The 1998–2001 data also include the jokes of Bill Maher. The 1990–1994 data also include the jokes of Arsenio Hall. The 1993 data also include the jokes of Jon Stewart.

Al Gore, Clinton's vice president and the 2000 Democratic nominee, never finished better than third in the late-night joke rankings, but he did so three times (in 1993, 1997, and 2000).

Further evidence of the role played by alternative media in setting the public agenda can be seen in the discussion of Michael Moore's movie *Fahrenheit 9/11*, a controversial anti-Bush documentary released in June 2004 and thought by some likely to encourage people to question Bush's competence and credibility during the upcoming presidential campaign (cf. Finnegan 2004; Shenon 2004). Late-night comic

David Letterman featured the film—and its attacks on Bush—with the "Top Ten George W. Bush Complaints about *Fahrenheit 9/11*."

10. That actor who played the president was totally unconvincing.
9. It oversimplified the way I stole the election.
8. Too many of them fancy college-boy words.
7. If Michael Moore had waited a few months, he could have included the part where I get him deported.
6. Didn't have one of them hilarious monkeys who smoke cigarettes and gives people the finger.
5. Of all Michael Moore's accusations, only 97% are true.
4. Not sure—I passed out after a piece of popcorn lodged in my windpipe.
3. Where the hell was Spiderman?
2. Couldn't hear most of the movie over Cheney's foul mouth.
1. I thought this was supposed to be about dodgeball! (*Late Show*, June 29, 2004)

## Conclusion

Twenty years of presidential scandals show how presidents remain the central focus of political news, even—perhaps especially—when things go wrong. But that intense media focus on the executive branch provides a key executive branch power: a president's ability to frame a story more successfully than his competitors and opponents. In scandal after scandal, whether Clinton-Lewinsky or Whitewater, the Abu Ghraib torture photos or the Iran-contra affair, presidents have been able to minimize immediate damage to themselves by working to frame the story in a way less hostile to the White House.

The plan for responding to a presidential scandal is simple, and it starts with a direct, consistent message that is echoed by all administration officials (Auletta 2004). For the G. W. Bush administration, for example, the September 11, 2001, terrorist attacks provided a way to frame other initiatives as linked to the war on terror. This process maximizes support for these linked policies and tends to keep the administration's opponents off balance (Fisher 2004).

But successful politicians are rarely content to stay on defense. Responding to scandals, especially, requires going on offense as well. Administrations respond to an emerging scandal by attacking their opponents, such as by presenting them as ideological fanatics blinded by their hatred of the president. If the scandal is of a sexual nature, no one can launch a more effective retaliatory strike than the First Lady. Depending on the issue, administration defenders may be able to counterattack by questioning the patriotism of opponents. Reporters love conflict, so countercharges are an effective way to stop playing defense and start playing offense. Sometimes the insults can even muddy the waters, obscuring relevant but—from the point of view of the White House—unhelpful evidence.

For the really big crises, triage is an important part of a president's media defense. During the Clinton-Lewinsky affair, Bill Clinton and his defenders frequently admitted to flaws in the president's character, thereby making the president and his team seem more reasonable to reporters and to viewers of television newscasts. While that approach did not draw investigative bloodhounds like Kenneth Starr and Republican members of the House Judiciary Committee off the scent, the public remained convinced throughout the yearlong spectacle that the president should not be removed from office. Though the intensely partisan House impeached the president on a near party-line vote, the less ideologically oriented Senate found it impossible to remove from office a figure receiving such high public approval ratings. The White House also employed triage in the wake of the Iran-contra and Whitewater disclosures. Key administration officials and presidential friends took the fall to protect Clinton and Reagan, a particularly effective strategy for relatively popular presidents.

Making things seem more complicated as a scandal progresses can also strengthen a president's position by depriving opponents of the opportunity to make a clear and simple case. The more justifications a president offers for doing something, the harder it will be for opponents to counter the arguments, particularly given the relatively small amount of television news time provided to voices from outside the executive branch. By moving from "weapons of mass destruction" to "weapons of mass destruction programs" to "weapons of mass destruction activities" to the mass graves found in Iraq, the Bush administration offered

a number of after-the-fact justifications for why the United States fought
in Iraq. If the question on the lips of reporters is, Does Saddam Hussein deserve to remain in power? then the answer about that brutal
tyrant is obvious. The more complicated alternative question offered
by the war's opponents—Is Saddam Hussein a greater threat to the
United States than, say, al Qaeda or North Korea or Iran?—is a question not likely to be answered effectively on time-pressured television
newscasts, which may mean the question will not even be asked by a
media-savvy politician.

Lying may seem to be an appealing presidential response to an unfolding scandal, but it is clearly a high-risk strategy. There is the substantial chance that one will be caught in the deceit—all the memos;
recalled conversations; and, in the case of Bill Clinton, even DNA samples can undermine the claim that one is telling the whole truth. If that
happens, videotape of the damning statements—like Nixon's famous "I
am not a crook" response to Watergate and Clinton's finger-wagging
denial of a sexual relationship with Monica Lewinsky—are shown over
and over again. Although Bill Clinton's presidency survived the scandal, his became a greatly weakened administration, just like the post–
Iran-contra Reagan presidency.

Every administration has its dissidents, and their inside views can be
very damaging, as a variety of insider books about recent presidents
illustrate (Clarke 2004; Reich 1998; Stephanopoulos 1999; Suskind
2004; Woodward 1994). While we do not know as this book goes to
press what the Bush administration officials knew and when they knew
it about Iraq, we do know that some former administration officials tell
a very different story than do current ones. We also know that the
doubts that have been sowed in the public's consciousness about the
Bush team's credibility seem, even after his reelection in November
2004, to be debilitating. While reporters may hesitate to say plainly that
a candidate is lying, today's intensely partisan politics provides a variety
of people willing to make such a charge. (The Democratic attacks in
January 2005 on the nomination of National Security Adviser Condo-
leezza Rice to be secretary of state demonstrate the depth of partisan
anger over the administration's alleged deceit on Iraq.) And if nobody
in the political mainstream will make that case against a president,

there's always Michael Moore on the left and Rush Limbaugh on the right!

The "scandals that weren't" had two key factors in common—the lack of both convincing evidence and good pictures to help tell the story. Economic news reports are notoriously difficult to present visually, and the lack of good pictures to illustrate the corporate crime issues—as well as the lack of "smoking guns" to simplify and illustrate a story—help explain why the Bush-Enron and Cheney-Halliburton issues did not receive more attention than they did. All that may change, of course, if and when the Enron executives go to trial and if Cheney's energy panel deliberations are made public. But neither of those things happened in time to affect the administration's central concern of 2004 the president's reelection campaign. And even if either potential scandal blossoms during Bush's second term, neither topic seems destined to provide many good pictures, which may also work against the future eruption of these potential scandals.

The Abu Ghraib scandal is another example of how the lack of visual images can influence news media coverage. The mass media were particularly slow to pick up on that story (the most famous incidents happened in November 2003), but reporters made up for lost time with saturation coverage after the pictures were published in April 2004. Once pictures become public, they stay public. Six years after the Clinton-Lewinsky scandal broke—when Bill Clinton started making the rounds of television news programs to peddle his autobiography—news reports illustrating the president's new book returned to the now vintage footage of President Clinton embracing a beret-clad former intern in a White House rope line.

One important possible consequence of heavy scandal coverage is that other stories may not be covered in sufficient depth. In a study of the health care reform debate of 1994, for example, researchers found that news coverage of the Whitewater scandal overshadowed reporting on the health care debate, an important and controversial topic that year (Jamieson and Cappella 1998). The consequences would be even greater for stories that received even more media attention—like the Clinton-Lewinsky matter four years later.

But there are limits to how effectively a president can change the subject in midscandal. Indeed, when Clinton sought to engage in foreign policy during scandal periods, some news accounts questioned whether he was doing so to distract the electorate and the press. Bush's efforts in mid-2004 to talk more about a proposed manned space mission to Mars and less about Iraq likewise largely fell flat.

The scandals examined in this chapter took place during a rapidly changing media environment. The rise of aggressively partisan media outlets online and elsewhere seems likely to increase scandal coverage rather than reduce it. There is no doubt that the Clinton-Lewinsky matter became a subject of great public concern in part because of the online reporting of Matt Drudge. Similarly, the criticisms of G. W. Bush found throughout the online world increasingly have become part of more mainstream media coverage of the problems the United States faces in Iraq.

We may be entering an age in which the online news media function as an immense echo chamber, allowing whispered stories to remain alive until mainstream media turn their attention to them. Stories may live longer than ever before, and unsubstantiated allegations may get more attention than ever before as media outlets "race to the bottom" in accuracy in order to be first in this highly competitive industry (cf. Orkent 2004).

In the past three chapters we have examined how television reports on three specific areas of presidential news: the economy, foreign policy, and scandals. In our next chapter we compare the coverage of network television with that of other media outlets—two elite newspapers (the *Washington Post* and the *New York Times*) and four regionally significant newspapers.

# CHAPTER 6

## COMPETING VOICES
### Network Television versus Newspapers

So far in this book, we have focused on the content of the evening network newscasts. To some readers, this emphasis may seem odd. Today's young adults in particular are more likely to be "news grazers," getting the news when they have a few minutes rather than deliberately sitting down to watch the national news at 6:30 p.m. or 7:00 p.m. as many members of older generations did—and in significant numbers still do (Pew 2004a).

The contrast in news consumption habits is striking. Once upon a time in America, much of the nation stopped to listen to these evening newscasts. During the 1970–1971 television season, for example, 75 percent of the homes with a television on during the evening newscast time slot were tuned to those network news programs (Kurtz 2002b). Even in the 1980s, more than two-thirds of the people watching television during the evening newscast time slot were tuned to Tom Brokaw, Peter Jennings, or Dan Rather (Kurtz 2002b). Even now, these newscasts draw tens of millions of viewers, or roughly 43 percent of the people watching television at that hour (Kurtz 2002b).

Although their influence has declined over the past quarter century, leading media sources like network television news, the *New York*

*Times*, and the *Washington Post*—along with the many news organizations around the country that follow their leads—remain the principal lenses through which most citizens view their government (T. Cook 1998; Graber 2002; Sparrow 1999). Newer media sources, including twenty-four-hour cable news, the Internet, and a revived talk radio, have not displaced the old; instead, they offer a wider range of choices for news consumers, many of whom continue to rely heavily on the evening network newscasts and the online offerings of media outlets that also dominate off-line (Davis 1999; Davis and Owen 1998; Farnsworth and Owen 2004; Farnsworth and Lichter 2003a; Seib 2001).

More than one-third of those surveyed in mid-2004 said they regularly watched a network evening newscast, up slightly from the 30 percent who said they regularly watched an evening newscast in a mid-2000 survey (Pew 2004a). Some media outlets—particularly local television news and newspapers taken collectively—have larger audiences than network television, as shown in table 6.1. Others do not. Network television evening newscasts are still considerably more popular than many network television news magazines (like *20/20* and *Dateline*). Likewise, the number of people regularly watching an evening newscast still exceeds the percentage getting their news online at least three days a week (Pew 2004a).

Thus, there are two reasons why we emphasize network news coverage in this book. First, network television is an important source of news for other media outlets. Cable newscasts frequently use the same news footage and sometimes, as with MSNBC (the joint venture of NBC and Microsoft), even the same correspondents. Similarly, some of the most popular news outlets on the Internet are the online versions (like cnn.com and nytimes.com) of the same media brand names that dominate off-line (Pew 2000b).

Second, network newscasts have been very popular throughout the past quarter century. During Ronald Reagan's first year as president, there was no CNN and virtually no public use of the Internet. While network news stars have dimmed over the past quarter century, network television started this period as *the* leading national news source, and today remains *a* leading national news source.

While network newscasts represent the most effective comparisons

| TABLE 6.1 | News Media Use Regularly Watch, Read, or Listen To: (In Percentages) | | |
|---|---|---|---|
| | 1996 | 2000 | 2004 |
| **Major News Sources** | | | |
| Local Television News | 65 | 56 | 59 |
| Network Evening News | 42 | 30 | 34 |
| Newspaper Yesterday | 50 | 47 | 42 |
| Network TV Magazines | 36 | 31 | 22 |
| Time/Newsweek/US News | 15 | 12 | 13 |
| **In-Depth News Sources** | | | |
| National Public Radio | 13 | 15 | 16 |
| *NewsHour* (PBS) | 4 | 5 | 5 |
| C-SPAN | 6 | 4 | 5 |
| *New Yorker/Atlantic* | — | 2 | 2 |
| **Specialized News** | | | |
| Weather Channel | — | 32 | 31 |
| ESPN | — | 23 | 20 |
| Entertainment TV | — | 8 | 10 |
| Business Magazines | 5 | 5 | 4 |
| Religious Radio | 11 | — | 11 |
| **Get News Online Three Or More Days per Week** | 2* | 23 | 29 |

*From June 1995.
  Options not asked in a particular survey are marked with dashes.
  Because many respondents use more than one media source, percentages do not add up to 100.
*Source:* Pew (2004a).

over time in a study spanning three decades, they were not the only media outlets we examined. In this chapter we compare network news coverage to that of two leading national newspapers: the *New York Times* and the *Washington Post*. As with television news, we examined the extent, focus, and tone of their coverage of the national government during the first year of the Reagan, Clinton, and George W. Bush administrations. For reasons of economy, we examined only front-page stories from the pivotal first years of this study—1981, 1993, and 2001. A story was included in this analysis if it began on the front page and at least one-third of its content dealt with the federal government. (As we do throughout this project, the 2001 data will be broken out before and after the terrorist attacks of 9/11.)

Our decision to limit this analysis to front-page stories captures what *Times* and *Post* editors considered the most important stories of a given day and the ones that were most likely seen by the largest number of readers. While this approach understates the breadth and depth of newspaper coverage, it provides a fairer comparison to the broadcast networks' flagship nightly newscasts, whose length—barely twenty minutes of actual news—approximates television's version of a front page.

The *Times* and the *Post* are almost certainly the most influential general circulation daily newspapers with national influence. Among other potential candidates, *USA Today*, a headline-oriented paper popular with travelers and known for its generally brief stories, did not exist in 1981. The *Wall Street Journal*, another possible candidate for comparison, focuses more on business news than on general government news. In addition, both of these papers publish only five days a week. Ranked by their Sunday circulations, the *New York Times* is the most popular paper in the country, with average Sunday sales of nearly 1.7 million copies. The *Washington Post* ranks third with roughly 1.1 million in average Sunday sales, trailing both its Interstate 95 rival and the *Los Angeles Times* (*Editor and Publisher* 2004).

While the *Times* and the *Post* set the tone for many of the nation's newspapers through their news content and their wire services, we wanted to look beyond these Washington-focused publications. Therefore, in this chapter, we also examine front-page stories of government from four highly regarded newspapers around the country: the *Austin American-Statesman*, the *Des Moines Register*, the *San Jose Mercury News,* and the *St. Petersburg Times*. The four papers range in average weekday circulation from just over 152,000 to nearly 334,000 copies (*Editor and Publisher* 2004). In addition to their geographical diversity, the first two are located in state capitals, while the others are also regionally influential papers located in major cities. These four papers are located in some of the most important states in terms of national politics: California (where Ronald Reagan had served as governor) is the nation's most populous state, and Texas (where George W. Bush was governor) ranks second, according to the 2000 U.S. Census. Florida is

the nation's fourth-largest state and a key swing state in national politics, as the 2000 presidential election demonstrated. The *Des Moines
Register* is one of the most influential papers in America's agricultural
Midwest and gains a national showcase during the Iowa caucuses. (See
table 6.2.)

Geographically, the papers represent the American heartland and
both the East and West Coasts. As such, we might expect different

| TABLE 6.2 | Top Daily Newspapers in the United States (Newspapers Ranked by Weekday Circulation as of September 30, 2002) | |
| --- | --- | --- |
| 1. *USA Today* (M–F) | 2,136,068 | |
| 2. *Wall Street Journal* (M–F) | 1,800,607 | |
| 3. **New York Times** | 1,113,000 | |
| 4. *Los Angeles Times* | 925,135 | |
| 5. **Washington Post** | 746,724 | |
| 6. *New York Daily News* | 715,070 | |
| 7. *Chicago Tribune* | 679,327 | |
| 8. *New York Post* | 590,061 | |
| 9. *Newsday* (Long Island, NY) | 578,809 | |
| 10. *Houston Chronicle* | 552,052 | |
| 11. *San Francisco Chronicle* | 512,129 | |
| 12. *Dallas Morning News* | 505,724 | |
| 13. *Chicago Sun-Times* | 479,584 | |
| 14. *Boston Globe* | 467,745 | |
| 15. *Arizona Republic* (Phoenix) | 448,782 | |
| 16. *Newark Star-Ledger* | 408,557 | |
| 17. *Philadelphia Inquirer* | 373,892 | |
| 18. *Atlanta Journal-Constitution* | 371,161 | |
| 19. *Detroit Free Press* | 368,839 | |
| 20. *Cleveland Plain Dealer* | 363,750 | |
| 24. **St. Petersburg Times** | 333,557 | (largest circulation in Florida) |
| 32. **San Jose Mercury News** | 272,682 | (sixth-largest circulation in California) |
| 60. **Austin American-Statesman** | 183,288 | (fifth-largest circulation in Texas) |
| 75. **Des Moines Register** | 152,633 | (largest circulation in Iowa) |

*Source: Editor and Publisher* website, www.editorandpublisher.com/eandp/
images/pdf/usd100cand10.pdf, accessed July 6, 2004.

coverage patterns based on the characteristics of the regions they represent. Immigration issues—particularly those involving Latin America—would likely be most interesting to readers in Texas, Florida, and California. The heavy concentration of retirees in Florida might suggest greater reader interest in issues of Social Security than in other regions, while Asian news may be of more interest to readers of a paper based in California.

Stories written by wire services were excluded from the analysis of the front-page stories published in the newspapers examined here. Wire service stories comprise a far larger share of the national news coverage of regional papers when compared to national papers. Rarely does a story written by someone other than a staff reporter appear anywhere in the national news sections of the *New York Times* or the *Washington Post*—much less on the front page. The exclusion of wire service stories from the analysis of regional papers allows for a more precise analysis of the news content prepared by a given regional newspaper.

Given this approach, we cannot make fair comparisons between the amount of government coverage in the national and the regional papers. But we can compare the tone of coverage among all media outlets, since externally generated wire service stories used routinely in the regional papers (but almost never in the national press) have been excluded. We also make news volume comparisons among the regional newspapers, since they all were subject to the same rules that excluded wire service reports.

These six newspapers, two with a national reach and the four regionally influential ones, are examined and compared to the network news coverage analyzed in earlier chapters. In particular, these papers are analyzed to determine whether previously identified patterns—including declining coverage of government, executive-focused news, and pervasive negativity—are characteristic only of television news or pertain to print as well.

## Amount of Coverage

### THE NATIONAL PRESS

We analyzed 6,480 front-page stories that dealt with the federal government during 1981, 1993, and 2001 in the *Post* and the *Times*—an average of about 1,000 per year or 3 per day for each newspaper. The first surprise: Based on our findings for television news, we expected the 9/11 terrorist attacks to push front-page coverage of government in 2001 well beyond the totals of 1993 and 1981. On the contrary, coverage of the Bush administration's first year in office barely exceeded that of the Clinton administration, and the greatest amount of reporting on the government occurred in Ronald Reagan's first year in office.

Television's trend toward less coverage over time was duplicated by the prestige press. As table 6.3 illustrates, the federal government was

| TABLE 6.3 | Amount of Government News Coverage during Presidential First Years | | | |
|---|---|---|---|---|
| | 2001 | 1993 | 1981 | Total |
| **Network News** | | | | |
| Number of Stories | 5,011 | 3,843 | 7,216 | 16,078 |
| Number of Hours | 138 | 107 | 178 | 422 |
| Avg Min per Night | 23 | 18 | 29 | 23 |
| | | | | |
| Number of Minutes ABC | 2,807 | 2,128 | 3,012 | 7,947 |
| Number of Minutes CBS | 2,110 | 2,065 | 3,931 | 8,106 |
| Number of Minutes NBC | 3,372 | 2,223 | 3,707 | 9,302 |
| **National Newspapers** | | | | |
| **Number of Stories** | **2,076** | **2,053** | **2,351** | **6,480** |
| *Washington Post* | 1,100 | 1,025 | 1,331 | 3,456 |
| *New York Times* | 976 | 1,028 | 1,020 | 3,024 |
| **Column Inches** | **64,561** | **36,911** | **58,919** | **187,390** |
| *Washington Post* | 33,845 | 33,142 | 35,845 | 102,832 |
| *New York Times* | 30,715 | 30,768 | 23,074 | 84,557 |
| **Regional Newspapers** | | | | |
| **Number of Stories** | **1,814** | **2,065** | **2,966** | **6,846** |
| *Austin American-Statesman* | 547 | 551 | 425 | 1,523 |
| *Des Moines Register* | 432 | 443 | 924 | 1,799 |
| *San Jose Mercury News* | 460 | 635 | 656 | 1,751 |
| *St. Petersburg Times* | 375 | 437 | 961 | 1,773 |
| **Column Inches** | **40,060** | **41,574** | **56,317** | **137,951** |
| *Austin American-Statesman* | 12,737 | 11,575 | 4,735 | 29,645 |
| *Des Moines Register* | 5,348 | 7,361 | 22,871 | 35,580 |
| *San Jose Mercury News* | 12,372 | 14,287 | 12,139 | 8,798 |
| *St. Petersburg Times* | 9,603 | 7,753 | 16,572 | 33,928 |

the focus of 2,351 front-page stories in these two papers in 1981, but only 2,053 in 1993 and 2,076 in 2001. Indeed, but for the transformation of the news agenda by the 9/11 attacks, 2001 would have finished a distant third. The combined daily rate of coverage for the two papers was only 5.3 stories prior to 9/11, which projects to less than 2,000 reports for the year. But the events and aftermath of September 11 boosted the actual daily average to 5.7. By contrast, the *Times* and *Post* combined for 6.4 governmental stories per day in 1981—almost as many as the 6.5 per day in the aftermath of 9/11.

It will surprise no one that the *Washington Post*'s coverage exceeded that of the *New York Times* by a margin of more than four hundred stories over these three years. After all, the *Post*'s location in the nation's capital provides it with an audience far more interested in the federal government than is the case elsewhere. To Washingtonians, the national government is also local. On closer inspection, however, the *Post* is getting increasing competition in its franchise on national politics. Most of the difference between the two papers came in 1981, when the *Post* averaged nearly a story per day more than the *Times*. In 1993, the *Times* actually published more front-page stories on government than did the *Post*, although the *Post* regained the lead in 2001. In terms of column inches, the *Post* led by a commanding 45 percent more coverage in 1981, but the margin dropped to 10 percent or less in the next two years. Thus, America's two most prestigious general interest newspapers have become nearly equal competitors in covering the federal government.

REGIONAL PAPERS

We found an even sharper decline in coverage at the four regional papers, though there was far more variation among them. Front-page coverage totals for 2001 for all four papers dropped from 1993, the first year of the Clinton administration. Once again, as table 6.3 shows, the heaviest coverage appeared in 1981 (Ronald Reagan's first year in office) when the federal government was the focus of 2,966 stories in these four publications, compared to 1,814 stories in 2001 and 2,065 in 1993. Likewise, three of the four regional papers had substantial declines in coverage from the first year of Reagan's presidency to the first year of George W. Bush's. Coverage of the national government during that time period fell by more than half at the *St. Petersburg Times* and the *Des Moines Register*, and by about a third at the *Mercury News*.

Among these four papers, only the *Austin American-Statesman* provided more front-page coverage of government in 2001 than it did in 1981, perhaps because George W. Bush had been governor of Texas and many members of the new administration were Texans. Having a home-state president meant different things to different papers, however. Despite having a Californian as president, the *San Jose Mercury News* did not dominate the 1981 coverage; among the four regional papers it finished third in the amount of coverage during Ronald Reagan's first year, behind both the *St. Petersburg Times* and the *Des Moines Register*.

One might expect that national government stories would frequently be front-page news in state capitals, with their concentration of state and federal government workers, contractors, and others deeply interested in policy decisions made in Washington. Yet it turned out that location in a state capital was not correlated with the amount of coverage. In 2001, the *Austin American-Statesman* had the most coverage of the national government, but the *Des Moines Register* ranked third out of the four. Eight years earlier, the state capital papers ranked second and third among the four regional papers, and in 1981 they ranked second and fourth. Overall, these findings remind us of how differently local newspapers, even highly regarded regionally influential ones, choose to allocate their resources in covering the federal government.

## THE 9/11 EFFECT ON NEWSPAPER COVERAGE

As table 6.4 illustrates, front-page stories about the national government became much more numerous after the 9/11 attacks. The *New York Times* printed only six fewer government stories than the *Post* from September 12 through December 31, as both averaged 3.3 stories per day. But even that total was well under the 3.6 that the *Post* averaged

| TABLE 6.4 | Amount of 2001 Government News Coverage Before and After 9/11 | | |
|---|---|---|---|
| | **Before 9/11** | **After 9/11** | **2001 Total** |
| **Network News** | | | |
| **Number of Stories** | **2,909** | **2,105** | **5,014** |
| Number of Hours | 84 | 54 | 138 |
| Avg Min per Night | 20 | 29 | 23 |
| | | | |
| Number of Minutes ABC | 1,775 | 1,032 | 2,807 |
| Number of Minutes CBS | 1,298 | 812 | 2,110 |
| Number of Minutes NBC | 1,984 | 1,388 | 3,372 |
| **National Newspapers** | | | |
| **Number of Stories** | **1,346** | **728** | **2,076** |
| *Washington Post* | 731 | 367 | 1,100 |
| *New York Times* | 615 | 361 | 976 |
| | | | |
| Column Inches | | | |
| *Washington Post* | 21,789 | 12,056 | 83,845 |
| *New York Times* | 19,514 | 11,201 | 30,715 |
| **Regional Newspapers** | | | |
| **Number of Stories** | **991** | **823** | **1,814** |
| *Austin American-Statesman* | 302 | 245 | 547 |
| *Des Moines Register* | 265 | 167 | 432 |
| *San Jose Mercury News* | 223 | 237 | 460 |
| *St. Petersburg Times* | 201 | 174 | 375 |
| **Column Inches** | **19,700** | **20,360** | **40,060** |
| *Austin American-Statesman* | 6,720 | 6,017 | 12,737 |
| *Des Moines Register* | 3,064 | 2,284 | 5348 |
| *San Jose Mercury News* | 4,950 | 7,442 | 12,372 |
| *St. Petersburg Times* | 4,976 | 4,627 | 9,603 |

two decades before. (In other words, over the past two decades the *Post*'s front-page coverage has fallen to the level of the *Times*.)

As we have seen elsewhere, the reduction in local newspaper coverage in 2001 would have been even greater had the terrorist attacks of 9/11 not taken place. As table 6.4 demonstrates, the four regional newspapers also provided disproportionately greater coverage after the attacks. In fact, the *San Jose Mercury News* provided more national government coverage in the sixteen weeks after the attacks than in the thirty-six weeks that preceded them.


## A Renewed Executive Branch Focus

### NATIONAL PAPERS

As we have done for network television news, we based the bulk of our analysis not on news stories as a whole but on the individual discussions of government that appear within each article. This allowed us to differentiate discussions of the three branches of government and their component parts, even when they were discussed within the same story. To qualify, an individual, group, issue, office, or organization related to the federal government had to be discussed for at least two full paragraphs within an article. This procedure yielded 15,800 government-related discussions in the *New York Times* and the *Washington Post*, or about 2.5 discussions per story.

Coverage of the executive branch dominated government news, receiving over 70 percent of the coverage in all three years. Coverage of the legislative branch stood at roughly one-quarter of the executive branch totals in all three years, dropping from a high of 1,687 discussions in 1981 to 1,031 in 2001. The terrorist strikes of September 11, 2001, contributed to the coverage gap. Coverage of the administration increased from roughly seven discussions to ten per day in these two papers in the months that followed the terrorist attacks, while coverage of Congress fell to barely over half its previous rate. Pollsters have long noted that citizens tend to gravitate toward the president and his administration in times of crisis, and we found that the executive branch became the focus of news coverage during the period of national anxiety that followed the attacks.

The competition for media attention exists within the legislative branch of government, as well as between it and the executive branch. Overall, the Senate received 50 percent more coverage in these two papers than did the House of Representatives (12 percent of all governmental coverage across the three years, versus 8 percent for the lower chamber). The gap has increased over the years, so that by 2001 the Senate was the subject of roughly double the amount of coverage afforded the House in these two papers. Why the Senate's advantage in coverage? First, news follows power. Individual members of a body of 100 typically wield more influence than members of a body numbering over 450. Senators also represent entire states rather than smaller districts, and they are more likely to carve out a sphere of national influence.

The internal composition of each chamber matters as well. The Republicans controlled the Senate for part of 2001, until the Democrats took over with the partisan defection of Sen. James Jeffords (I-VT); narrowly divided chambers are often subject to more contentious and uncertain battles than those in which one party has a clear, effective majority. In addition, the Senate rules also provide greater power for the minority party. The Senate's norms and procedures lead to a less organized chamber, and a more unpredictable one, when compared to the more tightly managed House (Binder and S. Smith 1997). All things being equal, such narrow partisan divisions and such loose procedures offer greater opportunities for conflict and uncertainty—two conditions that increase the likelihood of media and public attention.

## REGIONAL NEWSPAPERS

Discussions of government in these four regional newspapers also focused mainly on the White House, as the legislative branch received less than one-third as much coverage as the executive branch in all three years. The details are found in table 6.5.

The 2001 coverage became even more executive-dominated after the terrorist attacks. The 1,171 executive branch discussions in these four newspapers during the eight and a half months before the attacks were almost equaled by the 1,169 discussions during the final three and a half months of 2001. Conversely, coverage of the legislative branch fell sharply, and coverage of the judicial branch fell to a mere 11 discussions—fewer than 1 per paper per month after 9/11.

Given such coverage gaps similar to those we found for the national newspapers and television networks, a commander in chief faces very little questioning of his policies during the early months of military action. Even the controversial procedures undertaken by the Justice Department and the Defense Department regarding the incarceration of U.S. citizens and foreign nationals in the wake of the terrorist attacks did not trigger much discussion of the judiciary during this period.

Among the regional papers, the executive-dominated coverage was most evident in President Bush's home-state paper, the *Austin American-Statesman*. In 2001, the executive branch—which included Texans George W. Bush, Karl Rove, Karen Hughes, and many other figures from Bush's gubernatorial team—enjoyed a 3 to 1 margin favoring the executive branch in the Texas paper. This was particularly notable given the influential roles played in Congress by other Lone Star State political figures, including U.S. Rep. Dick Armey (R-TX), then House majority leader; U.S. Rep. Tom DeLay (R-TX), then House majority whip; and U.S. Sen. Phil Gramm (R-TX), who chaired the Senate Committee on Banking, Housing, and Urban Affairs until mid-2001.

| TABLE 6.5 | Number of 2001 Executive Branch Discussions | | |
|---|---|---|---|
| | **Before 9/11** | **After 9/11** | **2001** |
| **Total** | | | |
| **Network News** | | | |
| **Total Executive** | 2,597 (100%) | 1,327 (100%) | 3,924 (100%) |
| President | 914 (35) | 298 (22) | 1,212 (31) |
| White House & Cabinet | 544 (21) | 306 (23) | 850 (22) |
| Other Executive | 1,139 (44) | 723 (55) | 1,862 (47) |
| **National Newspapers** | | | |
| **Total Executive** | 1,870 (100%) | 1,061 (100%) | 2,841 (100%) |
| President | 611 (34) | 189 (18) | 800 (28) |
| White House & Cabinet | 499 (23) | 235 (22) | 644 (23) |
| Other Executive | 760 (43) | 637 (60) | 1,397 (49) |
| **Regional Newspapers** | | | |
| **Total Executive** | 1,171 (100%) | 1,1691 (100%) | 2,340 (100%) |
| President | 374 (32) | 186 (16) | 560 (24) |
| White House & Cabinet | 307 (26) | 315 (27) | 622 (27) |
| Other Executive | 490 (42) | 668 (57) | 1,158 (49) |

*Note:* More than one individual or institution may be featured in one story.

In other words, having an unusually large number of Texans in leadership positions in the House did not prevent legislative branch coverage from declining in the state's capital city newspaper. The greatest number of discussions involving Congress occurred in the *Austin American-Statesman* in 1993, when Texans were far less influential in Congress than the state's delegation in 2001.

The pattern seen with these regional papers again demonstrates the influence of administration media strategies in shaping coverage of government, particularly in times of crisis. Mr. Bush's managerial style of delegating day-to-day visibility to his cabinet, the White House staff, and other executive branch officials was reflected in increased airtime for Defense Secretary Donald Rumsfeld and Attorney General John Ashcroft, among others. The administration's media management efforts after 9/11 helped secure for Bush an extraordinarily large and lengthy "rally round the flag" effect in public opinion during at least the two years that followed those attacks (Gregg and Rozell 2004; Kumar 2003a, 2003b; Nincic 1997). The consistency of this pattern across these three media groups suggests a similar ability to influence the content of television, national newspapers, and regional newspapers during times of great public concern.

## News Topics

### NATIONAL NEWSPAPERS

The dramatically different political and media environments that Ronald Reagan, Bill Clinton, and George W. Bush faced upon taking office were reflected in the changing news agenda of the *Washington Post* and the *New York Times*. Not surprisingly, the war on terrorism was the leading news story in these two agenda-setting newspapers during 2001. The attacks attracted more than twice as many front-page discussions as any other topic. General discussions of defense, a category that refers to discussions about the need for a strong defense without mentioning specific defense topics such as weapons systems or the size and composition of the military, ranked second in both papers during 2001.

Coverage of the war in Afghanistan represents the only issue that was handled very differently by the *Post* and the *Times*. It placed third on the *Times*'s news agenda but only ninth at the *Post*, behind taxes, health care, the handling of 9/11 and the anthrax attacks, the economy, the environment, and the budget. The tax issue, which ranked third in the *Post* in 2001, was also the most heavily covered domestic issue in the *Times*, where it placed fifth. (President Bush succeeded in persuading Congress to pass a major tax cut in mid-2001.)

During Bill Clinton's first year as president, no single issue towered over the news agenda the way terrorism would eight years later. Three different issue areas—the federal budget, health care, and taxes—competed on an almost equal footing for the top spot. By a narrow margin, the federal budget was the number one story in these two papers.

The top stories in these two papers during Ronald Reagan's first year in office are another reminder of how much the world has changed over the past quarter century. Relations with the USSR finished second, flanked by the budget and taxes. These totals also indicate how much more discussion of issues there was in the prestige press two decades ago; the five most heavily covered issues in 1981 were all discussed more frequently than the top-ranked issue twelve years later.

## REGIONAL NEWSPAPERS

The war on terrorism was by far the leading news story during 2001 for the four regional papers as well. But even this topic illustrates the regional differences that appear in governmental coverage. Three of the papers focused on the war on terrorism itself, while the handling of the terrorist attacks on the United States (including the anthrax attacks) ranked first in the *St. Petersburg Times*—a topic of particularly high interest to readers in Florida, the state where the first death from mailed anthrax spores occurred.

The war in Afghanistan ranked third in the *St. Petersburg Times*, but it failed to make the top ten issues lists of the other three papers. This is likely the result of the heavy military presence found in the Tampa Bay region, which would lead to more locally oriented stories. (The other papers would likely have relied more extensively on wire service copy for this topic.) Social Security is also an important issue in Florida, which has a disproportionately high percentage of retirees. It ranked as the seventh most important issue at the *St. Petersburg Times* but was not on the top ten lists of the other three papers. Energy was the second most important issue at the *San Jose Mercury News*—a likely result of the blackout and severe energy price hikes in California during 2001—but did not make the top five stories in the other papers.

Eight years earlier, all four regional papers treated the federal budget as the top national government story, and all devoted a similar amount of time to it in 1993. But beyond the top national issue, the papers presented very different visions of the most important policy matters. Health care reform was the second most important issue in senior-rich St. Petersburg, but only fifth in the Iowa paper and seventh in its California counterpart. Agriculture ranked fourth and disaster relief seventh in the *Des Moines Register*, logical choices for a state economy highly dependent on farming and with considerable territory susceptible to flooding. Those two issues did not appear in the top ten stories covered by the other three regional papers. The Clinton administration's handling of the siege in Waco, Texas, was the seventh most important issue the *Austin American-Statesman*, but the out-of-state papers paid far less attention. The *Mercury News*—located in relatively gay-friendly northern California—made the "don't ask, don't tell" military personnel policy one of its leading stories, but that matter was not a leading topic of discussion in the other three papers.

During Ronald Reagan's first year in office, the budget was again the leading issue for all the regional papers, and the Soviet Union was the second most important topic for three of the four, while the *Austin American-Statesman* made taxes the second most important theme. Taxes ranked from third to fifth in importance at the remaining three papers. There was also broad agreement on several other international issues, including policy toward Iran and Israel. But some issues again demonstrated differing regional priorities. The status of the space shuttle program, parts of which are based in Florida, was a leading issue only for the *St. Petersburg Times*. Likewise, Social Security ranked third in the *St. Petersburg Times* but no higher than eighth elsewhere.

## Sources

### NATIONAL NEWSPAPERS

Just as the executive branch dominated prestige press coverage, executive branch officials served as the primary sources of information. They were cited nearly twice as frequently as congressional sources, by a margin of 37 to 19 percent of all sources. By contrast, only a smattering of sources came from the judiciary or state and local governments. When former officials were added to the mix, U.S. government sources of all types accounted for nearly two-thirds (65 percent) of all sources who were cited.

Private sector sources were dominated by members of interest groups (8 percent) and experts from academia and other research organizations (6 percent). In addition, foreign sources accounted for just less than one source in ten—about the same amount as our residual category general attributions (such as "sources tell us" or "critics charge") and other sources (such as ordinary citizens). There were no significant differences between the *Post* and *Times* on this dimension of coverage.

Away from the government, the *Times*'s and *Post*'s reliance on scholars and other expert sources tripled over time, from 3 percent in 1981 to 6 percent in 1993 and 9 percent in 2001. Interest groups were the source for information 9 percent of the time in 2001 and 1993, up from 6 percent in 1981. There was also an increase in the presence of pundits and commentators not designated as experts, along with citations of other news organizations.

Citations of foreign officials, citizens, and institutions dropped steadily from 11 percent of sources in 1981 to only 7 percent in 2001. Since the nation in 2001 became more heavily engaged with international affairs than at any time since the Cold War, the declining appearance of foreign sources in the *Times* and the *Post* proved unexpected. (Of course, our study does not include news stories about foreign topics that do not deal with U.S. policy or other government functions.) The *Times* and the *Post* both retain extensive news bureaus around the world, as well as skilled national reporting staffs who can do much to place U.S. foreign policy issues into context for readers.

Our findings also raise concerns about the possible parochialism in government coverage back home. Even with former governors heading all three administrations, there were fewer than six hundred citations of state and local government officials out of nearly forty-two thousand sources overall. The absence of state and local officials in the 2001 coverage is remarkable given the debate over the "devolution" of government functions from Washington, widespread anxiety over the supply of electricity in California and elsewhere, and the vital roles played by state and local officials in New York and elsewhere in the wake of the terrorist attacks. Yet the use of state and local government sources bottomed out in 2001 at only twenty-two sources, one-fifth of 1 percent of the overall total.

## REGIONAL NEWSPAPERS

Executive branch sources dominated in the four regionally influential papers as well. But this dominance diminished over time, dropping to 37 percent of sources under Bush and Clinton, down from 45 percent under Reagan. The somewhat reduced dependence on the executive branch did not lead to an increase in the use of Capitol Hill sources. The legislative branch accounted for only 14 percent of all sources used in 2001, and 16 percent for the three years combined. Instead, reporters at these papers increasingly turned to people outside government as sources. The largest proportionate gain was seen for experts and representatives of think tanks, who went from 2 percent of sources in 1981 to 8 percent in 2001. Still, the overall picture was one of stability over time.

National news sources are often attacked for being too "inside the Beltway," too focused on the goings-on inside the national capital. Critics urge reporters for the network newscasts and leading newspapers like the *New York Times* and the *Washington Post* to spend more time in the country to appreciate the world beyond the Potomac and the Hudson. But the same criticism can be leveled against the national news coverage of the four regional papers, all based far beyond the Washington Beltway. Even though two of the four papers are based in state capitals, state and local government officials were almost never used as sources in national government stories.

Of the 9,656 sources relied upon in 2001 by these four papers for the front-page stories examined here, only 35 were state and local government officials. Given the increasing attention paid to unfunded mandates, the "new federalism," and other issues of state/federal relations, this seems an unfortunate omission. These newspapers all had some degree of locally flavored coverage, yet they didn't take advantage of state and local officials in their communities when reporting on federal policy.

## Tone of Coverage

### NATIONAL NEWSPAPERS

For the press, as for television, we examined the tone of every evaluation or judgment of individuals or institutions involved with the federal government. To reiterate, this measure of tone did not include comments that simply dealt with either good or bad news (such as the passage or defeat of legislation) but only explicit statements of support or criticism.

This study provides two sets of comparisons to measure partisan tilt. The first is the treatment of the Democratic Clinton administration versus the Republican administrations of Reagan and Bush. This is less than ideal since two Republicans are compared to only one Democrat at different time points, with no way to determine whether any difference is based on personal rather than political or ideological factors. The second is a direct comparison of Democratic and Republican members of Congress. This is more satisfying since it compares large numbers of individuals who have only their party affiliations in common and who are evaluated at the same point in time.

As shown in table 6.6, the Bush and Clinton administrations received the same proportion of positive evaluations in the *Washington Post* (37 percent), with the Reagan administration third (31 percent). These results were reversed for personal evaluations of the presidents. Bush and Clinton again tied with 40 percent positive evaluations, but Reagan led both with 43 percent positive judgments. In the legislative branch, congressional Republicans fared better in the *Post* in 1981 and

| TABLE 6.6 | Tone of Coverage during Presidential First Years (Percent Positive) | | | | | |
|---|---|---|---|---|---|---|
| | 2001 | | 1993 | | 1981 | |
| **ABC News** | | | | | | |
| Executive Total | 35% | n = 939 | 38% | n = 1521 | 40% | n = 402 |
| President | 39 | n = 497 | 40 | n = 837 | 41 | n = 186 |
| White House & Cabinet | 40 | n = 167 | 54 | n = 222 | 40 | n = 129 |
| Other Executive | 26 | n = 275 | 23 | n = 462 | 37 | n = 87 |
| **CBS News** | | | | | | |
| Executive Total | 35% | n = 815 | 34% | n = 1645 | 32% | n = 601 |
| President | 35 | n = 506 | 35 | n = 903 | 35 | n = 253 |
| White House & Cabinet | 48 | n = 153 | 50 | n = 234 | 29 | n = 206 |
| Other Executive | 25 | n = 156 | 26 | n = 508 | 32 | n = 142 |
| **NBC News** | | | | | | |
| Executive Total | 38% | n = 784 | 40% | n = 1641 | 32% | n = 61 |
| President | 44 | n = 394 | 40 | n = 968 | 34 | n = 266 |
| White House & Cabinet | 44 | n = 135 | 56 | n = 283 | 29 | n = 272 |
| Other Executive | 27 | n = 255 | 28 | n = 390 | 34 | n = 74 |
| *New York Times* | | | | | | |
| Executive Total | 30% | n = 607 | 33% | n = 782 | 25% | n = 893 |
| President | 32 | n = 199 | 38 | n = 293 | 32 | n = 237 |
| White House & Cabinet | 33 | n = 260 | 35 | n = 336 | 23 | n = 468 |
| Other Executive | 21 | n = 148 | 20 | n = 153 | 22 | n = 188 |
| *Washington Post* | | | | | | |
| Executive Total | 37% | n = 600 | 37% | n = 779 | 31% | n = 1501 |
| President | 40 | n = 221 | 40 | n = 240 | 43 | n = 419 |
| White House & Cabinet | 41 | n = 219 | 43 | n = 346 | 28 | n = 684 |
| Other Executive | 26 | n = 160 | 23 | n = 193 | 24 | n = 398 |
| *San Jose Mercury News* | | | | | | |
| Executive Total | 26% | n = 317 | 29% | n = 341 | 20% | n = 189 |
| President | 31 | n = 106 | 32 | n = 188 | 14 | n = 29 |
| White House & Cabinet | 29 | n = 99 | 25 | n = 81 | 14 | n = 111 |
| Other Executive | 17 | n = 112 | 26 | n = 72 | 37 | n = 49 |
| *St. Petersburg Times* | | | | | | |
| Executive Total | 36% | n = 386 | 45% | n = 596 | 28% | n = 453 |
| President | 35 | n = 125 | 43 | n = 292 | 42 | n = 156 |
| White House & Cabinet | 39 | n = 136 | 53 | n = 223 | 21 | n = 208 |
| Other Executive | 34 | n = 125 | 26 | n = 81 | 17 | n = 89 |
| *Austin American-Statesman* | | | | | | |
| Executive Total | 31% | n = 221 | 33% | n = 410 | 21% | n = 211 |
| President | 32 | n = 104 | 33 | n = 211 | 24 | n = 101 |
| White House & Cabinet | 50 | n = 46 | 33 | n = 129 | 15 | n = 78 |
| Other Executive | 18 | n = 71 | 31 | n = 70 | 28 | n = 32 |
| *Des Moines Register* | | | | | | |
| Executive Total | 31% | n = 217 | 59% | n = 185 | 28% | n = 843 |
| President | 35 | n = 85 | 60 | n = 107 | 41 | n = 239 |
| White House & Cabinet | 39 | n = 51 | 72 | n = 57 | 22 | n = 501 |
| Other Executive | 22 | n = 81 | 24 | n = 21 | 24 | n = 103 |

Based on evaluations made by sources and reporters on the evening news and in front-page newspaper stories.

2001, while the Democrats led in 1993. Overall coverage of Republicans in this paper was 29 percent positive in tone during these three years, only slightly ahead of the Democrats' 26 percent positive rating. It would be difficult to discern any partisan advantage in this pattern of results.

By contrast, the *New York Times* displayed some tilt toward the Democrats. The *Times* gave more favorable (though still mainly negative) press to the Clinton administration (33 percent positive evaluations) than to the Reagan and Bush administrations, which received 25 and 30 percent positive comments, respectively. Bill Clinton also bested his rivals in his personal coverage, with 38 percent positive press versus 32 percent positive for both Ronald Reagan and George W. Bush.

To sum up, the data from two of America's leading newspapers provide a split decision on the question of bias. The evidence suggests that the *Times* tilts somewhat toward the Democrats, particularly in its congressional coverage, while any partisan differences at the *Post* are slight and balance out over time. However, any differences along a partisan or ideological spectrum exist within a journalistic milieu so negative in tone that the question will doubtless provide continued fodder for critics from both sides.

## REGIONAL NEWSPAPERS

The four regional papers were most positive toward the national government in 1993—Bill Clinton's first year in office. The executive branch received coverage that was positive in tone 40 percent of the time, compared to 30 percent positive during the first year of the Bush administration and 26 percent positive coverage for Ronald Reagan's first year.

The two most negative assessments of the executive branch found in table 6.6 are found among the regional papers in 1981—the *San Jose Mercury News* and the *Austin American-Statesman*. The *Mercury News* was also the most negative of all nine media outlets during 2001. The two most positive treatments were also found among the regional papers—the *Des Moines Register* and the *St. Petersburg Times*—and both during Bill Clinton's first year.

In the regional papers, Congress seemed to fare a bit better than elsewhere. Overall, the tone of Congress's coverage mirrored that of the executive branch—about two-to-one negative. But this parity conceals a gradual improvement in Congress's press, from only 28 percent positive evaluations in 1981 to 34 percent in 1993 and 37 percent in 2001. The legislative branch was treated more positively than the executive branch under Bush and Reagan but fell short of executive branch coverage in 1993 under Clinton. Since a significant amount of the regional coverage from Washington concerns the local congressional delegation—many national stories can be left to the wire services—the more evenhanded treatment of the branches may the be result of the more effective self-promotion efforts of legislators and their locally oriented papers (cf. Hess 1981, 1991, 1996).

Republicans and Democrats in the legislative branch received equally positive coverage in the *San Jose Mercury News*, where 32 percent of the coverage of lawmakers from each party was positive. The Democrats on Capitol Hill received modest coverage advantages in the *Des Moines Register* (36 percent positive to 31 percent for Republican lawmakers) and in the *St. Petersburg Times* (47 percent to 40 percent). By far the widest gap was found in the *Austin American-Statesman*, where Democrats on Capitol Hill were favored by a 44 percent positive to 19 percent positive margin—a 25 percentage point gap over the GOP.

COVERAGE DIFFERENCES: BEFORE AND AFTER 9/11

As table 6.7 shows, all three media groups treated the executive branch quite negatively during 2001—36 percent positive on television, 33 percent positive in the national newspapers, and 31 percent positive in the regional papers. But there was greater variation in the tone of coverage after 9/11. Coverage of President Bush became more positive across the board, going from roughly two-to-one negative on network news and in the regional papers to nearly two-to-one positive after the attacks. For all three outlets, coverage of Bush was considerably more positive than the coverage of the rest of executive branch after 9/11.

The results for individual outlets show some of the most positive coverage anywhere in our study, as shown in table 6.8. At CBS, coverage of Bush went from 32 percent to 69 percent positive. Three other outlets gave Bush more than 60 percent favorable ratings post-9/11—

| TABLE 6.7 | Tone of 2001 Executive Branch Coverage (Percent Positive) | | | | | |
|---|---|---|---|---|---|---|
| | **Before 9/11** | | **After 9/11** | | **2001 Total** | |
| *Network News* | | | | | | |
| **Executive Total** | **35%** | **n = 2,122** | **42%** | **n = 416** | **36%** | **n = 2,538** |
| President | 36 | n = 1,267 | 63 | n = 130 | 39 | n = 1,397 |
| White House & Cabinet | 48 | n = 351 | 31 | n = 104 | 44 | n = 455 |
| Other Executive | 23 | n = 504 | 34 | n = 182 | 26 | n = 686 |
| *National Newspapers* | | | | | | |
| **Executive Total** | **34%** | **n = 832** | **31%** | **n = 375** | **33%** | **n = 1,207** |
| President | 35 | n = 372 | 48 | n = 48 | 37 | n = 420 |
| White House & Cabinet | 42 | n = 275 | 30 | n = 204 | 37 | n = 479 |
| Other Executive | 21 | n = 185 | 27 | n = 123 | 23 | n = 308 |
| *Regional Newspapers* | | | | | | |
| **Executive Total** | **30%** | **n = 854** | **36%** | **n = 287** | **31%** | **n = 1,141** |
| President | 30 | n = 373 | 64 | n = 47 | 33 | n = 420 |
| White House & Cabinet | 37 | n = 267 | 39 | n = 65 | 38 | n = 332 |
| Other Executive | 21 | n = 214 | 27 | n = 175 | 24 | n = 389 |

the NBC *Nightly News*, the *San Jose Mercury News,* and the *St. Petersburg Times.* The most negative tone was found in the *New York Times* (43 percent positive)—the only outlet of the nine with a majority of negative coverage of Bush during the final sixteen weeks of 2001.

However, the coverage changes that followed 9/11 in these news outlets boosted Bush's personal coverage only. The period after the attacks included pointed questioning as to why the nation's intelligence services had not done more to protect the public, as well as the Justice Department's secretive and controversial detention procedures relating to possible terrorists. The administration's strategy of limiting the president's exposure on network news allowed Bush to concentrate on his commander-in-chief functions and to emphasize his role as the national leader in televised speeches to the nation and before Congress (Gregg and Rozell 2004).

## Conclusion

In many respects our findings for local and national newspapers echo the trends we found for the television networks. News coverage of gov-

| TABLE 6.8 | Tone of Executive Branch Coverage in 2001 by Outlet (Percent Positive) | | | | | |
|---|---|---|---|---|---|---|
| | **Before 9/11** | | **After 9/11** | | **2001 Total** | |
| **ABC News** | | | | | | |
| Executive Total | 35% | n = 771 | 39% | n = 168 | 35% | n = 939 |
| President | 38 | n = 449 | 54 | n = 48 | 39 | n = 497 |
| White House & Cabinet | 42 | n = 123 | 32 | n = 44 | 40 | n = 167 |
| Other Executive | 23 | n = 199 | 34 | n = 76 | 26 | n = 275 |
| **CBS News** | | | | | | |
| Executive Total | 35% | n = 714 | 53% | n = 101 | 35% | n = 815 |
| President | 32 | n = 467 | 69 | n = 39 | 35 | n = 506 |
| White House & Cabinet | 51 | n = 125 | 50 | n = 28 | 48 | n = 153 |
| Other Executive | 18 | n = 122 | 36 | n = 34 | 25 | n = 156 |
| **NBC News** | | | | | | |
| Executive Total | 39% | n = 637 | 37% | n = 147 | 38% | n = 784 |
| President | 41 | n = 351 | 67 | n = 43 | 39 | n = 394 |
| White House & Cabinet | 51 | n = 183 | 25 | n = 32 | 44 | n = 135 |
| Other Executive | 28 | n = 103 | 25 | n = 72 | 27 | n = 255 |
| *New York Times* | | | | | | |
| Executive Total | 32% | n = 401 | 27% | n = 206 | 30% | n = 607 |
| President | 30 | n = 171 | 43 | n = 28 | 32 | n = 199 |
| White House & Cabinet | 40 | n = 147 | 26 | n = 113 | 34 | n = 260 |
| Other Executive | 20 | n = 83 | 22 | n = 65 | 21 | n = 148 |
| *Washington Post* | | | | | | |
| Executive Total | 37% | n = 431 | 37% | n = 169 | 37% | n = 600 |
| President | 39 | n = 201 | 55 | n = 20 | 40 | n = 221 |
| White House & Cabinet | 45 | n = 128 | 35 | n = 91 | 41 | n = 219 |
| Other Executive | 23 | n = 102 | 33 | n = 58 | 26 | n = 160 |
| *San Jose Mercury News* | | | | | | |
| Executive Total | 23% | n = 240 | 34% | n = 77 | 26% | n = 317 |
| President | 27 | n = 94 | 67 | n = 12 | 31 | n = 106 |
| White House & Cabinet | 27 | n = 78 | 38 | n = 21 | 29 | n = 99 |
| Other Executive | 13 | n = 68 | 23 | n = 44 | 17 | n = 112 |
| *St. Petersburg Times* | | | | | | |
| Executive Total | 35% | n = 257 | 40% | n = 129 | 36% | n = 386 |
| President | 30 | n = 104 | 62 | n = 21 | 35 | n = 125 |
| White House & Cabinet | 41 | n = 106 | 33 | n = 30 | 39 | n = 136 |
| Other Executive | 32 | n = 47 | 36 | n = 78 | 34 | n = 125 |
| *Austin American-Statesman* | | | | | | |
| Executive Total | 33% | n = 168 | 26% | n = 53 | 31% | n = 221 |
| President | 31 | n = 98 | 50 | n = 6* | 32 | n = 104 |
| White House & Cabinet | 52 | n = 33 | 46 | n = 13 | 50 | n = 46 |
| Other Executive | 22 | n = 37 | 15 | n = 34 | 18 | n = 71 |
| *Des Moines Register* | | | | | | |
| Executive Total | 30% | n = 189 | 43% | n = 28 | 31% | n = 217 |
| President | 31 | n = 77 | 75 | n = 8* | 35 | n = 85 |
| White House & Cabinet | 38 | n = 50 | 100 | n = 1* | 39 | n = 51 |
| Other Executive | 21 | n = 62 | 26 | n = 19 | 22 | n = 81 |

*Too few evaluations for meaningful analysis.

ernment was mainly negative in tone, focused heavily on the executive branch, and declined over time. A pessimist might summarize national and regional newspaper coverage of the federal government as bad news and less of it. These findings reinforce our concern that the media inadvertently promote a pessimistic, if not cynical, perspective about government. Nonetheless, critics should take into account some positive findings as well.

At all six papers, and in all three years, the vast majority of evaluations of government officials were based on job performance criteria. Moreover, this issue-oriented coverage consistently included a significant amount of international news, regardless of whether the papers were located on one of the coasts or in the nation's heartland. Even so, we found a surprisingly strong focus on inside-the-Beltway sources for government information at all four regional papers. Even those papers located in state capitals almost never called on state and local government officials to discuss current national policy issues.

For all these newspapers, the president has the most decisive voice in American government, and that public role is inevitably heightened during times of crisis (Adams et al. 1994; Lowi 1985; Woodward 2002). But presidential media management strategies can shift at least some of the coverage away from the Oval Office toward other parts of the executive branch. In the wake of the 9/11 terrorist attacks, for example, George W. Bush received proportionately less attention than he had earlier in the year as the administration sought to shift day-to-day news coverage toward Bush's executive branch subordinates. The sustained presidential approval during this period suggests how media management strategies and leadership styles can be important weapons in the president's ongoing struggles with reporters and legislators over how to set and frame the public agenda. Deflecting potential criticism in the direction of subordinates can be an effective strategy for maintaining a president's public prestige in the aftermath of a major crisis.

The rally round the flag effect is frequently used to explain increases in public support for the president during crises (cf. Adams et al. 1994; Nincic 1997). We found similar tendencies in both newspaper and television coverage. CBS anchor Dan Rather's tearful public statement of support for President Bush after reporting for days on the death and devastation found in lower Manhattan may have reflected a widely shared view among U.S. reporters and editors at the time. Indeed, the content analysis suggests there was a rally round the flag effect that influenced reporters as well as citizens. Post-9/11 news reports were unusually supportive of the president, compared both to the rest of the executive branch and to Bush's coverage before the attacks. The effect, however, was less to diminish criticism than to deflect it away from the Oval Office onto other parts of the administration.

Our findings on the tone of news coverage belie overarching generalizations about alleged partisan bias in the mass media. While these data identify a pervasive negativism in news coverage during periods of normal politics, some outlets are more negative than others. Coverage of Bush was consistently negative in all the media outlets before the terrorist attacks, but sharp differences appeared in the coverage post-9/11. Coverage of Bush was far more negative in tone during the final weeks of 2001 in the *New York Times* (43 percent positive) than in any other news media outlet examined here.

The CBS *Evening News*, recently the subject of a critical book by former correspondent Bernard Goldberg (2002), was actually the second most positive media outlet (behind the *Des Moines Register*) in its treatment of Bush after the attacks (69 percent positive) and the most positive (53 percent positive) in its treatment of the executive branch as a whole post-9/11. But some other evidence suggests a more mixed decision for CBS. During the thirty-six weeks of 2001 before the terrorist attacks, the tone of Bush's coverage on CBS was 32 percent positive, which was below the 38 percent positive coverage of Bush on ABC and the 41 percent positive coverage of Bush on NBC. CBS was, however, still more positive than the *New York Times*, which was 30 percent positive in tone in its coverage of George W. Bush during the same preattack period. In general, we find more evidence of partisan tilt at the *New York Times* than at the *Washington Post*.

These differences suggest the importance of further research in the consideration of possible media bias—a topic that receives far less attention from media scholars than it does from media observers based outside university gates. The evidence here demonstrates why such analysis should take place at the level of individual news outlets. This content analysis demonstrates the considerable differences in executive branch coverage during 1981, 1993, and 2001 among the television networks; between the *New York Times* and the *Washington Post*; and among the four regional newspapers examined here. In summary, our content analysis suggests that the mainstream media environment is far more varied in tone than many of its critics are willing to admit.

We now turn to an overall assessment of news coverage of government—the subject of our final chapter. In addition to a summary of our findings, we discuss possible alterations in the presidency-media relationship, as well as how trends in using the media are likely to affect some of the patterns of coverage identified here.

# CHAPTER 7

## PRESIDENTIAL COVERAGE AND THE CHALLENGES OF A CHANGING MEDIA

The daily White House news briefings, televised presidential activities, and administration announcements are the most visible parts of today's tug-of-war over coverage of the president and his administration. In addition, there are many behind-the-scenes, off-the-record conversations designed to shape the daily news reports in ways favorable to the White House. The struggle among reporters and public officials over the framing of news is a constant feature of America's mediated government. While many of these efforts at spin are not visible to the public, today's generous buffet of news outlets increasingly allows Americans to become their own editors. Rather than being dependent on the corner newsstand, today's news consumers can point and click to get news online and use their remote controls to jump from one broadcast or cable newscast to another.

Our focus on news coverage of three presidential first years—Ronald Reagan in 1981, Bill Clinton in 1993, and George W. Bush in 2001—encompassed nearly thirty thousand news stories from nine national and local media outlets. We also examined tens of thousands of other television news stories over the past three decades to study news coverage of government beyond those three first years—particularly in the key areas of foreign and military policy, economic policy, and presidential scandals. The unusual breadth and depth of our content analyses allowed us to test some widely held assumptions about news coverage of the federal government. In some respects the results confirmed or built upon the findings of previous researchers. In others, they challenged misconceptions held by scholars, politicians, or journalists.

## What's News?

First of all, there is far less news about government than there used to be. From 1981 to 2001, the number of stories touching on the federal government dropped by 30 percent on network television news, by 12 percent in two leading national papers (the *New York Times* and the *Washington Post*), and by 34 percent in our sample of staff-written stories in four widely respected and regionally influential newspapers. Even more telling, the number of discussions of government within these stories dropped by over 40 percent in print and broadcast news alike. This decline extended to all three branches of government. The unprecedented terrorist attacks in 2001 reversed the trend, at least temporarily, though only for the executive branch. Before 9/11, the media were on track to produce less than half the annual coverage that they had twenty years earlier. George W. Bush's first term in office saw the growing attention paid to international crises and associated foreign policy issues, which continued throughout the 2004 presidential election.

### THE EXECUTIVE BRANCH'S ADVANTAGE IN THE AMOUNT OF NEWS COVERAGE

News coverage of government was apportioned very unevenly. Both print and broadcast media focused heavily on the executive branch. In 1981, 1993, and 2001, the presidential administration comprised more than 70 percent of all discussions of government in national and local newspapers, and even over 80 percent on network news. The legislative branch attracted most of the remaining coverage, while the judiciary made relatively rare appearances—a mere 3 percent of the coverage in print and broadcast outlets alike. Although new administrations naturally attract a great deal of coverage initially, content analyses of news in other years during the past quarter century confirmed this overall pattern of a huge executive branch advantage in media attention.

Many critics have complained that the legislative and judicial branches are given short shrift by the media. However, our findings challenge the related criticism that the focus of government news is becoming narrower and more personalized due to increased attention to the president as communicator in chief. We found a mild increase in the proportion of discussions about President Clinton above that of President Reagan, but there was no further increase in attention to President George W. Bush. In fact, due to the declining government coverage overall, coverage of the president himself fell by over a thousand stories in the five national media outlets from 1981 to 2001.

Since the presidency is the closest thing to a single decisive voice in American government, it is often assumed that the president's public role is inevitably heightened during times of tension in the vital areas of national defense and foreign policy. Yet, in the wake of the 9/11 terrorist attacks, President George W. Bush received proportionately less attention than he had earlier in the year as the media's focus shifted to his executive branch subordinates. The news media's attention was drawn away from the chief executive in a deliberate strategy by George W. Bush's subordinates to try to elevate the presidential office above the level of day-to-day political concerns. This was a sharp contrast from the behavior of Bill Clinton, whose personalized presidency was a gift that kept on giving to scandal-hungry reporters (Kumar 2003a, 2003b; Sabato et al. 2000).

A much clearer trend was the increased attention to the heads of executive agencies and other administration appointees outside the traditional power centers of the White House and the president's cabinet. The difference was most pronounced on the networks (where the proportion of presidential coverage rose only slightly from 1981 to 1993), while coverage of executive agencies outside the White House and the cabinet nearly doubled, rising to half of all national media coverage of the entire federal government.

The most significant victim of executive-centered news is Congress. The legislative branch may be a full partner in policymaking under the Constitution, but in news coverage it takes a backseat to the executive.

Congress accounted for less than one in four discussions of government in the press, and one in six on television. The total dropped as low as one out of ten televised discussions during the first year of the Clinton administration. The lack of legislative access to the nation's airwaves and leading newspapers makes it very difficult for lawmakers on Capitol Hill to be heard, much less "spin" the news as the White House does. In times of crisis, the legislative branch gets pushed even farther into the shadow of the president and his appointees. In the months after 9/11, for example, Congress received only about half as much coverage as it enjoyed before the terrorist attacks.

There are obvious reasons for these disparities in coverage in terms of the media's priorities. Individual members of the Senate, even the party leaders, are far less well known than presidents. Stories involving less visible figures are more difficult and time-consuming to present than is a report that focuses on the president as either commander in chief or legislator in chief. Members of the House are typically even less recognizable and nationally influential than senators, and they receive even less coverage.

Of course, the media spotlight is a mixed blessing. News audiences exposed to such executive-centered coverage may not fully appreciate the obstacles a president faces in trying to secure passage of his agenda. Thus, presidents may be blamed for things that they had little ability to influence. Further, the tone of the attention they receive makes much of that greater news attention unwelcome. Like football quarterbacks, presidents receive more credit from the media than they deserve when things go right and more blame than they deserve when things go wrong.

The judicial branch receives by far the least media attention of the three branches of government. The demands of daily journalism suggest why the judiciary can be described as "the forgotten branch." On a day-to-day basis, the federal court system generally handles issues of less immediate public concern than the central political issues of war and peace, taxes and the economy. The unwillingness of the Supreme Court to allow cameras and tape recorders to record oral arguments also helps shunt the judicial branch to third-class status on network television news. Thus, the media treated the courts as an afterthought, allotting the judicial branch only 3 percent of all coverage. Moreover, much of the coverage was directed to Supreme Court nominations rather than the sitting justices and their decisions.

Ironically, the judicial branch may actually benefit from being relegated to the sidelines. Since coverage of political institutions tends to be negative, its absence may be a blessing for an institution whose members do not run for reelection. And since federal judges serve for life, and generally have no larger political ambitions beyond the bench, they have little need for the individual coverage desired by House members who hope to become senators or governors, or by senators who dream of becoming president (cf. T. Cook 1989). In fact, the relative absence of judicial branch coverage—particularly the dearth of individually oriented coverage—may help instill public deference to and respect for the courts (O'Brien 1993).

It is not clear, though, how much the public benefits from such minimal coverage of the justices. Media distance—and the expectations of the Supreme Court's members that they are not subject to the media standards that apply to other parts of official Washington—can lead to serious gaps in the public's understanding of who the justices are and how important a role they play in contemporary politics (Epstein and Kobylka 1992; Kennedy 1997; O'Brien 1993; Tapper 2001; Toobin 2001). For example, while modern presidents and other elected officials can be subject to extensive public discussions of any health problems, Supreme Court justices refuse to provide detailed information on the state of their health.

When Chief Justice William Rehnquist disappeared from the Supreme Court for months in late 2004 and early 2005 as he battled thyroid cancer, little public information about his condition was disclosed, even though he led a court frequently divided by a 5–4 margin (Goodman 2005; Lane 2005). Rehnquist was only the last in a long line of justices who remained on the court despite a variety of severe and sometimes incapacitating health problems, including strokes, nervous breakdowns, and even chemical dependency (Goodman 2005). The Supreme Court's prohibition of television coverage decreases the opportunity for citizens to assess for themselves the fitness of these highly influential jurists—or even to see who is showing up for work and who is not.

THE EXECUTIVE BRANCH'S ADVANTAGE AS A SOURCE OF NEWS

Not surprisingly, the voices heard most often in the media were those of federal government officials. Almost two out of every three sources who were quoted or cited on television and in print were in government service. Executive branch employees accounted for a majority of all sources—roughly twice as many as the legislative branch provided. No other category even came close to these two groups. In all three administrations, executive branch officials were the source of more information on TV news than any other part of the government or any collection of voices outside the government. In two of the three, executive branch officials were cited twice as often as members of the legislative branch in both print and broadcast news. Nor was there any clear change over time; the executive branch was as dominant in 2001 as in 1981, apart from a slight drop in the local newspapers.

The national media also shared an increase in the use of independent "experts" outside the government, such as academics or think tank scholars. But television and print diverged in their attention to the voices of ordinary Americans. In 1981 the press cited ordinary people—individuals identified as voters, citizens, residents of areas affected by news events, and so forth—as one out of every eight sources, compared to fewer than one out of ten on television. By 2001 these figures were reversed, as television news increasingly made use of "person in the street" interviews and focus groups.

By contrast, state and local government officials were neglected as news resources, accounting for only 1 percent of all sources cited. For more than two decades presidents of both parties have proposed containing or shrinking the size of the national government and handing some of its responsibilities—particularly welfare—over to the states. (That has changed somewhat since 2001, as the federal government has increased its role in education through the No Child Left Behind legislation and through the creation of the Homeland Security Department.) Many other federal policy decisions have major consequences for the states, ranging from tax cuts that trigger cuts in state revenues to decisions over whether to intervene in state-level problems (such as California's 2001 electricity crisis or Florida's sequential hurricanes in 2004).

An increased visibility of sources in state capitals, just as those in foreign capitals, could broaden these perspectives and remind readers of how the U.S. government is connected to their everyday lives. The relative absence of international and state-level sources makes the president's voice even more dominant.

A more welcome trend was the growing tendency to identify the sources of information in news stories. The use of unnamed sources, which prevents news consumers from evaluating the credibility of the information they receive, has long been a rallying point for critics of political journalism. But the percentage of such sourcing has dropped sharply in the national press, from 30 percent of all sources in 1981 to 25 percent in 1993 and 20 percent in 2001. Television's need for pictures and a strong narrative may explain why only one out of six sources was not identified, compared to one out of four in print.

## News Media Bias?

### THE EXECUTIVE BRANCH'S ADVANTAGE IN TONE

Any discussion of partisan favoritism in coverage must carry the caveat that elected officials of both parties were subjected to far more criticism than praise. News coverage of all three presidencies combined was nearly two-to-one negative in tone, and evaluations of members of Congress were even more disparaging. The proportion of favorable comments toward the executive branch by the national media during the three first years of these administrations ranged from a high of only 40 percent positive (i.e., 60 percent negative) toward the Clinton administration on NBC News to a low of 25 percent positive (versus 75 percent negative) toward the Reagan administration in the *New York Times*. Overall, congressional Democrats received "only" two-to-one margins of criticism over praise, compared to an even worse three-to-one negative margin of opinions about Republicans.

The margin of negative over positive congressional evaluations at times exceeded ten to one for both parties, as in *New York Times* coverage of GOP legislators in 1993 (92 percent negative) and network news coverage of the Democrats in 1981 (93 percent negative). The only

good news for Congress is that the overall tone of congressional coverage improved over the course of the study period, from a more than
three-to-one negative margin in 1981 to just under two-to-one negative
in 2001, when it reached parity with the executive branch.

Only the judiciary, which received very little notice, managed to
attract balanced coverage. But even that finding reflects the chance oc-
currence that our sample period contained two noncontroversial Supreme Court nominations and none that were heavily contested. The
combined coverage of all three branches of government, during all three
of these first years of new presidential administrations, was almost ex-
actly two-to-one negative in tone—34 percent positive versus 66 percent negative evaluations.

Even the rally round the flag atmosphere that followed the terrorist
strikes on September 11, 2001, benefited only the president personally.
Coverage of executive agencies and presidential appointees, as well as
that of Congress, actually became more negative after the attacks. This
reflects recriminations over the government's failure to anticipate or
prevent this tragedy. Even Mr. Bush's post-9/11 "second honeymoon"
with the media proved short-lived. The tone of his coverage in 2002
returned to about the same two-to-one negative margin that greeted his
administration before the 9/11 tragedy (Media Monitor 2002).

The media portrayed the institutions of government even more harshly
than the individuals who temporarily embodied them. Evaluations of the
government, Congress, the White House, the courts, and so forth were
far more negative than judgments of particular presidents, congressmen, or judges. The difference was even greater for the judiciary—
nearly three out of four evaluations of individual judges were positive,
and over three out of five evaluations of the courts were negative.

If our portrayal of the media itself seems unrelentingly negative, we
did find a silver lining. In both television and print outlets, news coverage during the first year of each administration was heavily focused on
questions of policy and performance rather than personality or political
maneuvers. This substantive tendency increased over time, exceeding
three out of four evaluations of all branches in 2001. The downside is
that this sphere also attracted the heaviest criticism. Nonetheless, unlike
election news with its emphasis on ephemera and trivia over policy and

substance, coverage of governance offered relatively substantive and in-
formative treatment of important issues. Partisans of our system of government should applaud the difference.

## PARTISAN DIFFERENCES IN NEWS COVERAGE OF GOVERNMENT

Our findings on the tone of news coverage call into question any
sweeping generalizations about partisan bias. The tone differed from
one administration to another and from one outlet to another. Nonetheless, some provocative patterns emerged.

In our focused study of the first years of three recent presidents, the
only Democratic administration in the sample received slightly more
favorable coverage than its two Republican counterparts, but the differences were trivial. For network television, for example, coverage ranged
from 36 percent to 39 percent positive in tone, and their administrations received coverage that ranged only from 34 percent to 38 percent
positive. George W. Bush received the highest personal coverage and
Bill Clinton received the most positive coverage of his administration,
but these overall differences across 8,773 references to the executive
branch during 1981, 1993, and 2001 on three networks were far too
small to be detected by an ordinary news consumer.

Of course, partisan balance is not the same as ideological balance.
News coverage of any administration inevitably reflects the individual
personalities of the president and his advisors, as well as their relationships with the press. To improve the match between party affiliation
and political ideology, we looked at evaluations of each administration's
policies overall (including many general statements not linked to a specific policy), and of their domestic and foreign policies separately. This
eliminated comments that were directed toward personal virtues and
vices, resulting in a purer measure of how each administration's agenda
was judged. We then compared evaluations of the Clinton administration's policies with those of the Bush and Reagan administrations.

Table 7.1 summarizes the results of statistical significance tests per-
formed on these comparisons. (Following widely used procedures, we
employed the chi-square statistic, and set an acceptable level of significance at .05.) Policies of Clinton's administration were favored over
those of Reagan's to a significant degree in all news genres. In addition,

| TABLE 7.1 | Party Differences in Presidential Evaluations—Results of Significance Tests | | | | | |
|---|---|---|---|---|---|---|
| | Clinton vs. G. W. Bush | | | Clinton vs. Reagan | | |
| | All | Domestic Policy | Foreign Policy | All | Domestic Policy | Foreign Policy |
| **TV News** | — | — | — | D* | — | D** |
| **NY Times** | — | D* | — | D** | D** | D** |
| **Washington Post** | — | — | — | D** | D* | — |
| **Regional Papers** | D** | D** | — | D** | D** | D** |

*Significant at .05 level
**Significant at .01 level

Clinton's domestic policies were treated significantly better than Reagan's by all press outlets except network television, and his foreign policies fared significantly better everywhere but the *Washington Post*. (It should not be surprising that the tone of Clinton's coverage improves once personal evaluations are separated from coverage of policy matters, as is done here.)

By contrast, George W. Bush's presidency was treated about equally with Clinton's in the national media, except for a slight tilt toward the Clinton team's domestic policies in the *New York Times*. In the regional papers, however, the Clinton administration was favored overall as well as in the realm of domestic policy. Thus, out of the twenty-four paired comparisons represented in the table, the Democratic administration was favored in thirteen, and the two parties did not differ significantly in eleven. Ten of these thirteen statistically significant comparisons favored Clinton over Reagan, while the other three favored Clinton over George W. Bush. Five of the six regional paper comparisons favored Clinton over the two Republican presidents, as did four of the six comparisons in the *New York Times*. Only two of the six comparisons on network television and two of the six in the *Washington Post* favored the Democrats to a statistically significant degree. Neither Republican administration received significantly better coverage than Clinton's on any dimension for any of these media outlets.

When we applied the same tests to coverage of Congress, the results were not quite so one-sided, as table 7.2 shows. When evaluations of individual Democratic and Republican members were aggregated, Democratic legislators fared significantly better than Republicans in all media samples during Clinton's first year in office and on network news during that of George W. Bush. But Republicans fared significantly better on television news during Ronald Reagan's first year in office.

Thus, congressional Democrats were favored in five of twelve comparisons, congressional Republicans were favored in one, and there was no significant difference among the remaining six. (A separate set of comparisons established that the tone of congressional coverage did not vary consistently according to which party controlled the House and Senate.)

When these party differences in the executive and legislative branches were combined, Democrats received significantly better press in just under half of all comparisons (seventeen out of thirty-six), Republicans fared significantly better in one, and there were no statistically significant party differences in the other eighteen. Nearly half of the statistically significant differences emerged from evaluations of policies rather than individuals.

This pattern of findings suggests that differences in the media's treatment of the two parties was based not only on the personal traits and behavior of officials but also on judgments about their political and

| TABLE 7.2 | Party Differences in Congressional Evaluations— Results of Significance Tests | | |
|---|---|---|---|
| | **2001** | **1993** | **1981** |
| **TV News** | D** | D** | R** |
| **NY Times** | — | D** | — |
| **Washington Post** | — | D** | — |
| **Regional Papers** | — | D* | — |

*Significant at .05 level
**Significant at .01 level
Note: The Republicans controlled the House in 2001 and the Senate in 1981 and for the first five months of 2001, until Sen. James Jeffords (I-VT) left the GOP. Nineteen ninety-three was the only full year of one-party control on Capitol Hill of the three, as the Democrats controlled both the Senate and the House.

ideological convictions. In addition, the differences in tone at the various outlets show the importance of individual news judgment—a reminder that journalists' differing appraisals of government help shape the various versions of reality that readers and viewers receive.

However, this portrait of partisan tilt must be tempered by the recognition that what is statistically significant may not be substantively significant. The results of significance tests depend on the size of the samples as well as the magnitude of differences between groups. The larger the number of evaluations, the smaller the differences needed to attain a given level of significance. For example, the 14 percentage point advantage in good press that congressional Republicans enjoyed in the *Washington Post* in 2001 was not statistically significant because it was based on only eighty evaluations. Yet, the 14 percentage point advantage held by congressional Democrats on network news in 1993 was statistically significant because it was based on 364 evaluations.

Therefore, as an alternative measure, we reexamined all thirty-six comparisons while substituting a rule of thumb that defined double-digit percentage differences (i.e., 10 or more percentage points) between the two parties as substantively significant. As it turned out, this nonscientific "commonsense" standard produced results similar to those of the formal significance tests. GOP members of Congress bested their Democratic colleagues on television news and in the regional newspapers in 1981, as well as in the *Washington Post* in 2001. Overall, this procedure produced a total of seventeen "wins" for Democrats and three for Republicans in the paired comparisons; the remaining sixteen comparisons resulted in party differences below ten percentage points.

The magnitude of the partisan differences we found should not be exaggerated. For example, the competitive advantages enjoyed by congressional Democrats were clustered in 1993, and even the numerous double-digit percentage differences in good press rarely exceeded the teens in magnitude. In addition, the overall tone figures which may be most relevant to news consumers, differed less than did the tone of news coverage for the policy subgroups.

Nonetheless, our findings should give pause to those who categorically dismiss longstanding complaints of liberal media bias. And they present a challenge to recent complaints of a conservative media bias, insofar as they apply to traditional news outlets. The differences in tone among the outlets in our sample are also a reminder that "the media" was never a monolith, even before the recent profusion of new information sources that compete with traditional outlets. Our results suggest that charges of partisan bias are more of a concern for the regional newspapers we examined and the *New York Times* than the network television broadcasts and the *Washington Post*.

## Lessons

### FOR PRESIDENTS AND OTHER POLITICIANS

In today's news environment, the executive branch has all the advantages. The president has only to open his mouth to dominate the airwaves, and his administration should dominate the legislative branch with ease. In any struggle for "spin," the president is likely to win, even when the president is himself the topic of debate—as was the case with Bill Clinton's sexual scandals and impeachment. The president may not always emerge victorious in the battle to frame a story, but he can at least keep his adversaries on the defensive as well. During both the Clinton sexual misconduct scandal and the Iran-contra affair of Reagan's second term, critics who attacked the White House fared worse on network television than did those who were responsible for the scandal.

Scholars who study presidential image-making have suggested that presidents face a progressively more hostile media as time goes on. Above all, presidents have been thought to enjoy a "honeymoon" of favorable coverage upon entering office. But we found little evidence of a honeymoon for the last two presidents. George W. Bush and Bill Clinton faced heavy criticism from the news media virtually from their inauguration days. Some of the damage may be self-inflicted; new presidents sometimes make freshman-year mistakes, such as Bill Clinton's first two failed nominees for attorney general and his bumbling efforts to change the military's prohibition of "out" gay soldiers.

Ronald Reagan did enjoy a burst of favorable coverage after being shot in March 1981, but that clearly involved exceptional circumstances. In addition, the boost in coverage was brief. Despite the assassination attempt and the president's graceful and courageous recovery, Reagan's full first-year news coverage was actually a bit worse than Bill Clinton or George W. Bush later received.

We did find a positive upswing in media coverage during wartime. Regardless of the circumstances, recent presidents have received some of their best news coverage during times of international crisis, be it driving Saddam Hussein from Kuwait under George H. W. Bush, the NATO bombing campaign that rescued Bosnia on Bill Clinton's watch, or driving the Taliban from power in Afghanistan during the first term of George W. Bush.

Although coverage of the invasion of Iraq in the spring of 2003 was somewhat less positive than that of previous military actions, it was nevertheless far more positive than the media treatment the White House received in peacetime. A Pentagon program of "embedding reporters" into military units during the Iraqi war led to largely positive coverage for the military and for the Bush administration generally. It also led to criticisms from some who worried that the independence and judgment of some of these "embedded" reporters might be compromised (cf. Graber 2003; Norris et al. 2003).

But such periods of positive executive branch coverage during periods of hostilities like Iraq (1991), Kosovo (1999), Afghanistan (2001), and Iraq (2003) tend to be fleeting. News coverage of Iraq following George W. Bush's announcement that major combat operations had concluded became considerably more negative as armed resistance grew in strength and as the president's claims that Iraq possessed weapons of mass destruction could not be confirmed during the U.S. occupation.

Indeed, no one knows more clearly how short-lived such positive coverage can be than the elder President Bush, who saw his highly positive coverage regarding Kuwait turn into heavily negative coverage regarding the economy. He might have been wise to follow the strategy employed by his successors—when in trouble with the press, change the subject. Clinton received a burst of favorable publicity in the middle of the Clinton-Lewinsky scandal when he traveled to China, and the younger President Bush erased nearly all talk of any personal connection to the corporate financial scandals of 2002 by drawing attention to the weapons of mass destruction allegedly in Iraq.

While researchers disagree over the extent to which favorable press can help a president, a strategy of "going public" is commonly employed by presidential administrations. The evidence here suggests that there is great advantage for an administration in doing so, particularly regarding foreign policy and military issues. Such matters often are less contentious than domestic policy concerns—and often are a lesser priority on Capitol Hill—so there likely will be fewer potential critics with the stature necessary to gain a media platform.

The executive branch controls the State Department and the Pentagon, and it exerts considerable influence over the Central Intelligence Agency, which puts the president in a very good position to control the release of information—which can shape public debate over international matters to the president's liking. In addition, if the president chooses to go public on a national security matter, the White House may be able to portray its political or media critics as disloyal to the commander in chief, if not the nation itself. Even the threat of such a retaliatory public relations strike by the president or his supporters may be sufficient to silence would-be critics.

But this short-term executive branch advantage comes with long-term risks for an administration. A White House may eventually be found to be wrong on the facts, which can hurt a president's credibility. Or, some would note, being wrong may not matter that much to a White House in wartime. After all, Bush was reelected in 2004 despite heavy criticism of his administration's handling of Iraq. A week before Inauguration Day for his second term, the president publicly admitted that no weapons of mass destruction existed in Iraq (cf. Diamond 2005; Dowd 2005).

The early wagging of doubting tongues can raise problem areas for a government, but the effort to silence critics from the start may blind the White House to problems that become obvious later on. "Groupthink" seems strengthened, not undermined, during times of national crisis, even though these are the times when one-sided debate can have the most dangerous consequences.

In another initiative designed to build public support for the chief executive, recent administrations have invested considerable resources in cultivating positive media coverage from local media outlets. The content analysis of these four regional newspapers suggests limitations to the utility of that approach. The four regional papers analyzed here operated in very similar ways in their coverage of the White House—and in some cases were even more negative than the network news.

(They were also more hostile to GOP presidents than the national press or network television.)

While one cannot generalize from such a small sample, other research examining local television coverage also suggests very similar coverage from one local news outlet to another in the same media markets (Farnsworth and Lichter 2004a, 2004c). Further research into local news coverage would be particularly useful for scholars, given the important role local news plays in media consumption (Pew 2000b, 2004c). It may be that smaller papers than those examined here offer different, and perhaps more supportive, coverage patterns.

Finally, in terms of media management, our story is a tale of two Washingtons; comparatively speaking, it is the best of times at 1600 Pennsylvania Avenue and the worst of times on Capitol Hill. Congress simply cannot compete effectively with the president before the national media. By a margin of three to one and sometimes more, presidents command more media attention. Presidents and their teams not only get to do most of the talking, the media often treat them more positively. Even when Congress is trying to do its job and investigate allegations of executive branch wrongdoing, as in the Iran-contra scandal, the executive branch gets better press. When Congress is at its most vulnerable—when a president asserts his constitutional authority as commander in chief of the armed forces—the legislative branch is treated particularly harshly. If a member of Congress wants better media coverage, the best way to get it may be to run for president!

## FOR REPORTERS

Washington reporters are subject to intense scrutiny. Politicians, interest groups, and media watchdog organizations all cast a critical eye on news stories of interest to them. So do many ordinary viewers. However, a reporter who has angered a member of Congress often faces relatively modest consequences. Congress leaks from every office, and if one disgruntled member refuses to talk to you, there are many, many other places to go for help with the next story.

Angering the White House proves more dangerous to a reporter's future prospects. While nearly every member of the House and Senate has his or her own press secretary, the White House coordinates the administration's entire message dissemination operation from the West Wing. The White House can keep particularly close control over the release of information on foreign and military policy, where lawmakers and reporters have few alternative sources for information. This may lead to relatively positive stories about the president's foreign policy initiatives—as was the case in the run-up to the war in Iraq. In the months before the 2003 Iraq war, the Bush administration made many statements about the existence of weapons of mass destruction in that country and predicted that U.S. troops would be welcomed as liberators. Few people were in a position to disagree, or at least few chose to do so publicly.

But such positive early coverage—influenced by the limited information available at the time—may be supplanted by very negative information available later on that contradicts the administration's predictions and early reports. In the case of news coverage leading up to the Iraq war, several key media outlets eventually criticized their own performance as too accepting of the administration's earlier assertions.

Most reporters, regardless of their personal beliefs, do try to be fair in their news coverage. While the evidence here and elsewhere suggests they do not always succeed in treating candidates and officials of different parties equally, the national media coverage of the first year of recent presidential administrations was generally similar in tone.

Reporters may need to pay attention to a second type of media bias—one far more pervasive than political partisanship. Our evidence suggests that reporters frequently favor the White House over Congress in their coverage. There were disparities in the amount of coverage each branch received and periods of disparities in the tone of coverage of the two branches. Indeed, the modern media environment gives the president such advantages that renewed journalistic vigilance against institutional bias may be necessary to maintain the balance the Founders intended by vesting substantial authority in the legislative branch.

Critics have long maintained that journalists fail at the vital mission of holding government officials to account in a timely way (cf. Entman 1989). In the wake of the 2003 Iraqi war, even editors at the *New York Times* and *Washington Post* raised similar concerns. Reporters certainly could be more careful to hedge their news stories with clearer attributions of where material from anonymous sources came from and whose interests it serves. But ultimately reporters are not likely to air criticisms of proposed administration foreign policy matters unilaterally. Such concerns can be raised if there is widespread public opposition from citizens or within the government, or if a reporter can obtain evidence at the time that contradicts the president's position. But such critics do not always choose to disagree publicly with a popular president. Even so, reporters certainly could do more to contextualize information, making news reports more thematic and less episodic (Iyengar 1991). A key question being debated in newsrooms today is how much initiative reporters should take in raising questions about government policy when few newsmakers or public officials are doing so. To go too far raises questions of possible bias; to do too little may mean failing to uphold their public trust as watchdogs over those in power.

## FOR CITIZENS

While effective citizenship depends on high-quality, independent journalism, news organizations likewise need audiences of sophisticated citizens if they are to stay in business while offering such coverage (Entman 1989). Do the American media possess such an audience? Maybe. There is some evidence the public is able to distinguish among news outlets of varying quality. When asked to grade sources of presidential campaign news, for example, voters award higher scores to news sources that offer more substance in the information provided as measured by content analysis (Farnsworth and Lichter 2003a). News consumers pay more attention to media outlets—including cable television and newspapers—that provide more substantive coverage of recent presidential elections, moving away from the horse-race-dominated coverage found on network television (Pew 2000b, 2004c).

Or maybe not. Evidence also demonstrates that large numbers of Americans continued into 2004 to believe the discredited prewar George W. Bush administration claims that Saddam Hussein was connected to the September 11, 2001, terrorist attack and that the defeated Iraqi regime possessed weapons of mass destruction. This demonstrates how powerful the "bully pulpit" of presidential communication can be in the public debate. It also demonstrates the utility of a varied media diet, since the content analysis across these chapters has identified a number of differences in how different media outlets have covered the same story.

Citizenship in the modern political environment is particularly challenging. The huge amount of information available far exceeds what any observer of political life can consume. While network newscasts each offer one version of the world's top events, modern media consumers may find it necessary to search far beyond the boundaries of ABC, CBS, and NBC to find the information they need to follow politics and policy debates. The increased opportunity to select one's own menu of news requires citizens to be vigilant about the accuracy of the contents. But today's media environment offers great opportunities for learning about public policy issues and debates. Whether that potential is actualized is a function of how ready citizens are to exercise their responsibilities, as well as their privileges, in the expanding marketplace of ideas.

## Final Thoughts

The portrait of government presented by the news outlets we studied was frequently less than attractive. The coverage was heavily weighted toward a single branch, largely negative in tone, imbalanced enough to keep alive questions of partisan bias, and lacking a wide diversity of sources.

Notwithstanding such positive signs as the substantive focus of coverage and the declining use of unnamed sources, the results help to explain why so many Americans view both the media and the government with either suspicion or outright disdain. Further research on the mediated presidency should take a more extensive look at other media sources, including the newer media outlets like Fox News and the plethora of online media outlets.

Because of our historical focus, we have not traced the rise of new media outlets in this study. The Internet only became a major source of information for citizens in the past few years, and it—along with both CNN and the Fox News Channel—did not exist as a mass media outlet during the early years of this study. As these "upstart" media outlets become more established, they can be subject to long-term comparisons like those we applied to network news.

The clearest lesson to be drawn from our study is that journalists should apply the same critical scrutiny to their own performance that they do to the workings of government. Although it has taken scandals like those of Jayson Blair at the *New York Times* and the forged George W. Bush National Guard records at CBS News to trigger a rise in such introspection, more careful consideration of media content by both reporters and news consumers can only encourage better news coverage and more informed citizens.

# APPENDIX

---

Content analysis is a technique that allows researchers to classify statements objectively and systematically according to explicit rules and clear criteria. The goal is to produce valid measures of program content, and the hallmark of success lies in reliability. Other investigators who apply similar procedures to the same material should obtain similar results, although their interpretations of those results may differ. Clear rules and standards have to be set for identifying, measuring, and classifying each news story.

Evaluations were coded as positive or negative if they conveyed an unambiguous assessment or judgment about an individual, an institution, or an action. Only explicit evaluations were coded, in which both the target of the evaluation and its direction were clear. A positive example was provided by a voter quoted on ABC: "I think that Bill Clinton represents the best hope that this nation has for a brighter future" (January 17, 1993). A negative example came from NBC reporter Lisa Myers: "The president already had a reputation on the Hill for making contradictory promises and not keeping commitments. Now House members say even if he tells them the truth, they can't trust the president not to cave later under pressure" (June 10, 1993).

A description of events that reflected well or badly on some political actor was not coded for its tone unless it contained an evaluative comment. For example, an account of the passage of a bill supported by the White House would be coded as positive only if a source or reporter explicitly described it as a victory for the White House, a validation of the president's views or efforts on its behalf, and so on.

A minimum reliability of 80 percent was achieved for all variables retained in the final analysis.

# REFERENCES

Abrams, Burton A. 1980. "The Influence of State-Level Economic Conditions on Presidential Elections." *Public Choice* 35:623–31.

Abramson, Paul R., John H. Aldrich, and David W. Rohde. 1982. *Change and Continuity in the 1980 Elections*. Washington, DC: CQ Press.

———. 1999. *Change and Continuity in the 1996 and 1998 Elections*. Washington, DC: CQ Press.

———. 2002. *Change and Continuity in the 2000 Elections*. Washington, DC: CQ Press.

Adams, William C., Dennis J. Smith, Allison Salzman, Ralph Crossen, Scott Hieber, Tom Naccarato, William Valentine, and Nine Weisbroth. 1994. "Before and After 'The Day After': The Unexpected Results of a Televised Drama." In *Media Power in Politics*, ed. Doris Graber. 3rd ed. Washington, DC: CQ Press.

Adatto, Kiku. 1990. "Sound Bite Democracy." Research paper, Kennedy School Press Politics Center, Harvard University, June.

Adler, David G. 2003. "Presidential Greatness as an Attitude of Warmaking." *Presidential Studies Quarterly* 33 (3): 466–83.

Aitken, Jonathan. 1993. *Nixon: A Life*. Washington, DC: Regnery.

Alford, C. Fred. 1988. "Mastery and Retreat: Psychological Sources of the Appeal of Ronald Reagan." *Political Psychology* 9 (4): 571–89.

Alger, Dean. 1996. *The Media and Politics*. 2nd ed. Belmont, CA: Wadsworth.

Allen, Craig. 2001. *News Is People: The Rise of Local TV News and the Fall of News from New York.* Ames: Iowa State University Press.

Allen, Mike. 2003. "Bush Cites 9/11 on All Manner of Questions." *Washington Post,* September 11, A12.

Allen, Mike, and Susan Schmidt. 2004. "Document on Prison Tactics Disavowed." *Washington Post,* June 23, A1.

Alterman, Eric. 2000. *Sound and Fury: The Making of the Punditocracy.* Ithaca, NY: Cornell University Press.

———. 2003. *What Liberal Media?* New York: Basic Books.

Andolina, Molly W., and Clyde Wilcox. 2000. "Public Opinion: The Paradoxes of Clinton's Popularity." In *The Clinton Scandals and the Future of American Government,* ed. Mark J. Rozell and Clyde Wilcox. Washington, DC: Georgetown University Press.

Anyaegbunam, Chike, and Leland Ryan. 2003. "Students as Citizens: Experiential Approaches to Reflexive Thinking on Community Journalism." *Journalism and Mass Communication Educator* 58 (1): 64–73.

Arnold, R. Douglas. 2004. *Congress, the Press, and Public Accountability.* New York: Russell Sage.

Asher, Herb, and Mike Barr. 1994. "Popular Support for Congress and Its Members." In *Congress, the Press, and the Public,* ed. Thomas E. Mann and Norman Ornstein. Washington, DC: American Enterprise Institute and Brookings Institution.

Auletta, Ken. 2004. "Fortress Bush: How the White House Keeps the Press Under Control." *New Yorker,* February 19.

Baker, Nancy V. 2002. "The Impact of Anti-Terrorism Policies on Separation of Powers: Assessing John Aschroft's Role." *Presidential Studies Quarterly* 32 (4): 765–78.

Barber, James David. 1992. *Presidential Character: Predicting Performance in the White House.* Englewood Cliffs, NJ: Prentice Hall.

Bartels, Larry. 1988. *Presidential Primaries and the Dynamics of Public Choice.* Princeton, NJ: Princeton University Press.

Baum, Matthew A., and Samuel Kernell. 1999. "Has Cable Ended the Golden Age of Presidential Television?" *American Political Science Review* 93 (1): 99–114.

Bennett, W. Lance. 1994. "Toward a Theory of Press-State Relations in the United States." *Journal of Communication* 40:103–27.

———. 2005. *News: The Politics of Illusion.* 6th ed. New York: Pearson/Longman.

Berman, Larry, and Emily O. Goldman. 1996. "Clinton's Foreign Policy at Midterm." In *The Clinton Presidency: First Appraisals,* ed. Colin Campbell and Bert A. Rockman. Chatham, NJ: Chatham House.

Berman, William C. 2001. *From the Center to the Edge: The Politics and Policies of the Clinton Presidency*. Lanham, MD: Rowman & Littlefield.

Bernstein, Carl, and Bob Woodward. 1974. *All the President's Men*. New York: Warner Books.

Beschloss, Michael. 2002. *The Conquerors: Roosevelt, Truman, and the Destruction of Hitler's Germany, 1941–1945*. New York: Simon & Schuster.

Binder, Sara A., and Steven S. Smith. 1997. *Politics or Principle? Filibustering in the United States Senate*. Washington, DC: Brookings Institution.

Biskupic, Joan. 1995. "Has the Court Lost Its Appeal?" *Washington Post*, October 12, A23.

Blaney, Joseph R., and William L. Beniot. 2001. *The Clinton Scandals and the Politics of Image Restoration*. Westport, CT: Praeger.

Blumenthal, Sidney. 2003. *The Clinton Wars*. New York: Farrar, Straus & Giroux.

Bond, Jon R., Richard Fleisher, and B. Dan Wood. 2003. "The Marginal and Time-Varying Effect of Public Approval on Presidential Success in Congress." *Journal of Politics* 65 (1): 92–110.

Boorstin, Daniel. 1961. *The Image: A Guide to Pseudo-Events in America*. New York: Harper Colophon.

Booth, William. 2002. "Economic Anxiety Worries Politicians." *Washington Post*, July 21, A1.

Bowles, Nigel. 2003. "Comparing the Core Executive in Britain, France, and the United States." In *The Presidency and the Political System*, ed. Michael Nelson. 7th ed. Washington, DC: CQ Press.

Bozell, L. Brent, and Brent H. Baker. 1990. *And That's the Way It Wasn't*. Alexandria, VA: Media Research Center.

Brinkley, Douglas. 1998. *The Unfinished Presidency: Jimmy Carter's Journey Beyond the White House*. New York: Penguin.

Brody, Richard A. 1991. *Assessing the President: The Media, Elite Opinion, and Public Support*. Stanford, CA: Stanford University Press.

Brown, Jane Delano, Carl R. Bybee, Stanley T. Wearden, and Dulcie Murdock Straughan. 1987. "Invisible Power: Newspaper News Sources and the Limits of Diversity." *Journalism Quarterly* 64:45–54.

Brown, Cynthia, ed. 2003. *Lost Liberties: Ashcroft and the Assault on Personal Freedom*. New York: New Press.

Brown, Robin. 2003. "Clausewitz in the Age of CNN: Rethinking the Military-Media Relationship." In *Framing Terrorism: The News Media, the Government, and the Public*, ed. Pippa Norris, Montague Kern, and Marion Just. New York: Routledge.

Bugliosi, Vincent. 2001. *The Betrayal of America: How the Supreme Court*

*Undermined the Constitution and Chose Our President.* New York: Avalon/Nation Books.

Bumiller, Elisabeth. 2004. "Lawyer for Bush Quits over Links to Kerry's Foes." *New York Times,* August 26, A1.

Burger, Timothy J. 2001. "In the Driver's Seat: The Bush DUI." In *Overtime: The Election 2000 Thriller,* ed. Larry Sabato. New York: Longman.

Burke, John P. 2003. "The Institutional Presidency." In *The Presidency and the Political System,* ed. Michael Nelson. 7th ed. Washington, DC: CQ Press.

Burke, John P., and Fred Greenstein. 1989. *How Presidents Test Reality.* New York: Russell Sage.

Burnham, Walter Dean. 1996. "Realignment Lives: The 1994 Earthquake and Its Implications." In *The Clinton Presidency: First Appraisals,* ed. Colin Campbell and Bert A. Rockman. New York: Chatham House.

Burns, James MacGregor, and Susan Dunn. 2001. *The Three Roosevelts: Patrician Leaders Who Transformed America.* New York: Atlantic Monthly Press.

Busch, Andrew E. 2004. "On the Edge: The Electoral Career of George W. Bush." In *Considering the Bush Presidency,* ed. Gary Gregg II and Mark J. Rozell. New York: Oxford University Press.

Califano, Joseph A. 2001. "Too Many Federal Cops." *Washington Post,* December 6, A39.

Campbell, Colin, and Bert A. Rockman, eds. 1996. *The Clinton Presidency: First Appraisals.* Chatham, NJ: Chatham House.

Campbell, James. E. 1992. "Forecasting the Presidential Vote in the States." *American Journal of Political Science* 36 (2): 386–407.

———. 2001. "The Referendum That Didn't Happen: The Forecasts of the 2000 Presidential Election." *PS: Political Science & Politics* 34 (1): 33–38.

Cameron, Carl. 2002. "Studying the Polarized Presidency." *Presidential Studies Quarterly* 32 (4): 647–63.

Cantril, Hadley, Hazel Gaudet, and Herta Herzog. 1940. *The Invasion from Mars.* Princeton, NJ: Princeton University Press.

Cappella, Joseph N., and Kathleen Hall Jamieson. 1997. *Spiral of Cynicism: The Press and the Public Good.* New York: Oxford University Press.

Carey, George W. 1989. *The Federalist: Design for a Constitutional Republic.* Urbana: University of Illinois Press.

Carter, Ralph G. 1986. "Congressional Foreign Policy Behavior: Persistent Patterns of the Postwar Period." *Presidential Studies Quarterly* 16 (2): 333–34.

Ceaser, James. 1988. "The Reagan Presidency and American Public Opinion." In *The Reagan Legacy: Promise and Performance*, ed. Charles O. Jones. Chatham, NJ: Chatham House.

Ceaser, James, and Andrew Busch. 1993. *Upside Down and Inside Out: The 1992 Elections and American Politics*. Lanham, MD: Rowman & Littlefield.

———. 1997. *Losing to Win: The 1996 Elections and American Politics*. Lanham, MD: Rowman & Littlefield.

———. 2001. *The Perfect Tie: The True Story of the 2000 Presidential Election*. Lanham, MD: Rowman & Littlefield.

Chernow, Ron. 2004. "Leader of a Nation, Not a Party." *New York Times*, February 22.

Clancey, Maura, and Michael J. Robinson. 1985. "General Election Coverage." In *The Mass Media in Campaign '84*, ed. Michael J. Robinson and Austin Ranney. Washington, DC: American Enterprise Institute Press.

Clark, Terry N. 2002. "The Presidency and the New Political Culture." *American Behavioral Scientist* 46 (4): 535–52.

Clark, Wesley K. 2003. *Winning Modern Wars: Iraq, Terrorism, and the American Empire*. New York: Public Affairs.

Clarke, Richard A. 2004. *Against All Enemies. Inside America's War on Terror*. New York: Free Press.

Clinton, Bill. 2004. *My Life*. New York: Knopf.

Cochran, Clarke E., Lawrence C. Mayer, T. R. Carr, and N. Joseph Cayer. 2003. *American Public Policy: An Introduction*. 7th ed. Belmont, CA: Wadsworth/Thomson.

Cohen, Jeffrey E. 2002a. "The Polls: Policy-Specific Presidential Approval, Part I." *Presidential Studies Quarterly* 32 (3): 600–609.

———. 2002b. "The Polls: Policy-Specific Presidential Approval, Part II." *Presidential Studies Quarterly* 32 (4): 779–88.

Cohen, Richard. 2004. "A Grim Graduation Day." *Washington Post*, June 29, A23.

Cook, Corey. 2002. "The Contemporary Presidency: The Permanence of the 'Permanent Campaign': George W. Bush's Public Presidency." *Presidential Studies Quarterly* 32 (4): 753–64.

Cook, Timothy E. 1989. *Making Laws and Making News*. Washington, DC: Brookings Institution.

———. 1998. *Governing with the News: The News Media as a Political Institution*. Chicago: University of Chicago Press.

Cooper, John M., Jr. 1983. *The Warrior and the Priest: Woodrow Wilson and Theodore Roosevelt*. Cambridge, MA: Harvard University Press.

Cornfield, Mike. 2000. "The Internet and Democratic Participation." *National Civic Review* 89 (3): 235–41.

Craig, Stephen C. 1993. *The Malevolent Leaders*. Boulder, CO: Westview.

———. 1996. "The Angry Voter: Politics and Popular Discontent in the 1990s." In *Broken Contract? Changing Relationships between Americans and Their Government*, ed. Stephen C. Craig. Boulder, CO: Westview.

Cronin, Thomas E., and Michael A. Genovese. 2004. *The Paradoxes of the American Presidency*. 2nd ed. New York: Oxford University Press.

Dautrich, Kenneth, and Thomas H. Hartley. 1999. *How the News Media Fail American Voters: Causes, Consequences, and Remedies*. New York: Columbia University Press.

Davie, William R., and Jung-Sook Lee. 1993. "Television News Technology: Do More Sources Mean Less Diversity?" *Journal of Broadcasting and Electronic Media* 37 (4): 453–64.

Davis, Richard. 1987. "'Whither the Congress and the Supreme Court?' The Television News Portrayal of American National Government." *Television Quarterly* 22 (4): 55–61.

———. 1994. *Decisions and Images: The Supreme Court and the Press*. Englewood Cliffs, NJ: Prentice Hall.

———. 1999. *The Web of Politics: The Internet's Impact on the American Political System*. New York: Oxford University Press.

Davis, Richard, and Diana Owen. 1998. *New Media and American Politics*. New York: Oxford University Press.

Deakin, James. 1983. *Straight Stuff: The Reporters, the White House, and the Truth*. New York: William Morrow.

Dellinger, Walter, and Christopher H. Schroeder. 2001. "The Case for Judicial Review." *Washington Post,* December 6, A39.

Diamond, Larry. 2005. "How a Vote Could Derail Democracy." *New York Times,* January 9, 4:13.

Dickinson, Matthew. 2003. "The President and Congress." In *The Presidency and the Political System*, ed. Michael Nelson. 7th ed. Washington, DC: CQ Press.

Dimock, Michael. 2004. "Bush and Public Opinion." In *Considering the Bush Presidency*, ed. Gary Gregg II and Mark J. Rozell. New York: Oxford University Press.

Domino, John C. 1994. *Civil Rights and Liberties: Toward the 21st Century*. New York: HarperCollins.

Dowd, Maureen. 2005. "Defining Victory Down." *New York Times,* January 9, 4:13.

Downie, Leonard, Jr., and Robert G. Kaiser. 2002. *The News about the News: American Journalism in Peril*. New York: Knopf.

Drew, Elizabeth. 1994. *On the Edge: The Clinton Presidency*. New York: Simon & Schuster.

Druckman, James N. 2003. "The Power of Television Images: The First Kennedy-Nixon Debate Revisited." *Journal of Politics* 65 (2): 559–71.

Drudge, Matt. 2000. *Drudge Manifesto.* New York: New American Library.

Easton, David. 1975. "A Reassessment of the Concept of Political Support." *British Journal of Political Science* 5:435–57.

Easton, David, and Jack Dennis. 1969. *Children in the Political System.* New York: McGraw-Hill.

Easton, Nina, Michael Kranish, Patrick Healy, Glen Johnson, Anne E. Komblut, and Brian Mooney. 2004. "On the Trail of Kerry's Failed Dream." *Boston Globe,* November 14.

Edelman, Murray 1985. *The Symbolic Uses of Politics.* Urbana: University of Illinois Press.

*Editor and Publisher.* 2004. Web site, accessed July 6, 2004. www.editorand publisher.com/eandp/images/pdf/usd100cand10.pdf.

Edwards, George C., III. 1989. *At the Margins: Presidential Leadership of Congress.* New Haven, CT: Yale University Press.

———. 1996. "Frustration and Folly: Bill Clinton and the Public Presidency." In *The Clinton Presidency: First Appraisals,* ed. Colin Campbell and Bert A. Rockman. New York: Chatham House.

———. 1997. "Aligning Tests with Theory: Presidential Approval as a Source of Influence in Congress." *Congress & the Presidency* 24 (2): 113–30.

———. 2000. "Campaigning Is Not Governing: Bill Clinton's Rhetorical Presidency." In *The Clinton Legacy,* ed. Colin Campbell and Bert A. Rockman. New York: Chatham House.

———. 2003. *On Deaf Ears: The Limits of the Bully Pulpit.* New Haven, CT: Yale University Press.

———. 2004. "Riding High in the Polls: George W. Bush and Public Opinion." In *The George W. Bush Presidency: Appraisals and Prospects,* ed. Colin Campbell and Bert A. Rockman. Washington, DC: CQ Press.

Edwards, George C., III, William Mitchell, and Reed Welch. 1995. "Explaining Presidential Approval: The Significance of Issue Salience." *American Journal of Political Science* 39 (1): 108–34.

Edwards, George C., III, and Stephen J. Wayne. 2003. *Presidential Leadership: Politics and Policy Making.* 7th ed. Belmont, CA: Thomson/Wadsworth.

Edwards, George C., III, and B. Dan Wood. 1999. "Who Influences Whom? The President, Congress, and the Media." *American Political Science Review* 93 (2): 327–44.

Egan, Timothy. 2004. "Wounds Opened Anew as Vietnam Resurfaces." *New York Times,* August 26, A25.

Eggerton, John. 2004. "Howard Dean: Scream Never Happened." *Broadcasting & Cable,* June 14.

Entman, Robert M. 1989. *Democracy without Citizens*. New York: Oxford University Press.

———. 2000. "Declarations of Independence." In *Decision-Making in a Glass House: Mass Media, Public Opinion, and American and European Foreign Policy in the 21st Century*, ed. B. L. Nacos, R. Y. Shapiro, and P. Isernia. Lanham, MD: Rowman & Littlefield.

Epstein, Lee, and Joseph F. Kobylka. 1992. *The Supreme Court and Legal Change: Abortion and the Death Penalty*. Chapel Hill: University of North Carolina Press.

Ericson, David. 1977. "Newspaper Coverage of the Supreme Court: A Case Study." *Journalism Quarterly* 54: 605–7.

Erikson, Robert S., Michael B. MacKuen, and James A. Stimson. 2000. "Bankers or Peasants Revisited: Economic Expectations and Presidential Approval." *Electoral Studies* 19: 295–312.

Fair, Ray C. 1982. "The Effects of Economic Events on Votes for President: The 1980 Results." *Review of Economics and Statistics* 64: 322–25.

Fallows, James. 2004. "Blind into Baghdad." *Atlantic Monthly*, January/February.

Farah, Barbara G., and Ethel Klein. 1989. "Public Opinion Trends." In *The Election of 1988*, ed. Gerald M. Pomper. Chatham, NJ: Chatham House.

Farnsworth, Stephen J. 2001. "Patterns of Political Support: Examining Congress and the Presidency." *Congress & the Presidency* 28 (1): 45–60.

———. 2003a. *Political Support in a Frustrated America*. Westport, CT: Praeger.

———. 2003b. "Congress and Citizen Discontent: Public Evaluations of the Membership and One's Own Representative. *American Politics Research* 31 (1): 66–80.

Farnsworth, Stephen J., and S. Robert Lichter. 2003a. *The Nightly News Nightmare: Network News Coverage of U.S. Presidential Elections, 1988–2000*. Lanham, MD: Rowman & Littlefield.

———. 2003b. "The *Manchester Union Leader*'s Influence in the 1996 New Hampshire Republican Primary." *Presidential Studies Quarterly* 33 (2): 291–304.

———. 2004a. "Increasing Candidate-Centered Televised Discourse: Evaluating Local News Coverage of Campaign 2000." *Harvard International Journal of Press/Politics* 9 (2): 76–93.

———. 2004b. "New Presidents and Network News: Covering the First Year in Office of Ronald Reagan, Bill Clinton, and George W. Bush." *Presidential Studies Quarterly* 34 (3): 674–90.

———. 2004c. "Local Television News and Campaign 2000: Assessing Efforts to Increase Substantive Content." Paper delivered at the Annual Meeting of the Western Political Science Association. Portland, Oregon. March.

———. 2005. "The Mediated Congress." *Harvard International Journal of Press/Politics* 10 (2): 94–107.

Farnsworth, Stephen J., and Diana Owen. 2004. "The Internet and the 2000 Elections." *Electoral Studies* 23 (3): 415–29.

Farrell, John A. 2001. *Tip O'Neill and the Democratic Century*. Boston: Little, Brown.

Fenno, Richard F., Jr. 1975. "If, As Ralph Nader Says, Congress Is 'the Broken Branch,' Then How Come We Love Our Congressmen So Much?" In *Congress and Change: Evolution and Reform*, ed. Norman J. Ornstein. New York: Praeger.

Ferrell, Robert H. M. 2003. "Who Are These People?" *Presidential Studies Quarterly* 32 (4): 664–71.

Finnegan, Michael. 2004. "Film and Election Politics Cross in *Fahrenheit 9/11*." *Los Angeles Times*, June 11, A1.

Fiorina, Morris P. 1981. *Retrospective Voting in American National Elections*. New Haven, CT: Yale University Press.

Fisher, Louis. 2004. "The Way We Go to War: The Iraq Resolution." In *Considering the Bush Presidency*, ed. Gary Gregg II and Mark J. Rozell. New York: Oxford University Press.

Fishkin, James S. 1991. *Democracy and Deliberation: New Directions for Democratic Reform*. New Haven, CT: Yale University Press.

———. 1995. *The Voice of the People: Public Opinion and Democracy*. New Haven, CT: Yale University Press.

Fitzwater, Marlin. 1995. *Call the Briefing! Bush and Reagan, Sam and Helen: A Decade with Presidents and the Press*. New York: Times Books/Random House.

Fleisher, Richard, and Jon R. Bond. 2000a. "Congress and the President in a Polarized Era." In *Polarized Politics: Congress and the President in a Partisan Era*, ed. Jon R. Bond and Richard Fleisher. Washington, DC: CQ Press.

———. 2000b. "Partisanship and the President's Quest for Votes on the Floor of Congress." In *Polarized Politics: Congress and the President in a Partisan Era*, ed. Jon R. Bond and Richard Fleisher. Washington, DC: CQ Press.

Franken, Al. 1999. *Rush Limbaugh Is a Big, Fat Idiot: And Other Observations*. New York: Delacorte.

Frum, David. 2003. *The Right Man: The Surprise Presidency of George W. Bush, an Inside Account*. New York: Random House.

Gaines, Brian J. 2002. "Where's the Rally? Approval and Trust of the President, Cabinet, Congress, and Government since September 11." *PS: Political Science & Politics* 35 (3): 531–36.

Gallup Organization. 2002. "Bush Approval Drops below 80% Level." *Gallup Poll News Service*. Poll Analyses, March 8. Available at www.gallup.com.

Gans, Herbert J. 1979. *Deciding What's News*. New York: Pantheon.

Gellman, Irwin F. 1999. *The Contender: Richard Nixon, the Congress Years*. New York: Free Press.

Genovese, Michael A. 2001. *The Power of the American Presidency, 1789–2000*. New York: Oxford University Press.

Georges, Christopher. 1993. "Perot and Con: Ross's Teledemocracy Is Supposed to Bypass Special Interests and Take the Money Out of Politics; It Won't." *Washington Monthly* 25 (June): 38–43.

Gergen, David. 2000. *Eyewitness to Power: The Essence of Leadership*. New York: Simon & Schuster.

Germond, Jack, and Jules Witcover. 1993. *Mad as Hell: Revolt at the Ballot Box, 1992*. New York: Warner.

Gilbert, Robert E. 1989. "President versus Congress: The Struggle for Public Attention." *Presidential Studies Quarterly* 16 (3): 83–102.

Gilliam, Frank D., Jr., and Shanto Iyengar. 2000. "Prime Suspects: The Influence of Local Television News on the Viewing Public." *American Journal of Political Science* 44 (3): 560–73.

Gillon, Steven M. 2002. "Election of 1992." In *History of American Presidential Elections, 1789–2001*, vol. 11, ed. Arthur M. Schlesinger Jr. and Fred L. Israel. Philadelphia: Chelsea House.

Gingrich, Newt. 1995. *To Renew America*. New York: HarperCollins.

Ginsberg, Benjamin. 1986. *The Captive Public: How Mass Opinion Promotes State Power*. New York: Basic Books.

Gitlin, Todd. 1980. *The Whole World Is Watching: Mass Media and the Making and Unmaking of the New Left*. Berkeley and Los Angeles: University of California Press.

Glad, Betty. 1995. "How George Bush Lost the Presidential Election of 1992." In *The Clinton Presidency: Campaigning, Governing, and the Psychology of Leadership*, ed. Stanley A. Renshon. Boulder, CO: Westview.

Glass, Andrew. 1996. "On-Line Elections: The Internet's Impact on the Political Process." *Harvard International Journal of Press/Politics* 1 (4): 140–46.

Glasser, Theodore L. 1999. "The Idea of Public Journalism." In *The Idea of Public Journalism*, ed. Theodore L. Glasser. New York: Guilford Press.

Gold, Victor. 1994. "George Bush Speaks Out." *Washingtonian Magazine*, February.

Goldberg, Bernard. 2002. *Bias: A CBS Insider Exposes How the Media Distort the News*. Washington, DC: Regnery.

Goldberg, Robert, and Gerald J. Goldberg. 1995. *Citizen Turner*. New York: Harcourt Brace.

Goldman, Emily O., and Larry Berman. 2000. "Engaging the World: First Impressions of the Clinton Foreign Policy Legacy." In *The Clinton Legacy*, ed. Colin Campbell and Bert A. Rockman. New York: Chatham House.

Goodman, Ellen. 2005. "The High Court's Unhealthy Secrecy." *Washington Post,* January 8, A19.

Goodwin, Doris Kearns. 1994. *No Ordinary Time*. New York: Simon & Schuster.

Graber, Doris. 1987. "Kind Words and Harsh Pictures." In *Elections in America*, ed. Kay Lehman Schlozman. Boston: Alwin & Unwin.

———. 1988. *Processing the News*. 2nd ed. New York: Longman.

———. 2002. *Mass Media and American Politics*. 6th ed. Washington, DC: CQ Press.

———. 2003. "Terrorism, Censorship, and the First Amendment: In Search of Policy Guidelines." In *Framing Terrorism: The News Media, the Government, and the Public*, ed. Pippa Norris, Montague Kern, and Marion Just. New York: Routledge.

Granato, Jim, and George A. Krause. 2000. "Information Diffusion within the Electorate: The Asymmetrical Transmission of Political-Economic Information." *Electoral Studies* 19:519–37.

Greenberg, David. 2003. "Calling a Lie a Lie." *Columbia Journalism Review,* September/October.

Greenstein, Fred. 1982. *The Hidden-Hand Presidency: Eisenhower as Leader*. New York: Basic Books.

Gregg Gary, L. 2004. "Dignified Authenticity: George W. Bush and the Symbolic Presidency." In *Considering the Bush Presidency*, ed. Gary Gregg II and Mark J. Rozell. New York: Oxford University Press.

Gregg, Gary, II, and Mark J. Rozell, eds. 2004. *Considering the Bush Presidency*. New York: Oxford University Press.

Groeling, Tim, and Samuel Kernell. 1998. "Is Network News Coverage of the President Biased?" *Journal of Politics* 60 (4): 1063–87.

———. 2000. "Congress, the President, and Party Competition via Network News." In *Polarized Politics: Congress and the President in a Partisan Era*, ed. Jon R. Bond and Richard Fleisher. Washington, DC: CQ Press.

Grossman, Lawrence K. 1995. *The Electronic Republic: Reshaping Democracy in the Information Age*. New York: Penguin.

Grossman, Michael B., and Martha Joynt Kumar. 1981. *Portraying the President*. Baltimore: Johns Hopkins University Press.

Habermas, Jurgen. 1973. *Legitimation Crisis,* trans. Thomas McCarthy. Boston: Beacon Press.

Halberstam, David. 1979. *The Powers That Be*. New York: Alfred A. Knopf.

Halderman, H. R. 1994. *The Halderman Diaries: Inside the Nixon White House*. New York: G. P. Putnam's Sons.

Hall, Jim. 2001. *Online Journalism: A Critical Primer*. London: Pluto Press.

Hallin, Daniel C. 1984. "The Media, the War in Vietnam, and Political Support: A Critique of the Thesis of an Oppositional Media." *Journal of Politics* 46 (1): 2–24.

Hamilton, Alexander, James Madison, and John Jay. 1990. *The Federalist*. Edited by George W. Carey and James McClellan. Dubuque, IA: Kendall-Hunt Publishing. Originally published 1787–1788.

Han, Lori Cox. 2001. *Governing from Center Stage: White House Communication Strategies during the Television Age of Politics*. Cresskill, NJ: Hampton Press.

Hart, Roderick P. 1994. *Seducing America: How Television Charms the Modern Voter*. New York: Oxford University Press.

Harwood Group, The. 1991. *Citizens and Politics: A View from Main Street America*. Dayton, OH: Kettering Foundation.

———. 1993. *College Students Talk Politics*. Dayton, OH: Kettering Foundation.

Herman, Edward S., and Noam Chomsky. 1988. *Manufacturing Consent: The Political Economy of the Mass Media*. New York: Pantheon.

Hershey, Marjorie Randon. 1989. "The Campaign and the Media." In *The Election of 1988*, ed. Gerald M. Pomper. Chatham, NJ: Chatham House.

———. 1997. "The Congressional Elections." In *The Election of 1996*, ed. Gerald M. Pomper. New York: Chatham House.

———. 2001. "The Campaign and the Media." In *The Election of 2000*, ed. Gerald M. Pomper. New York: Chatham House.

Hertsgaard, Mark. 1989. *On Bended Knee: The Press and the Reagan Presidency*. New York: Schocken.

———. 2003. *The Eagle's Shadow: Why America Fascinates and Infuriates the World*. New York: Picador.

Hess, Stephen. 1981. *The Washington Reporters*. Washington, DC: Brookings Institution.

———. 1986. *The Ultimate Insiders: U.S. Senators in the National Media*. Washington, DC: Brookings Institution.

———. 1991. *Live From Capitol Hill!* Washington, DC: Brookings Institution.

———. 1996. *Presidents and the Presidency*. Washington, DC: Brookings Institution.

———. 2000a. "Critical Information Not Covered by the Media." *USA Today*, September 25.

———. 2000b. "Viewers Seek Fairness in TV Political News." *USA Today*, October 23.

Hetherington, Marc. 2001. "Declining Trust and a Shrinking Policy Agenda: Why Media Scholars Should Care." In *Communication in U.S. Elections: New Agendas*, ed. Roderick P. Hart and Daron R. Shaw. Lanham, MD: Rowman & Littlefield.

Hetherington, Marc, and Suzanne Globetti. 2003. "The Presidency and Political Trust." In *The Presidency and the Political System*, ed. Michael Nelson. 7th ed. Washington, DC: CQ Press.

Hetherington, Marc, and Michael Nelson. 2003. "Anatomy of a Rally Effect: George W. Bush and the War on Terrorism." *PS: Political Science & Politics* 36 (1): 37–42.

Hibbing, John R., and Elizabeth Theiss-Morse. 1995. *Congress as Public Enemy: Public Attitudes towards American Political Institutions.* Cambridge: Cambridge University Press.

Hines, Cragg. 1992. "Queries on Infidelity Infuriate First Lady." *Houston Chronicle,* August 13, A1.

Hofstetter, C. Richard. 1976. *Bias in the News.* Columbus: Ohio State University Press.

Hollihan, Thomas A. 2001. *Uncivil Wars: Political Campaigns in a Media Age.* Boston: Bedford/St. Martin's.

Howe, Neil, and Bill Strauss. 1993. *13th Gen: Abort, Retry, Ignore, Fail?* New York: Vintage.

Hunt, Albert R. 1981. "The Campaign and the Issues." In *The American Elections of 1980*, ed. Austin Ranney. Washington, DC: American Enterprise Institute.

Isikoff, Michael. 2000. *Uncovering Clinton: A Reporter's Story.* New York: Three Rivers Press.

Iverson, Dave, and Tom Rosenstiel. 2003. "Local TV Eye-Opener: Politics Aren't Poison." *American Journalism Review* (March). Available at www .ajr.org/Article.asp?id = 2798.

Iyengar, Shanto. 1991. *Is Anyone Responsible? How Television Frames Political Issues.* Chicago: University of Chicago Press.

Iyengar, Shanto, and Donald R. Kinder. 1987. *News That Matters.* Chicago: University of Chicago Press.

Iyengar, Shanto, Helmut Norpoth, and Kyu S. Hahn. 2004. "Consumer Demand for Election News: The Horserace Sells." *Journal of Politics* 66 (1): 157–75.

Jacobs, Lawrence R. 2003. "The Presidency and the Press: The Paradox of the White House Communications War." In *The Presidency and the Political System*, ed. Michael Nelson. 7th ed. Washington, DC: CQ Press.

Jacobs, Lawrence R., and Robert Y. Shapiro. 1995. "Public Opinion of President Clinton's First Year: Leadership and Responsiveness." In *The Clin-*

*ton Presidency: Campaigning, Governing, and the Psychology of Leadership*, ed. Stanley A. Renshon. Boulder, CO: Westview.

Jacobson, Gary. 2001. *The Politics of Congressional Elections.* 5th ed. New York: Addison Wesley Longman.

———. 2003. "The Bush Presidency and the American Electorate." *Presidential Studies Quarterly* 33 (4): 701–29.

Jamieson, Kathleen Hall. 1996. *Packaging the Presidency.* 3rd ed. New York: Oxford University Press.

———. 2000. *Everything You Think You Know about Politics and Why You're Wrong.* New York: Basic Books.

Jamieson, Kathleen Hall, and Joseph N. Cappella. 1998. "The Role of the Press in the Health Care Reform Debate of 1993–1994." In *The Politics of News, The News of Politics,* ed. Doris Graber, Denis McQuail, and Pippa Norris. Washington, DC: CQ Press.

Janis, Irving L. 1982. *Groupthink: Psychological Studies of Policy Decisions and Fiascoes.* 2nd ed. Boston: Houghton Mifflin.

Janowitz, Morris. 1983. *The Reconstruction of Patriotism: Education for Civic Consciousness.* Chicago: University of Chicago Press.

Jasperson, Amy, and Mansour O. El-Kikhia. 2003. "CNN and al Jazeera's Coverage of America's War in Afghanistan." In *Framing Terrorism: The News Media, the Government, and the Public,* ed. Pippa Norris, Montague Kern, and Marion Just. New York: Routledge.

Jeffords, James M. 2003. *An Independent Man: Adventures of a Public Servant.* New York: Simon & Schuster.

Jennings, M. Kent, and Richard G. Niemi. 1974. *The Political Character of Adolescence.* Princeton, NJ: Princeton University Press.

———. 1981. *Generations and Politics: A Panel Study of Young Adults and Their Parents.* Princeton, NJ: Princeton University Press.

Jones, Charles O. 1994. *The Presidency in a Separated System.* Washington, DC: Brookings Institution.

———. 1995. *Separate but Equal Branches: Congress and the Presidency.* Chatham, NJ: Chatham House.

Jones, Jeffrey P. 2001. "Forums for Citizenship in Popular Culture." In *Politics, Discourse, and American Society: New Agendas,* ed. Roderick P. Hart and Bartholomew H. Sparrow. Lanham, MD: Rowman & Littlefield.

Just, Marion R., Ann N. Crigler, Dean E. Alger, and Timothy E. Cook. 1996. *Crosstalk.* Chicago: University of Chicago Press.

Kaid, Lynda Lee, and Joe Foote. 1985. "How Network Television Coverage of the President and Congress Compare." *Journalism Quarterly* 62:59–65.

Kaniss, Phyllis. 1991. *Making Local News.* Chicago: University of Chicago Press.

Kaplan, Martin, and Matthew Hale. 2001. "Local TV Coverage of the 2000 General Election." Report of the Normal Lear Center Campaign Monitoring Project, University of Southern California, Annenberg School for Communication, February.

Kassop, Nancy. 2003. "The War Power and Its Limits." *Presidential Studies Quarterly* 33 (3): 509–29.

Kellner, Douglas. 2002. "Presidential Politics: The Movie." *American Behavioral Scientist* 46 (4): 467–86.

———. 2003. *From 9/11 to Terror War: The Dangers of the Bush Legacy.* Lanham, MD: Rowman & Littlefield.

Kennedy, Randall. 1997. *Race, Crime, and the Law.* New York: Vintage.

Kerbel, Matthew Robert. 1995. *Remote and Controlled: Media Politics in a Cynical Age.* Boulder, CO: Westview.

———. 1998. *Edited for Television: CNN, ABC, and American Presidential Elections.* 2nd ed. Boulder, CO: Westview.

———. 2001. "The Media: Old Frames in a Times of Transition." In *The Elections of 2000*, ed. Michael Nelson. Washington, DC: CQ Press.

Kerbel, Mathew R., Sumaiya Apee, and Marc Howard Ross. 2000. "PBS Ain't So Different: Public Broadcasting, Election Frames, and Democratic Empowerment." *Harvard International Journal of Press/Politics* 5 (4): 8–29.

Kernell, Samuel. 1997. *Going Public: New Strategies of Presidential Leadership.* 3rd ed. Washington, DC: CQ Press.

Key, V.O., Jr. 1966. *The Responsible Electorate: Rationality in Presidential Voting, 1936–1960.* Cambridge, MA: Harvard University Press.

Kiewiet, D. Roderick. 1983. *Macroeconomics and Micropolitics: The Electoral Effects of Economic Issues.* Chicago: University of Chicago Press.

Kinsley, Michael. 2003. "An Apology Would Help." *Washington Post,* September 12, A31.

Kinzer, Stephen 2004. "Candidate, under Pressure, Quits Senate Race in Illinois." *New York Times,* June 26, A8.

Klapper, Joseph. 1960. *The Effects of Mass Media.* Glencoe, IL: Free Press.

Klein, Joe. 2002. *The Natural: The Misunderstood Presidency of Bill Clinton.* New York: Doubleday.

Klotz, Robert J. 2004. *The Politics of Internet Communication.* Lanham, MD: Rowman & Littlefield.

Kohut, Andrew. 2002. "Increasingly, It's the Economy That Scares Us." *New York Times,* July 14.

Kovach, Bill, and Tom Rosenstiel. 1999. *Warp Speed: America in the Age of Mixed Media.* New York: Century Foundation Press.

Kristof, Nicholas D. 2004. "Dithering As Others Die." *New York Times,* June 26.

Krosnick, Jon A., and Laura A. Brannon. 1993. "The Impact of the Gulf War on the Ingredients of Presidential Evaluations: Multidimensional Affects of Political Involvement." *American Political Science Review* 87 (4): 963–75.

Krosnick, Jon A., and Donald R. Kinder. 1990. "Altering the Foundations of Support for the President through Priming." *American Political Science Review* 84 (2): 497–512.

Kumar, Martha Joynt. 2001. "The Office of the Press Secretary." *Presidential Studies Quarterly* 31 (2): 296–322.

———. 2002. "Recruiting and Organizing the White House Staff." *PS: Political Science & Politics* 35 (1): 35–40.

———. 2003a. "The Contemporary Presidency: Communications Operations in the White House of President George W. Bush: Making News on His Terms." *Presidential Studies Quarterly* 33 (2): 366–93.

———. 2003b. "Source Material: The White House and the Press: News Organizations as a Presidential Resource and as a Source of Pressure." *Presidential Studies Quarterly* 33 (3): 669–83.

Kurtz, Howard. 1992. "Bush Angrily Denounces Report of Extramarital Affair as 'A Lie'; Tabloid Story on Rumored Relationship with Ex-Aide Called 'Sleaze.'" *Washington Post*, August 12, A12.

———. 1994. *Media Circus: The Trouble with America's Newspapers*. New York: Times Books.

———. 1998. *Spin Cycle: Inside the Clinton Propaganda Machine*. New York: Free Press.

———. 2002a. "At ABC, a Shaken News Dynasty." *Washington Post*, March 6.

———. 2002b. "Troubled Times for Network Evening News." *Washington Post*, March 10.

———. 2005. "Network Fires Four in Wake of Probe." *Washington Post*, January 11.

Lane, Charles. 2003. "Draft Bill Expands Anti-terror Powers." *Washington Post*, February 8.

———. 2005. "Rehnquist's Absences to Continue." *Washington Post*, January 8, A6.

Langman, Lauren. 2002. "Suppose They Gave a Culture War and No One Came." *American Behavioral Scientist* 46 (4): 501–34.

Laufer, Peter. 1995. *Inside Talk Radio: America's Voice or Just Hot Air?* Secaucus, NJ: Carol Publishing.

Lawrence, Regina G. 2001. "Defining Events: Problem Definition in the Media Arena." In *Politics, Discourse, and American Society: New Agendas*, ed. Roderick P. Hart and Bartholomew H. Sparrow. Lanham, MD: Rowman & Littlefield.

Lazare, Daniel. 1996. *The Frozen Republic: How the Constitution Is Paralyzing Democracy*. New York: Harcourt Brace.

Lengel, Allan, and Petula Dvorak. 2002. "Rep. Condit Subpoenaed by Grand Jury." *Washington Post*, March 26, B1.

Lesher, Stephan. 1982. *Media Unbound: The Impact of Television Journalism upon the Public*. Boston: Houghton Mifflin.

Lewis, Charles. 2004. *The Buying of the President 2004*. New York: Harper-Colllins.

Lewis, David A., and Roger P. Rose. 2002. "The President, the Press, and the War-Making Power: An Analysis of Media Coverage Prior to the Persian Gulf War." *Presidential Studies Quarterly* 32 (3): 559–71.

Lewis-Beck, Michael S., and Tom W. Rice. 1992. *Forecasting Elections*. Washington, DC: CQ Press.

Lewis-Beck, Michael S., and Charles Tien. 2001. "Modeling the Future: Lessons from the Gore Forecast." *Political Science and Politics* 34 (1): 21–23.

Liebovich, Louis W. 2001. *The Press and the Modern Presidency*. 2nd rev. ed. Westport, CT: Praeger.

Lichter, S. Robert. 1988. "Misreading Momentum." *Public Opinion* 11 (1): 15–17.

———. 1996. "Consistently Liberal: But Does It Matter?" *Forbes Media Critic* (Fall): 26–39.

———. 2001. "A Plague on Both Parties: Substance and Fairness in TV Election News." *Harvard International Journal of Press/Politics* 6 (3): 8–30.

Lichter, S. Robert, and Daniel Amundson. 1994. "Less News Is Worse News: Television News Coverage of Congress." In *Congress, the Press, and the Public*, ed. Thomas E. Mann and Norman Ornstein. Washington, DC: American Enterprise Institute and Brookings Institution.

Lichter, S. Robert, Daniel Amundson, and Richard Noyes. 1988. *The Video Campaign*. Washington, DC: American Enterprise Institute.

———. 1989. "Election '88: Media Coverage." *Public Opinion* 11 (5): 18–19.

Lichter, S. Robert, and Stephen J. Farnsworth. 2003. "Government in and out of the News." A Report to the Council for Excellence in Government. Washington, DC: Center for Media and Public Affairs.

Lichter, S. Robert, and Richard E. Noyes. 1995. *Good Intentions Make Bad News: Why Americans Hate Campaign Journalism*. 2nd ed. Lanham, MD: Rowman & Littlefield.

———. 1998. *Why Elections Are Bad News*. New York: Markle Foundation.

Lichter, S. Robert, Stanley Rothman, and Linda S. Lichter. 1990. *The Media Elite*. New York: Hastings House.

Lichter, S. Robert, Mary Carroll Willi, and Stephen J. Farnsworth. 2002.

"Evaluation of Alliance for Better Campaigns and Wisconsin Public Television Election 2000 Projects." Center for Media and Public Affairs, Washington, DC.

Lind, Rebecca A., and David R. Rarick. 1999. "Viewer Sensitivity to Ethical Issues in TV Coverage of the Clinton-Flowers Scandal." *Political Communication* 16 (2): 169–81.

Lindsay, James M. 2003. "Deference and Defiance: The Shifting Rhythms of Executive-Legislative Relations in Foreign Policy." *Presidential Studies Quarterly* 33 (3): 530–46.

Lopez, Steve. 2001. "You Gotta Admire TV's Commitment to Meaninglessness." *Los Angeles Times,* November 26.

Loth, Renee. 1992. "Bush's Denial of Infidelity Rumor Sparks Stories, Déjà Vu." *Boston Globe,* August 13, 20.

Lowi, Theodore J. 1985. *The Personal President: Power Invested, Promise Unfulfilled.* Ithaca, NY: Cornell University Press.

Lowi, Theodore J., Benjamin Ginsberg, and Kenneth Shepsle. 2002. *American Government: Power and Purpose.* 7th ed. New York: Norton.

Margolis, Michael, and David Resnick. 2000. *Politics as Usual: The Cyberspace "Revolution."* Thousand Oaks, CA: Sage.

Maltese, John Anthony. 2000. "The New Media and the Lure of the Clinton Scandal." In *The Clinton Scandals and the Future of American Government,* ed. Mark J. Rozell and Clyde Wilcox. Washington, DC: Georgetown University Press.

Massing, Michael. 2004. "Now They Tell Us." *New York Review of Books,* February 26.

Mayer, Jane, and Doyle McManus. 1988. *Landslide: The Unmaking of a President, 1984–1988.* Boston: Houghton Mifflin.

McChesney, Robert W. 1999. *Rich Media, Poor Democracy: Communication Politics in Dubious Times.* New York: New Press.

McCombs, Maxwell E., and Donald L. Shaw. 1977. *The Emergence of American Political Issues: The Agenda-Setting Function of the Press.* St. Paul, MN: West Publishing.

———. 1993. "The Evolution of Agenda-Setting Research: Twenty-five Years in the Marketplace of Ideas." *Journal of Communication* 43(2): 58.

McDonald, Greg. 1992. "Outraged Bush Calls Adultery Story 'A Lie'; President Rips Report as Wife Looks On." *Houston Chronicle,* August 12, A4.

McGinniss, Joe. 1969. *The Selling of the President, 1968.* New York: Trident Press.

McLeod, Jack M., Gerald M. Kosicki, and Douglas M. McLeod. 1994. "The Expanding Boundaries of Political Communication Effects." In *Media*

*Effects: Advances in Theory and Research*, ed. Jennings Bryant and Dolf Zillmann. Hillsdale, NJ: Lawrence Erlbaum Associates.

McManus, Doyle. 2004. "Wartime President Is Again Outflanked." *Los Angeles Times,* June 29.

McQuail, Denis. 2000. "The Influence and Effects of Mass Media." In *Media Power in Politics*, ed. Doris Graber. 4th ed. Washington, DC: CQ Press.

Media Monitor. 1987. "The Iran/Contra Story." Washington, DC: Center for Media and Public Affairs. March.

———. 1997. "What Do the People Want from the Press?" Washington, DC: Center for Media and Public Affairs. May/June.

———. 1998a. "Internal Affairs: TV News Coverage of the White House Sex Scandal." Washington, DC: Center for Media and Public Affairs. March/April.

———. 1998b. "Covering the Clinton Scandals." Washington, DC: Center for Media and Public Affairs. May/June.

———. 1998c. "Sex, Lies, and TV News." Washington, DC: Center for Media and Public Affairs. September/October.

———. 2001. "News in a Time of Terror." Washington, DC: Center for Media and Public Affairs. November/December.

———. 2002. "Scandalous Business: TV News Coverage of the Corporate Scandals." Washington, DC: Center for Media and Public Affairs. July/August.

———. 2004. "The 2004 Primaries." Washington, DC: Center for Media and Public Affairs. March/April.

Mermin, Jonathan. 1997. "Television News and the American Intervention in Somalia: The Myth of a Media-Driven Foreign Policy." *Political Science Quarterly* 112 (Fall): 385–402.

Mcyrowitz, Joshua. 1985. *No Sense of Place: The Impact of Electronic Media on Social Behavior*. New York: Oxford University Press.

Milbank, Dana. 2003. "Amid Iraq Policy Shift: Refusal to Admit Change Is a Constant." *Washington Post,* September 9, A21.

———. 2004a. "Bush Was Surprised at Lack of Arms." *Washington Post,* February 9, A1.

———. 2004b. "The Administration versus the Administration." *Washington Post,* June 29, A21.

Milbank, Dana, and Mike Allen. 2004. "Many Gaps in Bush's Guard Records." *Washington Post,* February 14, A1.

Milbank, Dana, and Claudia Deane. 2003. "Hussein Link to 9/11 Lingers in Many Minds." *Washington Post,* September 6, A1.

Milbank, Dana, and Walter Pincus. 2003. "Cheney Defends U.S. Actions in Bid to Revive Public Support." *Washington Post,* September 15, A1.

Milbank, Dana, and Jim VandeHei. 2004. "From Bush, Unprecedented Negativity." *Washington Post,* May 31, A1.

Miller, Arthur. 1999. "Sex, Politics, and Public Opinion: What Political Scientists Really Learned from the Clinton-Lewinsky Scandal." *PS: Political Science & Politics* 32 (4): 721–29.

Minutaglio, Bill. 1999. *First Son: George W. Bush and the Bush Family Dynasty.* New York: Times Books.

Miroff, Bruce. 2003. "The Presidential Spectacle." In *The Presidency and the Political System,* ed. Michael Nelson. 7th ed. Washington, DC: CQ Press.

Mooney, Chris. 2004. "Did Our Leading Newspapers Set Too Law a Bar for a Preemptive Attack?" *Columbia Journalism Review,* March/April.

Morin, Richard, and Dan Balz. 2003. "Public Says $87 Billion Too Much." *Washington Post,* September 14, A1.

Morin, Richard, and Dana Milbank. 2004. "Domestic Issues Hurt Bush in Poll." *Washington Post,* January 20, A1.

Morris, Dick. 1997. *Behind the Oval Office: Winning the Presidency in the Nineties.* New York: Random House.

Morris, Irwin L. 2002. *Votes, Money, and the Clinton Impeachment.* Boulder, CO: Westview.

Mueller, John. 1973. *War, Presidents, and Public Opinion.* New York: Wiley.

Mucciaroni, Gary, and Paul J. Quirk. 2004. "Deliberations of a 'Compassionate Conservative': George W. Bush's Domestic Presidency." In *The George W. Bush Presidency: Appraisals and Prospects,* ed. Colin Campbell and Bert A. Rockman. Washington, DC: CQ Press.

Mutz, Diana. 1992. "Mass Media and the Depoliticization of Personal Experience." *American Journal of Political Science* 36 (2): 483–508.

Nader, Ralph. 2002. *Crashing the Party: Taking On the Corporate Government in An Age of Surrender.* New York: St. Martin's.

Nagrourney, Adam. 2004. "Kerry Might Pay Price for Failing to Strike Back Quickly." *New York Times,* August 21, A10.

Nagourney, Adam, and Janet Elder. 2004. "Bush's Rating Falls to Its Lowest Point, New Survey Finds." *New York Times,* June 29.

Nelson, Michael. 2003. "Evaluating the Presidency." In *The Presidency and the Political System,* ed. Michael Nelson. 7th ed. Washington, DC: CQ Press.

———. 2004. "George W. Bush and Congress." In *Considering the Bush Presidency,* ed. Gary Gregg II and Mark J. Rozell. New York: Oxford University Press.

Neuman, W. Russell. 1986. *The Paradox of Mass Politics: Knowledge and Opinion in the American Electorate.* Cambridge, MA: Harvard University Press.

Neustadt, Richard. 1990. *Presidential Power and the Modern Presidents.* New York: Free Press.

Newman, Brian. 2002. "Bill Clinton's Approval Ratings: The More Things Change the More They Stay the Same." *Political Research Quarterly* 55 (4): 781–804.

Nickelsburg, Michael, and Helmut Norpoth. 2000. "Commander-in-Chief or Chief Economist? The President in the Eye of the Public." *Electoral Studies* 19:313–32.

Nieves, Evelyn. 2001. "Condit Is Quietly Heading toward Run for an Eighth Term." *New York Times,* October 27, A8.

Nincic, Miroslav. 1997. "Loss Aversion and the Domestic Context of Military Intervention." *Political Research Quarterly* 50 (1): 97–120.

Niven, David. 2001. "Bias in the News: Partisanship and Negativity in Media Coverage of Presidents George Bush and Bill Clinton." *Harvard International Journal of Press/Politics* 6 (3): 31–46.

Norris, Pippa. 1996. "Does Television Erode Social Capital? A Reply to Putnam." *PS: Political Science & Politics* 29 (3): 474–80.

Norris, Pippa, Montague Kern, and Marion Just. 2003. "Framing Terrorism." In *Framing Terrorism: The News Media, the Government, and the Public,* ed. Pippa Norris, Montague Kern, and Marion Just. New York: Routledge.

Nye, Joseph S., Jr. 2002. *The Paradox of American Power: Why the World's Only Superpower Can't Go It Alone.* Oxford: Oxford University Press.

O'Brien, David M. 1993. *Storm Center: The Supreme Court in American Politics.* 3rd ed. New York: Norton.

———. 1996. "Clinton's Legal Policy and the Courts: Rising from Disarray or Turning Around and Around?" In *The Clinton Presidency, First Appraisals,* ed. Colin Campbell and Bert A. Rockman. Chatham, NJ: Chatham House.

O'Connor, Karen, and Larry J. Sabato. 2002. *American Government: Continuity and Change.* New York: Longman.

Oldfield, Duane, and Aaron Wildavsky. 1989. "Reconsidering the Two Presidencies." *Society* 26 (July/August): 54–59.

Orkent, Daniel. 2004. "Weapons of Mass Destruction? Or Mass Distraction?" *New York Times,* May 30.

Ornstein, Norman, and Michael Robinson. 1986. "Where's All the Coverage: The Case of Our Disappearing Congress." *TV Guide,* January 11, 4–10.

Owen, Diana. 1991. *Media Messages in American Presidential Elections.* Westport, CT: Greenwood Press.

———. 1995. "The Debate Challenge: Candidate Strategies in the New Media Age." In *Presidential Campaign Discourse: Strategic Communication*

*Problems*, ed. Kathleen E. Kendall. Albany: State University of New York Press.

———. 1996. "Who's Talking? Who's Listening? The New Politics of Talk Radio Shows." In *Broken Contract? Changing Relationships between Americans and Their Government*, ed. Stephen Craig. Boulder, CO: Westview.

———. 1997. "The Press' Performance." In *Toward The Millennium: The Elections of 1996*, ed. Larry Sabato. Boston: Allyn & Bacon.

———. 2000. "Popular Politics and the Clinton/Lewinsky Affair: The Implications for Leadership." *Political Psychology* 21 (1): 161–77.

———. 2002. "Media Mayhem: Performance of the Press in Election 2000." In *Overtime: The Election 2000 Thriller*, ed. Larry Sabato. New York: Longman.

Page, Benjamin I., and Robert Y. Shapiro. 1992. *The Rational Public: Fifty Years of Trends in American Policy Preferences*. Chicago: University of Chicago Press.

Page, Benjamin I., Robert Y. Shapiro, and Glenn R. Dempsey. 1987. "What Moves Public Opinion." *American Political Science Review* 81 (1): 23–43.

Paletz, David L. 2002. *The Media in American Politics: Contents and Consequences*. 2nd ed. New York: Addison Wesley Longman.

Paletz, David L., and Robert M. Entman. 1981. *Media Power Politics*. New York: Free Press.

Paletz, David L., and K. Kendall Guthrie. 1987. "The Three Faces of Ronald Reagan." *Journal of Communication* 37:7–23.

Patterson, Thomas E. 1980. *The Mass Media Election: How Americans Choose Their President*. New York: Praeger.

———. 1994. *Out of Order*. New York: Vintage.

———. 2000. "Doing Well and Doing Good." Research paper, Kennedy School Press Politics Center, Harvard University, December.

———. 2002. *The Vanishing Voter: Public Involvement in an Age of Uncertainty*. New York: Knopf.

Pear, Robert. 2004. "U.S. Videos, for TV News, Come under Scrutiny." *New York Times*, March 15, A1.

Pear, Robert, and Sheryl Gay Stolberg. 2004. "Inquiry Ordered on Medicare Official's Charge." *New York Times*, March 17, A16.

Perlstein, Rick. 2001. *Before the Storm: Barry Goldwater and the Unmaking of the American Consensus*. New York: Hill & Wang.

Peterson, Jonathan, and Dawn Wotopka. 2004. "Lockyer Sues Enron: FERC to Review Tapes." *Los Angeles Times,* June 18, C1.

Peterson, Mark A. 2004. "Bush and Interest Groups: A Government of

Chums." In *The George W. Bush Presidency: Appraisals and Prospects*, ed. Colin Campbell and Bert A. Rockman. Washington, DC: CQ Press.

Pew Research Center for the People and the Press. 2000a. "Voters Unmoved by Media Characterizations of Bush and Gore." July 27.

———. 2000b. "Media Seen as Fair, but Tilting to Gore." October 15.

———. 2000c. "Campaign 2000 Highly Rated." November 16.

———. 2000d. "Internet Election News Audience Seeks Convenience, Familiar Names." December 3.

———. 2000e. "Some Final Observations on Voter Opinions." December 21.

———. 2001. "Terror Coverage Boosts News Media's Image." November 28.

———. 2003a. "America's Image Further Erodes, Europeans Want Weaker Ties." March 18.

. 2003b. "War with Iraq Further Divided Global Publics." June 3.

———. 2004a. "News Audiences Increasingly Politicized." June 8.

———. 2004b. "Public Support for War Resilient." June 17.

———. 2004c. "Voters Liked Campaign 2004, But Too Much 'Mud-Slinging.'" November 11.

Pfiffner, James P. 1988. *The Strategic Presidency: Hitting the Ground Running*. Chicago: Dorsey Press.

———. 2000. "Presidential Character: Multidimensional or Seamless?" In *The Clinton Scandals and the Future of American Government*, ed. Mark J. Rozell and Clyde Wilcox. Washington, DC: Georgetown University Press.

———. 2004a. *The Character Factor: How We Judge America's Presidents*. College Station: Texas A&M University Press.

———. 2004b. "Introduction: Assessing the Bush Presidency." In *Considering the Bush Presidency*, ed. Gary Gregg II and Mark J. Rozell. New York: Oxford.

Pious, Richard M. 2002. "Why Do Presidents Fail?" *Presidential Studies Quarterly* 32 (4): 724–42.

Pollack, Kenneth M. 2004. "Spies, Lies, and Weapons: What Went Wrong." *Atlantic Monthly*, January/February.

Polsby, Nelson. 1983. *Consequences of Party Reform*. Oxford: Oxford University Press.

Polsby, Nelson, and Aaron Wildavsky. 2000. *Presidential Elections: Strategies and Structures of American Politics*. 10th ed. New York: Chatham House/Seven Bridges.

Pomper, Gerald M. 1985. "The Presidential Election." In *The Election of 1984: Reports and Interpretations*, ed. Gerald M. Pomper. Chatham, NJ: Chatham House.

———. 1997. "The Presidential Election." In *The Election of 1996: Reports and Interpretations*, ed. Gerald M. Pomper. Chatham, NJ: Chatham House.

Popkin, Samuel. 1991. *The Reasoning Voter*. Chicago: University of Chicago Press.

Postman, Neil. 1985. *Amusing Ourselves to Death*. New York: Penguin.

Power, Samantha. 2002. *"A Problem from Hell": America and the Age of Genocide*. New York: Basic Books.

Powers, William. 1998. "News at Warp Speed: Coverage of the Scandal Has Turned the Press on Itself—With a Vengeance." *National Journal* 30 (January 31): 220–23.

Putnam, Robert D. 1995. "Tuning In, Tuning Out: The Strange Disappearance of Social Capital in America." *PS: Political Science & Politics* 28 (4): 664–83.

———. 2000. *Bowling Alone*. New York: Simon & Schuster.

Priest, Dana, and Bradley Graham. 2004. "U.S. Struggled over How Far to Push Tactics." *Washington Post*, June 24, A1.

Ranney, Austin. 1983. *Channels of Power*. New York: Basic Books.

Rash, Wayne, Jr. 1997. *Politics on the Nets*. New York: W. H. Freeman.

Rasmussen, Jim. 2004. "Shame on the Swift Boat Veterans for Bush." *Wall Street Journal*, August 10, A10.

Reich, Robert. 1998. *Locked in the Cabinet*. New York: Vintage.

Remini, Robert V. 1967. *Andrew Jackson and the Bank War*. New York: Norton.

Renshon, Stanley A. 1995. "Character, Judgment, and Political Leadership: Promise, Problems, and Prospects for the Clinton Presidency." In *The Clinton Presidency: Campaigning, Governing, and the Psychology of Leadership*, ed. Stanley A. Renshon. Boulder, CO: Westview.

Rich, Frank. 2003. "Tupac's Revenge on Bennett." *New York Times*, May 16, 2:1.

Rimer, Sara, Ralph Blumenthal, and Raymond Bonner. 2004. "Portrait of George W. Bush in '72: Unanchored in a Turbulent Time." *New York Times*, September 20, A1.

Roberts, Robert N., and Anthony J. Eksterowicz. 1996. "Local News, Presidential Campaigns, and Citizenship Education: A Reform Proposal." *PS: Political Science & Politics* 29 (1): 66–72.

Robinson, Michael. 1976. "Public Affairs Television and the Growth of Political Malaise: The Case of 'The Selling of the Pentagon.'" *American Political Science Review* 70:409–32.

———. 1981. "Three Faces of Congressional Media." In *The New Congress*, ed. Thomas E. Mann and Norman Ornstein. Washington, DC: American Enterprise Institute.

Robinson, Michael J., and Margaret Sheehan. 1983. *Over the Wire and on TV.* New York: Russell Sage Foundation.

Robinson, Piers. 2002. *The CNN Effect: The Myth of News, Foreign Policy, and Intervention.* London: Routledge.

Rockman, Bert A. 1996. "Leadership Style and the Clinton Presidency." In *The Clinton Presidency: First Appraisals,* ed. Colin Campbell and Bert A. Rockman. Chatham, NJ: Chatham House.

Roig-Franzia, Manuel, and Lois Romano. 2004. "Few Can Offer Confirmation of Bush's Guard Service." *Washington Post,* February 15, A1.

Romano, Lois. 2004. "New Federal Trial of 1995 Okla. Bombing Suspect to Open." *Washington Post,* February 29, A15.

Roselle, Laura. 2003. "Local Coverage of the 2000 Election in North Carolina: Does Civic Journalism Make a Difference?" *American Behavioral Scientist* 46 (5): 600–616.

Rosenstiel, Tom, and Bill Kovach. 2002. "Why We Need 'Nightline.'" *Washington Post,* March 6, A19.

Rozell, Mark. 1994. "Press Coverage of Congress, 1946–1992. In *Congress, the Press, and the Public,* ed. Thomas E. Mann and Norman Ornstein. Washington, DC: American Enterprise Institute and Brookings Institution.

Rusher, William A. 1988. *The Coming Battle for the Media.* New York: William Morrow.

Rutenberg, Jim. 2004a. "CBS News Concludes It Was Misled on Guard Memos, Network Officials Say." *New York Times,* September 20, A20.

———. 2004b. "Broadcast Group to Pre-empt Programs for Anti-Kerry Film." *New York Times,* October 11, A19.

Rutenberg, Jim, and Kate Zernike. 2004. "CBS Apologized for Report on Bush Guard Service." *New York Times,* September 21, A1.

Rutkus, Denis Steven. 1991. *Newspaper and Television Network News Coverage of Congress during the Summers of 1979 and 1989: A Content Analysis.* Washington, DC: Congressional Research Service. 91–238 GOV.

Sabato, Larry. 1993. *Feeding Frenzy: How Attack Journalism Has Transformed American Politics.* New York: Free Press.

———. 2002. "The Perfect Storm: The Election of the Century." In *Overtime: The Election 2000 Thriller,* ed. Larry Sabato. New York: Longman.

Sabato, Larry, Mark Stencel, and S. Robert Lichter. 2000. *Peepshow: Media and Politics in an Age of Scandal.* Lanham, MD: Rowman & Littlefield.

Sanford, Bruce. 1999. *Don't Shoot the Messenger: How Our Growing Hatred of the Media Threatens Free Speech for All of Us.* New York: Free Press.

Schechter, Danny. 2003. *Media Wars: News at a Time of Terror.* Boulder, CO: Rowman & Littlefield.

Schneider, William. 1981. "The November 4 Vote for President: What Did It Mean?" In *The American Elections of 1980*, ed. Austin Ranney. Washington, DC: American Enterprise Institute.

Schneider, William, and I. A. Lewis. 1985. "Views on the News." *Public Opinion* 8 (4): 6–11.

Schudson, Michael. 1978. *Discovering the News*. New York: Basic Books.

Scott, Ian. 2000. *American Politics in Hollywood Film*. Chicago: Fitzroy Dearborn.

Seelye, Katharine Q. 2004. "Both Sides' Commercials Create a Brew of Negativity, at a Boil." *New York Times,* September 22, A23.

Seelye, Katharine Q., and Ralph Blumenthal. 2004. "Documents Suggest Guard Gave Bush Special Treatment." *New York Times,* September 9, A1.

Seib, Philip. 2001. *Going Live: Getting the News Right in a Real-Time, Online World*. Lanham, MD: Rowman & Littlefield.

Shenon, Philip. 2004. "Will Michael Moore's Facts Check Out?" *New York Times,* June 20.

Simon, Adam. 2001. "A Unified Method for Analyzing Media Framing." In *Communication in U.S. Elections: New Agendas*, ed. Roderick P. Hart and Daron R. Shaw. Lanham, MD: Rowman & Littlefield.

Sinclair, Barbara. 2000. "Hostile Partners: The President, Congress, and Lawmaking in the Partisan 1990s." In *Polarized Politics: Congress and the President in a Partisan Era*, ed. Jon R. Bond and Richard Fleisher. Washington, DC: CQ Press.

Skocpol, Theda. 1997. *Boomerang: Health Care Reform and the Turn Against Government*. New York: Norton.

Slevin, Peter. 2004. "New 2003 Data: 625 Terrorism Deaths, Not 307." *Washington Post,* June 23, A1.

Slotnick, Elliot, and Jennifer Segal. 1998. *Television News and the Supreme Court: All the News That's Fit to Air?* New York: Cambridge University Press.

Smith, Culver H. 1977. *The Press, Politics, and Patronage*. Athens: University of Georgia Press.

Smith, Richard N. 2001. "'The President Is Fine' and Other Historical Lies." *Columbia Journalism Review* 40 (3): 30–32.

Smith, Ted J., III, S. Robert Lichter, and Louis Harris and Associates Inc. 1997. *What the People Want from the Press*. Washington, DC: Center for Media and Public Affairs.

Smoller, Fred. 1986. "The Six O'clock Presidency: Patterns of Network News Coverage of the President." *Presidential Studies Quarterly* 16: 31–49.

Soroka, Stuart N. 2003. "Media, Public Opinion and Foreign Policy." *Harvard International Journal of Press/Politics* 8 (1): 27–48.

Sparrow, Bartholomew. 1999. *Uncertain Guardians: The News Media as a Political Institution.* Baltimore: Johns Hopkins University Press.

Spitzer, Robert J. 1999. "Clinton's Impeachment Will Have Few Consequences for the Presidency." *PS: Political Science & Politics* 32 (3): 541–45.

Starobin, Paul. 2004. "The Angry American." *Atlantic Monthly,* January/February.

Steinberg, Jacques, and Bill Carter. 2004. "Rather Quitting as CBS Anchor in Abrupt Move." *New York Times,* November 24, A1.

Stephanopoulos, George. 1999. *All Too Human: A Political Education.* Boston: Little, Brown.

Stevenson, Richard W. 2002. "White House Says It Expects Deficit to Hit $165 Billion." *New York Times,* July 12, A1.

———. 2003. "Remember 'Weapons of Mass Destruction'? For Bush, They Are a Non-issue." *New York Times,* December 18.

———. 2004. "With 9/11 Report, Bush's Political Thorn Grows More Stubborn." *New York Times,* June 17.

Stevenson, Richard, and Janet Elder. 2002. "Poll Finds Concerns That Bush Is Overly Influenced by Business." *New York Times,* July 18, A1.

Stuckey, Mary. 1991. *The President as Interpreter-in-Chief.* Chatham, NJ: Chatham House.

Sullivan, Terry. 1991. "A Matter of Fact: The Two Presidencies Thesis Revisited." In *The Two Presidencies: A Quarter Century Assessment,* ed. Steven Shull. Chicago: Nelson-Hall.

Sunstein, Cass R. 2001. *Republic.com.* Princeton, NJ: Princeton University Press.

Sunstein, Cass R., and Richard A. Epstein. 2001. *The Vote: Bush, Gore, and the Supreme Court.* Chicago: University of Chicago Press.

Suskind, Ron. 2004. *The Price of Loyalty: George W. Bush, the White House, and the Education of Paul O'Neill.* New York: Simon & Schuster.

Tapper, Jake. 2001. *Down and Dirty: The Plot to Steal the Presidency.* Boston: Little, Brown.

———. 2002. "Down and Dirty, Revisited: A Postscript on Florida and the News Media." In *Overtime: The Election 2000 Thriller,* ed. Larry Sabato. New York: Longman.

Taylor, P. 2000. "The New Political Theater." *Mother Jones,* November/December.

Taylor, Paul. 2002. *The Case for Free Air Time.* Washington, DC: Alliance for Better Campaigns.

Tenpas, Kathryn Dunn, and Stephen Hess. 2002. "The Contemporary Presidency: The Bush White House, First Appraisals." *Presidential Studies Quarterly* 32 (3): 577–85.

Terwilliger, George J., III. 2002. "A Campout for Lawyers: The Bush Recount Perspective." In *Overtime: The Election 2000 Thriller*, ed. Larry
Sabato. New York: Longman.

Tocqueville, Alexis de. 1960. *Democracy in America*. New York: Vintage.
Originally published in 1835.

Toobin, Jeffrey. 2001. *Too Close To Call: The 36 Day Battle to Decide the 2000
Election*. New York: Random House.

Tribe, Lawrence. 2000. *American Constitutional Law*, vol. 1. 3rd ed. New
York: Foundation Press.

Tulis, Jeffrey K. 1987. *The Rhetorical Presidency*. Princeton, NJ: Princeton
University Press.

VandeHei, Jim. 2005. "Bush Paints his Goals as 'Crises.'" *Washington Post*,
January 8, A1.

Waldman, Paul, and Kathleen Hall Jamieson. 2003. "Rhetorical Convergence
and Issue Knowledge in the 2000 Presidential Election." *Presidential
Studies Quarterly* 33 (1): 145–63.

Waterman, Richard W., Robert Wright, and Gilbert St. Clair. 1999. *The
Image-Is-Everything Presidency*. Boulder, CO: Westview.

Wayne, Stephen J. 2000. "Presidential Personality and the Clinton Legacy."
In *The Clinton Scandals and the Future of American Government*, ed.
Mark J. Rozell and Clyde Wilcox. Washington, DC: Georgetown Univer-
sity Press.

———. 2001. *The Road to the White House, 2000: The Politics of Presidential
Elections*. Boston: Bedford/St. Martin's.

———. 2003. *Is This Any Way to Run a Democratic Election?* 2nd ed. Boston:
Houghton Mifflin.

Weisman, Jonathan. 2002. "Remember Fiscal Discipline?" *Washington Post*,
August 9, A1.

Weisman, Jonathan, and Nell Henderson 2004. "Quality of News Jobs Caught
in Election-Year Debate." *Washington Post*, June 23, E1.

West, Darrell M. 2001. *Air Wars: Television Advertising in Election Campaigns, 1952–2000*. Washington, DC: CQ Press.

West, Darrell M., and Burdett A. Loomis. 1999. *The Sound of Money: How
Political Interests Get What They Want*. New York: Norton.

White, Theodore H. 1961. *The Making of the President, 1960*. New York:
Atheneum House.

———. 1978. *In Search of History*. New York: Warner Books.

Wildavsky, Aaron. 1966. "The Two Presidencies." *Transaction* 4 (December): 7–14.

Wilgoren, Jodi. 2004. "Truth Be Told, the Vietnam Crossfire Hurts Kerry
More." *New York Times*, September 24, A24.

Wlezien, Christopher. 2001. "On Forecasting the Presidential Vote." *PS: Political Science & Politics* 34 (1): 25–31.

Woo, W. F. 2000. "Public Journalism: A Critique." In *Public Journalism and Political Knowledge*, ed. Anthony J. Eksterowicz and Robert N. Roberts. Lanham, MD: Rowman & Littlefield.

Woodward, Bob. 1994. *The Agenda: Inside the Clinton White House.* New York: Simon & Schuster.

———. 1999. *Shadow: Five Presidents and the Legacy of Watergate.* New York: Simon & Schuster.

———. 2000. Maestro: *Greenspan's Fed and the American Boom.* New York: Simon & Schuster.

———. 2002. *Bush at War.* New York: Simon & Schuster.

Wright, Robin. 2004. "Iraq Occupation Erodes Bush Doctrine." *Washington Post*, June 28.

Zaller, John R. 1998. "Monica Lewinsky's Contribution to Political Science." *PS: Political Science & Politics* 31 (2): 554–57.

Zernike, Kate, and Jim Rutenberg. 2004. "Friendly Fire: The Birth of an Attack on Kerry." *New York Times*, August 20, A1.

# INDEX

# ABOUT THE AUTHORS

**Stephen J. Farnsworth** is associate professor of political science at the University of Mary Washington and a former newspaper journalist.

**S. Robert Lichter** is professor of communication at George Mason University, where he directs the Center for Media and Public Affairs, a nonprofit, nonpartisan media research organization.